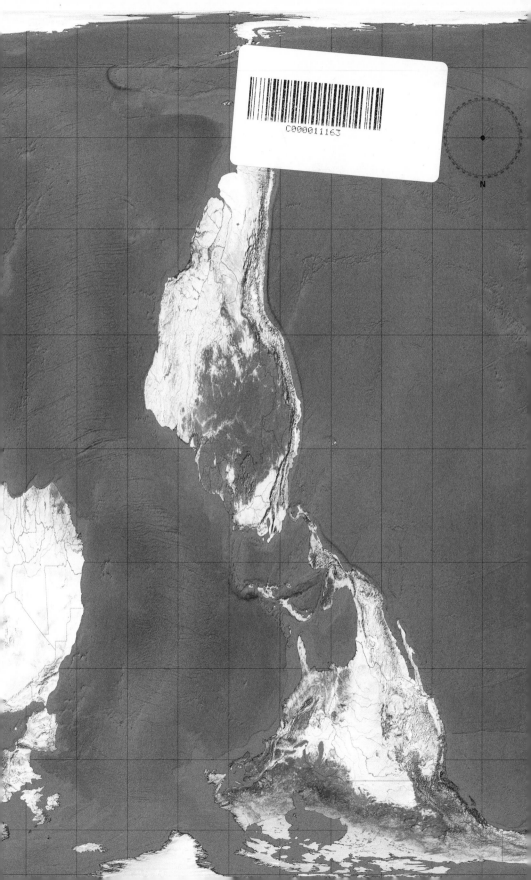

Lilian Thuram

White Thinking

Behind the Mask of Racial Identity

Translated by
David Murphy, Aedín Ní Loingsigh
and Cristina Johnston

Hero, an imprint of
Legend Times Group Ltd, 51 Gower Street, London, WC1E 6HJ
hero@hero-press.com | www.hero-press.com

First published in French in 2020 by Éditions Philippe Rey

© Éditions Philippe Rey, 2020
This edition is published by arrangement with Éditions Philippe Rey in
conjunction with its duly appointed Agent Books And More #BAM, Paris,
France

Translation © David Murphy, Aedín Ní Loingsigh and Cristina Johnston, 2021

This work is published with support from the French Ministry of Culture/
Centre national du livre.

Print ISBN: 9781-8-0031-344-6
Ebook ISBN: 9978-1-80031-345-3
Set in Times. Printed in the United Kingdom by Clays Ltd

To my first star, my mother, Marianna
To my sisters, Martine and Liliana
To my brothers Gaëtan and Antonio
To my two eagles, Marcus and Khephren
To Kareen
And to all the world's children
who carry the ancestors' hopes and dreams

To Elisabeth Caillet and Lionel Gauthier
who guided and supported me
at every step of the journey to publish this book

CONTENTS

CONTENTS

TRANSLATORS' NOTE

Translating discussions of race from one language to another is often fraught with difficulties. The idealised French vision of a colour-blind Republic of citizens raises specific challenges where this task is concerned. Attempts by minorities in France to speak about the discrimination to which they are subjected can often lead to accusations of *communautarisme*, or communitarianism. Such accusations are essentially a criticism of these groups for self-segregating and identifying according to specific group identities in a way that undermines the imagined unity of the Republic.

Debates about race have evolved in recent years and the Black Lives Matter movement of 2020 led to significant protests and important public debate. There is clearly an appetite for conversations about race, and commercially successful French translations of popular English-language books, not least Reni Eddo-Lodge's *Why I'm No Longer Talking to White People About Race*, have recently introduced common terms such as 'people of colour' into the French lexicon of race. Lilian Thuram's *La Pensée blanche* consciously avoids use of 'people of colour', however. As he writes in the introduction, White people generally do not perceive themselves to have a colour, although they clearly do, for every human being does. In light of this, he argues, why should we consider that only 'people of colour' have a 'racial' identity?

One of the main arguments of *La Pensée blanche* is thus that all racial identities are constructed. And White identity has constructed a non-White identity. This does not mean that Lilian Thuram believes there is a homogeneous 'non-White' identity. What he does believe is that White thinking has imagined the existence of a non-White identity, and we have followed this lexical choice in our translation in order to respect the author's conception of the ways in which racial identities are constructed, that is, as a mask we are obliged to wear (but from which we can ultimately escape).

Finally, in *La Pensée blanche*, although French usage would not typically capitalise anything other than proper nouns, Thuram also capitalises the words '*Blanc*' (White) and '*Noir*' (Black) when used as nouns (generally in the plural). In line with standard French usage, 'white' and 'black' are not capitalised by him when used as adjectives in expressions including 'white thinking' (*pensée blanche*). For this translation, however, we have opted to capitalise all instances where 'White' and 'Black' are used in order to signal Thuram's problematisation of these categories.

– David Murphy, Aedín Ní Loingsigh and Cristina Johnston

'The white race, the most perfect of [all] the human races.'

School textbook from 1877, reprinted annually with only minor changes right up until 1977[1]

'The White made a man of the Black.'

Victor Hugo, 'Discours sur l'Afrique', *Actes et paroles*[2]

'Yes, there is without doubt a war between the races: But who started it? And who is prosecuting it?'

Georges Clemenceau[3]

'It is possible to give greater importance to the ideal of liberty than one gives to one's own life. [...] In my opinion, an individual can't be free if others aren't.'

Denis Goldberg[4]

---

1 G. Bruno, *Le Tour de la France par deux enfants* (Paris: Belin, 1877).

2 Victor Hugo, *Actes et paroles*, Volume 4, 1879.

3 *Le Temps*, 29 November 1867.

4 Interview with Marie Boëton for the French newspaper *La Croix*: 'Denis Goldberg: Mon combat auprès de Mandela', 12 June 2019.

INTRODUCTION

A few years ago, I was invited to discuss a proposal for a major exhibition on the question of racism. The organisers wanted me to serve as the general curator of the exhibition, and I was deeply honoured to be entrusted with delivering its anti-racist message to the public. I planned to take an approach born of a situation I had experienced at a meeting in a government ministry: when it was time for those around the table to introduce themselves, I was asked about my work and that of my anti-racism foundation. I told them that we analysed how domination works within society. For instance, around that table, there were a lot more women than men. The chair of the meeting said: 'Indeed, there are very few women.' I replied: 'To be honest, that's not the issue; the problem is that there are too many men.' And, right there, in that moment, I could feel all those men staring at me, as though I had attacked them, rather than simply making an observation.

This is why I explained that, as curator of the exhibition, I wanted to adopt a different perspective. For far too long, whenever we speak about racism, we have concentrated on those on the receiving end of discrimination. And now, I was saying that we should instead focus on those who profit from this discrimination, often unconsciously and unintentionally. We needed to ask questions about something that is never questioned: Whiteness. What does it mean 'to be White'? How does one become White? Because people aren't born

White, they become White. Have you ever seen someone whose skin is genuinely the same colour as a sheet of white paper? No, I'm sure you haven't. Then, why do we say that a person is White? At what age does someone become White? When you think about it, isn't becoming White pretty similar to becoming a man in a society where men are educated to believe they should be dominant? As I developed these ideas at the meeting, I could feel a growing disquiet around the room. People perceived to be 'White' aren't used to being questioned about their skin colour and its potential meaning.

I went on: 'If we want to make progress in our fight for equality, then we need White visitors to the exhibition to realise that they have been educated to see the colour of their skin as politically neutral.'

I could sense a feeling of incomprehension, maybe even hostility. It was as though a 'we' had been formed, a 'we' that was asking itself: 'What has he got against us?' I realised that they felt attacked by my words. And maybe this is the point at which I should reveal that I was the only Black person in the room. They felt attacked in the same way that men do when told that men have a superiority complex in relation to women. I hadn't accused anyone of being a horrible racist. But speaking about *White domination*, well, no, that just wasn't on. Unfortunately, the discussion of my role in the exhibition ended right there.

This book is born of that unfinished dialogue. Why do most White people refuse to question this constructed identity? What's more, they don't even seem aware that they have a colour. Aren't Black people described as 'people of colour'? There's the proof that White people don't have a colour. So, what colour are White people? In France, we talk about 'visible minorities'. Does that mean White people are an 'invisible majority'? The word 'White' is almost never used in France to describe a particular segment of the population, as though it had no basis in social reality. And, when it is used, it leads to a form of tension and annoyance in those designated by it.

Ten years before that, I had come across a special issue of a magazine, titled 'Black Thinking', which had set my mind racing: if 'Black thinking' exists, does that mean there is such a thing as 'White thinking'?[1] This special issue contained texts by and

1 'La Pensée noire: les textes fondamentaux', *Le Point*, special issue, April–May 2009.

2

about Toni Morrison, Maryse Condé, Martin Luther King, James Baldwin, Aimé Césaire and Frantz Fanon, amongst others. But what did all of these Black people write about? About a world that treats Black people as inferior. About the need for liberation from this violence, so they might gain the same rights as White people. It is rarely noted, however, that deep down King, Baldwin and the others were writing in opposition to a system. But the outlines of this system are never entirely clear. Who constructed a discourse giving White people pride of place in the hierarchy of humankind? Who is it that claims Black people are less competent? Who decided that Black people should enjoy fewer opportunities than White men and women? The answer is racialised White thinking.

This is the centuries-old matrix that most White people don't dare even to contemplate. Why has no magazine devoted a special issue to this 'White thinking', which in many ways produced this 'Black thinking'? Why do the very words 'White thinking' appear so shocking?

In my opinion, the mechanisms at work here are comparable to those that lead to the domination of women by men. The great French anthropologist Françoise Héritier writes that:

> Sexual differences, categorised under the labels of masculine and feminine, exist within a hierarchical relationship, in the sense that the values associated with one of these two poles (the masculine) are considered superior to those of the other. [...] Western societies have developed an explanatory model that connects masculine strength to an innate male superiority. [...] Our interpretive framework is immutable and archaic, drawn from categories elaborated at a time when our ancestors' knowledge was limited to what their senses could apprehend.[1]

Might we not say that the history of male resistance to the emancipation of women is more revealing than the history of the emancipation of women? And wouldn't the history of White elite resistance to the emancipation of non-Whites be just as enlightening?

---

1 Françoise Héritier, *Masculin/Féminin II: Dissoudre la hiérarchie* (Paris: Odile Jacob, 2002), pp. 34–37.

Isn't it time to question this desire to maintain this colour line, this domination, generation after generation?

Today, we can study Black art, Black thinking, Black literature, Black music. We examine them, we exhibit them, we dissect them. Why then should it be forbidden to study White thinking, White literature, White music? Some areas of existence seem able to escape the bounds of their colour, while others can't. Why is that?

In White-dominated societies all around the world, Black people are constantly made aware of their Blackness, whether in the workplace or in the media. When they walk in public, they are reminded of their colour by sideways glances, which express the suspicion of those who always seem to look at Black people for evidence of some imagined misdemeanour. If you haven't been a victim of such discrimination, then this sensation will be alien to you as it's not part of your experience of the world. As for White people, they can go anywhere they like without becoming trapped within a negative vision of their skin colour. Are White people conscious of this sense of security, of freedom, of being at home wherever they are? I always remind my two sons that, whether they're in France or the US, they must never forget the colour of their skin. I tell them: 'You are perceived as Blacks, not as Whites.' This fills me with a deep sadness but there is no escaping that, sometimes, it's a matter of life and death.

If I am ever to escape the colour of my skin, for it to become an insignificant physical detail, then White people must also escape the colour of *their* skin. But how can this be achieved? Paradoxically, they must begin by acknowledging their colour and the system it demands they perpetuate.

One evening, I decided to call my childhood friend Pierre.

> 'Hi Pierre? How're things?'
> 'Hi Lilian. I'm fine, and you?'
> 'Listen, can I ask you a question?'
> 'Go ahead.'
> 'Pierre, do you feel White?'

I could sense his hesitation at the other end of the line.

'What? I don't understand you.'

'Pierre, would you agree that I'm Black?'

'Well, yeah.'

'If I'm Black, then what are you?'

'Well... I'm normal.'

I began to laugh. 'You're normal? So, does that mean I'm not normal?'

'No, that's not what I mean... don't you understand?'

Pierre's odd, spontaneous reply helped me to put my finger on something fundamental and profoundly rooted in society: even if you're an exceptional human being, a blood brother, you might, without even realising, be hiding behind the White mask of normality. Those who enjoy a dominant position in society feel so entitled – always at the heart of things, never feeling out of place – that they believe themselves to be the norm. This is the position White people find themselves in, the same position as men in relation to women.

Women know perfectly well that they're women, that they belong to a gender that has historically been dominated by men who have decided what they can and can't do. How much time and energy will it take for men to recognise that they too are trapped within a system of domination, trapped within their own masculinity and all the obligations that this entails? Similarly, I have known since the age of nine – when I arrived in Paris after leaving Guadeloupe, in the French Caribbean – what it means to be perceived as Black, and I know that it's not a trivial matter. Thinking White has made me wear a mask of Blackness.

But White people, who make up the majority, would like to live 'colour-free': and they would really rather not ask difficult questions about the meaning of this colour. Does this situation suit them? Are they afraid of confronting reality? As the Black British journalist, Reni Eddo-Lodge, has rightly said: 'Their skin colour is the norm and all others deviate from it'.[1] *To be Black is to not*

1 Reni Eddo-Lodge, *Why I'm No Longer Talking to White People about Race* (London: Bloomsbury, 2018), p.ix.

be White. On the other hand, to be White is not something to be questioned. Eddo-Lodge calls this 'white denial':[1] as for White people, their Whiteness is a simple fact, a basic reality with no particular meaning, so why question something that benefits them?

Academics in the social sciences, particularly in English-speaking countries, have increasingly opened up a field called 'whiteness studies' to attempt to answer some of these questions: what does it mean to Whites, who represent just 16.6% of the world's population, to enjoy a dominant position in relation to non-Whites, both within their own countries and in international relations? How has the form taken by this domination changed over the centuries? My country, France, has been reluctant to engage meaningfully with these questions. France wants to remove the word 'race' from its constitution, but what would that achieve? For I believe that there's a profound sense of racial belonging in my country.

In this book, I want to take my own observations, reflections and questions and explore them in the light of the writings of those who have sought to understand the White condition. For example, Reni Eddo-Lodge states that: 'I am only acutely aware of race because I've been rigorously marked out as different by the world I know'.[2] And she later bemoans the fact that: 'My blackness has been politicised against my will'.[3] I want White people to understand that their skin colour is a political construct. And I insist on this point: no one is born White. Whiteness happens *to them*, whether they like it or not, but unlike for non-Whites it acts in their favour.

This book will focus on neglected, sometimes actively dismissed areas of history, which have in fact contributed to the construction of White identity. The aim is not to denounce racism in a general sense. It won't point out racism in those places where we usually expect to find it, in the outrageous words and actions of extremist parties, but in the everyday aspects of our societies. The French philosopher Étienne Balibar has written of a 'racism without races' to describe the continued existence of discriminatory behaviour and practices in a modern society where it should be common knowledge by now that the concept of separate human races has no basis in scientific

---

1 Eddo-Lodge, *Why I'm No Longer Talking*, p. 10.

2 Eddo-Lodge, *Why I'm No Longer Talking*, p. xvi.

3 Eddo-Lodge, *Why I'm No Longer Talking*, p. 81.

fact.[1] The everyday racism to which non-Whites are subjected in Western societies is made up of a whole series of small acts, some well known, others less so, and some not at all: the ignorance of certain facts means they are never spoken about publicly, which is to the advantage of *some* individuals. When these small acts are taken as a whole, they comprise a set of habits. It's these habits that have led Whites to keep non-Whites below them in the pecking order. Originally, this was done in a very open fashion, but in recent decades it has become more subtle, in the same way that men have maintained their dominance over women.

We will discover in later chapters that White thinking is not exclusively the product of White people. Non-Whites have also internalised this tendency to 'think White'. As Frantz Fanon famously wrote, the *White mask* can be worn just as readily by non-Whites as by Whites.[2] Thinking White is not a question of skin colour. It's a way of being in the world that has existed since the Crusades, at least. The Franco-Colombian essayist and activist Rosa Amelia Plumelle-Uribe writes that:

> The conquest of America and its colonisation profoundly altered relationships between Europeans and other peoples. They soon bridged the gap between difference and superiority. […] [F]or centuries, there was ideological justification and cultural acceptance of the idea that these 'inferior' beings could be exploited at will, treated as objects and even removed if necessary. The material and psychological benefits deriving from being part of the superior group worked in favour of the acceptance of these givens that over the centuries became deep-seated cultural elements of Western civilisation.[3]

I would like this book to serve as an opportunity for dialogue. No bigotry, no hatred, no bad faith, all of which prevent a genuine

1 Étienne Balibar, 'La construction du racisme', *Actuel Marx*, 38.2 (2005), pp. 11–28.

2 Frantz Fanon, *Black Skin, White Masks*, trans. by Richard Philcox (London: Penguin, 2021 [1952]).

3 Rosa Amelia Plumelle-Uribe, *White Ferocity: The Genocides of Non-Whites and Non-Aryans from 1492 to Date*, trans. by Virginia Popper (Dakar: CODESRIA, 2020), pp. 97–98.

exchange of ideas. I have absolutely no desire to set one group against another. What I want is for all people of good will to acknowledge a simple fact. Namely, that there exists a system – economic, cultural and social – that has a devastating effect not only on non-Whites but on White people themselves. If we want to change our reality, then we have to begin by speaking the same language. We have to be aware of our own position within society. To acknowledge that I'm a man, I'm a woman, I'm Black, I'm White, I'm mixed race, I'm Catholic, I'm Muslim, I'm Jewish, I'm an atheist, etc., is the first step towards understanding that we can't speak in an entirely objective way about the so-called 'discovery' of the Americas, or slavery, or colonisation, or racism, or globalisation. We all engage with the past through the prism of extremely powerful historical and cultural forces that have shaped us in different ways. I will explore these different prisms and attempt to understand how they work. What's your assumed historical identity? What role does this assumed identity oblige you to take on today? I'm not making accusations, these are just questions. And these questions only ask one thing of us all: that we open our eyes to certain facts. State-sponsored racism no longer exists. But the fact that it did exist in my country and others for more than 250 years has shaped the reality we live in today. I dream of the day when we can show the maturity needed to resist the legacies of the past so that our thinking is no longer dictated by the colour of our skin. I dream that we can face up to what White economic thinking has done to humanity and our burned-out planet.

Don't confuse this book with the work of a 'spokesperson'. A White person can take on the universal mantle of the humanist, who speaks on behalf of humankind. A non-White person is typically cast as a spokesperson for their community. My aim in this book is to analyse the construction of a form of a dominant White thinking over the past few centuries. To do that, we need to trace that history, as we can't understand or solve the problems of the present without engaging with the long historical path that led us to where we are today. An understanding of history can shine a light on the true nature of racism. More importantly, it can provide us with the tools to construct a shared future.

Deep down, what is the purpose of racism? Who really benefits from it? Can we speak about racism without tackling the relationship between humankind and the other species that we share this planet with?

1

HISTORY

1. IN THE REALM OF OUR IMAGINATIONS

Take a look at the map at the start of this book.

No, it's not upside down. The traditional world map that we're all so familiar with is very different, so it's no surprise if you're confused. If you always look at something from the same angle, it's easy to forget that this isn't the only way of looking at it. The Earth is round like a football, so there's no top, no bottom, no upside down nor right side up. If you want to create a two-dimensional version of a sphere (aka the Earth), you can't be entirely faithful to reality: even if you include every island and don't forget a single sea, what you produce is just a representation. It highlights some parts, moves some to the centre and pushes others to the margins.

On the traditional map that all Europeans know, the Mercator projection, the continents are all out of proportion. Gerardus Mercator was a Flemish cartographer and geographer in the sixteenth century. His map was designed to support maritime trade. What mattered to him was the size of the oceans, not the continents. On the traditional maps that we still use today, Europe is always placed at the top and in a central position. Is that a coincidence? Europe is represented as far larger than it is in reality, as is North America; by contrast, the African continent is shrunk so much that it appears smaller than Russia. Does this matter? South America has been shrunk too. It seems incredible to me that the way in which most people view the world is biased without them even realising. On the map in this book, we have placed Africa at the centre as a reminder that, no matter where we are in the world today, we are all migrants who originally hailed from Africa. This map invites us to question our habits: to challenge the way in which we represent the world and the hierarchies that shape our worldview. If we respect the true proportions of the continents, maybe we can start to ask ourselves some searching questions: not least, why did a continent as small as Europe set out to colonise the world?

This belief in our own self-importance is a long-held, deep-seated conviction in the West. This discourse was patiently constructed over centuries and it owes nothing to chance. You can see many similarities in the way that China has, since 2002, reimagined mapmaking practices:[1] placing your own culture at the centre, isn't that what all 'imperial' visions seek to do?

History as understood by the West and Christianity places White people at the centre of the world. This history has been taught in schools, propagated through public debate, and sown in our collective unconscious. It tells its story solely from the Western perspective. It neglects some elements of the past and omits others. It promotes and maintains the idea that thinking White is the global norm. It is vital that we learn to show awareness that we always speak from a particular perspective, which we sincerely believe to be truthful. We forget though that it is just one perspective, which gives voice to a certain vision of the world marked by its own specific delusions, fears and social conditioning.

Have you ever heard of the word *agnotology*? It literally means the 'science of ignorance' (from the Greek *agnosia*, 'ignorance'). It was coined in 1992 by the historian Robert N. Proctor to describe 'the cultural production of ignorance' (a concept he subsequently

---

1 See Hao Xiaoguang's map (www.hxgmap.com).

developed with Londa Schiebinger in a landmark volume).[1] You might not be aware of this, but some institutions invest a lot of money and effort so that the public remains ignorant about certain facts. For example, multinational tobacco and sugar companies have spent and continue to spend millions of dollars to mislead the general public about the devastating effects of their products on public health. They have confused the debate by producing biased scientific studies in order to sow doubt. Indeed, 'manufacturing doubt' is a deliberate policy pursued by lobbyists for certain industries who attempt to make reality appear so complex that the ordinary citizen becomes lost ('these stories are too complicated to understand') and is blinded to the truth, while the multinationals bank the profits.[2]

In recent years, a lot has been written and spoken about *fake news*, as though this were something entirely new. The nonsense that clogs up social media often has a very clear target (Jews, Muslims, immigration, the European ideal) and, equally, historical facts have for centuries been hijacked, twisted and filtered with the aim of defending certain points of view and, thus, certain interests. We know that history can bring enlightenment. Knowledge of the past can allow us to understand our present and to construct a better future. But history can also serve as a powerful tool, used by the State to promote a sanitised version of the past that glosses over certain harsh realities (now that's *agnotological* work). At a certain point in their history, all societies produce a set of ideas and stories about their past that are deemed obvious, visions that can be traced back to mythical origins. These are the grand narratives that we tell ourselves and none of them is objective. It's always useful to discover what has been preserved, what has been redacted, and why, in these grand narratives.

Of course, research on this subject already exists. If you read serious historical works that aren't designed to contribute to these grand narratives and thus escape their pitfalls, then you can begin to see things more clearly. You can find them in bookshops and libraries, and they offer analysis of various realities, some of which you've never even heard of. These books help you understand that

---

1 Robert N. Proctor & Londa Schiebinger (eds), *Agnotology: The Making and Unmaking of Ignorance* (Stanford University Press, 2008).

2 Stéphane Horel, *Lobbytomie: comment les lobbies empoisonneront nos vies et la démocratie* (Paris: La Découverte, 2018).

the accepted truths of one era can be revealed as myths in the next. But most people don't read these academic studies. Their insights aren't included in schoolbooks or covered in the media. When you think about it, are many of the things taught in school not just the truth as perceived in that specific country? It's not by chance that these grand narratives are created, then propagated. They defend the interests of the dominant class and the ideas that underpin White thinking. This poison slowly works its way through society, persuading us to see others as enemies and presenting injustice as inevitable.

There have always been free thinkers, those who show intellectual integrity. But few are those prepared to dispute, to question, to challenge the consensus. Their warnings are not always heeded. They are often persecuted, just like those who sound the alarm on various topics today. Each era constructs a way of thinking in which certain ideas are deemed acceptable while others are rejected. There are 'just' wars and illegal wars; some countries contribute to a struggle on behalf of the 'values of democracy' or 'civilisation', while others belong to the infamous 'axis of evil'. Remember Saddam Hussein's alleged 'weapons of mass destruction', which led to the war in Iraq in 2003. Don't get me wrong, I'm not claiming that the 'enemies of the West' are always right. Their *fake news* and their myths are often just as deceitful and manipulative as those produced by thinking White. But these beliefs or this propaganda are produced in specific circumstances and are fairly young in ideological terms, unlike White thinking, which has constructed an entire worldview over five centuries. How are dominant discourses created? What is their purpose? And why is it crucial that we maintain a critical distance in relation to them? As Oscar Wilde's Dorian Gray declares, history shows that the powerful act 'in hypocrisy' and '[wear] the mask of goodness'.[1]

Before we examine some key moments in our history and the myths that surround them, I would like to anticipate a criticism that I'm sure some people will level at me. In the following pages, I'm not looking to put certain historical figures on trial. I'm fully aware of how anachronistic it would be to expect that Aristotle,

---

1 Oscar Wilde, *The Picture of Dorian Gray* (1890), in Oscar Wilde, *Plays, Prose Writings and Poems* (London: Everyman, 1967), p. 253.

or great French figures such as the eighteenth-century political philosopher Montesquieu, or the nineteenth-century politician Jules Ferry, should think like people from our era. I'll focus on what they wrote in order to trace the violence and injustice that it reveals not only for people of their era but also as a legacy for us today. If someone justifies slavery or colonialism, it's not simply a question of formulating a few abstract ideas. You're effectively justifying the cruelty and humiliation heaped upon human beings. I will try, whenever possible, to recall those who sought to challenge the dominant ideas of their era. There was another path open to those who used arguments normalising violence, which is why I choose to criticise them.

Right at the heart of the era of the Atlantic slave trade, when Montesquieu wrote that 'Our colonies in the Antilles are magnificent',[1] or when the German philosopher Immanuel Kant stated that 'Humanity exists in its greatest perfection in the white race',[2] they were steering the thinking of their times in a certain direction. Now, Montesquieu and Kant may well have sincerely believed in what they wrote and the direction of travel they promoted, but I can't help noticing that their sincere beliefs happen to coincide with some of the dominant economic and ideological interests of their eras. And not just any old interests. We need to be aware that, as privileged, White Europeans (it goes without saying that White thinking was not made by or for the European peasantry), Montesquieu and Kant were positioning themselves at the top of a scale of historical and moral values. We also need to assess just how much their vision permeated their society, as well as future generations of schoolchildren, students and adults. It's not what Montesquieu and Kant should have thought that matters here. What I want to underline here is the need not to lose sight of the fact that they contributed to the development of a set of ideas that justified violence and the systematic exploitation of human beings.

History is an intellectual building block; it's one of the social sciences that allow us to construct our understanding of the

---

1 Cited in Louis Sala-Molins, *Le Code Noir ou le calvaire de Canaan* (Paris: PUF, 2015, 12th edition [1987]), p. xi.

2 Cited in Emmanuel Chukwudi Eza (ed.), *Postcolonial African Philosophy: A Critical Reader* (Oxford: Blackwell, 1997), p. 118.

present. When this construction material is defective, the entire story that we build with it is incomplete, flawed, shocking even. History should force us to confront this fundamental question: what is the position from which we are speaking? Do we have the courage to fully take on board the fact that we all approach history from a specific point of view? Are we able to accept that this will decentre our worldview? What would happen if we decided no longer to think White, just like those historians who have approached their subject from the viewpoint of the working classes rather than the monarchy, or from the viewpoint of women rather than through the lens of the 'great men' of history? Greater and cleverer people than me have already begun this task. For example, at the end of the 1990s, the Indian economist Sanjay Subrahmanyam told the story of Vasco da Gama from the point of view of the African sultans, the Mamelukes and the Indians that he encountered.[1] Needless to say, this change of perspective turns our understanding of this story on its head. Amin Maalouf's book about the Crusades, as perceived by the Arab world, is another example.[2]

Subrahmanyam's appropriately named concept of 'connected history' involves the multiplication of viewpoints, instead of seeing everything through the lens of the West. We can see a similar approach at work in the writings of the political scientist Louis Sala-Molins: 'I try to understand this whole tragedy [slavery], not by slipping into the smooth, oiled skin of the intellectual in Paris, Geneva or Bordeaux [...] but rather by slipping into the flayed skin and mutilated body of the black slave in the Caribbean.'[3]

Unfortunately, this approach is still often labelled as dissident or marginal, the preserve of a few scholars with family backgrounds directly connected to these troubled histories. This state of affairs isn't good enough. We should be taught history in a way that arms us against the manipulation of history. This history should allow us to approach the past as human beings and not enclose us within our perceived identity, skin colour or nationality.

---

1 Sanjay Subrahmanyam, *The Career and Legend of Vasco da Gama* (Cambridge: Cambridge University Press, 1997).

2 Amin Maalouf, *The Crusades through Arab Eyes* (NY: Al Saqi Books, 1984).

3 *Le Code Noir ou le calvaire de Canaan*, p. x

2. FAKING ANTIQUITY

From the Renaissance onwards, European countries and from a later period, the West more widely, identified with the classical civilisation of Greece and Rome. Then they imposed this vision of their 'origins' on the whole world. The French historian Serge Gruzinski explains: 'Much of the world still writes the past in the same way, the European way. For example, in a Japanese textbook, the teaching of history begins with the Egyptians, just like in Europe!'[1] The aim of all this is firstly to affirm that the Greeks and the Romans form the basis of civilisation, and secondly to include Egypt as part of the White world. As a result, Europe and the West are incapable of seeing ancient Asian, American or African civilisations as foundational in the creation of 'who we are today'.

OK, so the Mayans or the Babylonians of Mesopotamia might be peoples that we recall today, and they might even be fascinating to some. But they are always held at one remove from 'the origins of humanity'. They are 'exotic' civilisations and they should stay that way. The people of these civilisations are not *our* ancestors. You'd be hard pressed to claim that Greeks and Romans look like their Northern European counterparts. But that's precisely what the West has done. The American historian Nell Irvin Painter has shown the ways in which the West has whitewashed Antiquity, transforming the 'classics into a lily-white field complete with pictures of blond ancient Greeks'.[2] If you think White, then Africa has no Antiquity. First of all because it's assumed that Egypt is 'White', forgetting that it is part of the African continent. As I wrote in *My Black Stars*: 'Until the 1950s and 1960s, Western, European, and Arab historians always perceived ancient Egypt as integral to their own societies, but not as part of Africa itself. As a result, ancient Egypt was set apart from black Africa.'[3] The second reason is that we are ignorant of key elements of this history: who knows about the Kingdom of Kerma in the south of Ancient Egypt? Who knows the story of the great African empires of Ghana, Songhai or

1 'L'Europe a construit sa domination en écrivant l'histoire des autres', *BiblioObs. com*, 22 December 2017.

2 Nell Irvin Painter, *The History of White People* (NY & London: W.W. Norton & Company, 2010), p.x.

3 Lilian Thuram, *My Black Stars: from Lucy to Barack Obama*, trans. by Laurent Dubois (Liverpool: Liverpool University Press, 2021), p. 12.

Benin? It is this ignorance that saw a French President, Nicolas Sarkozy, declare that 'the tragedy of Africa is that the African *has not fully entered into history*'.[1] This sentence is typical of the process that leads to thinking White. It was a statement made in Africa by a powerful man defending the West's interests and underlines the sense of superiority that White people are supposed to feel in relation to Black people.

Whether we like it or not, we are beginning to see how thinking White functions. If you walk into any museum and look closely at the artefacts from Egypt, it's immediately obvious that they're African. It takes particularly bad faith to argue that Egypt was not an African civilisation. Already at the end of the eighteenth century, right in the middle of the era of the slave trade, the French writer Volney stood alone amongst his peers and refused to think White, affirming that:

> the ancient Egyptians were true Negroes of the same type as all native-born Africans. That being so, we can see how their blood, mixed for several centuries with that of the Greeks and Romans, must have lost the intensity of its original colour, while retaining nonetheless the imprint of its original mould. [...] Just think [...] that this race of Black men, today our slave and the object of our scorn, is the very race to which we owe our arts, sciences, and even the use of speech! Just imagine, finally, that it is in the midst of people who call themselves the greatest friends of liberty and humanity that one has approved the most barbarous slavery, and questioned whether Black men have the same kind of intelligence as whites![2]

When the Senegalese anthropologist Cheikh Anta Diop published *Nations Nègres et culture* (*Negro Nations and Culture*) in 1954,

---

1 'Le discours de Dakar de Nicolas Sarkozy' [Nicolas Sarkozy's Dakar Speech], *Le Monde*, 9 November 2007 [my italics].] For the unofficial English translation of Sarkozy's speech, see: https://www.africaresource.com/essays-a-reviews/essays-a-discussions/437-the-unofficial-english-translation-of-sarkozys-speech?start=1.

2 Constantin François de Chassebœuf, comte de Volney, *Travels through Syria and Egypt in the Years 1783, 1784 and 1785*, Vol. 1 (London: G.G.J. and J. Robinson, 1787), pp. 80–83.

it turned Egyptology on its head, but still today in the collective unconscious, Egypt is mostly seen as White.

Our history still always begins with Greek and Roman Antiquity: in Athens and Rome there were great thinkers, people who invented an entire civilisation and organised society in pioneering ways. The 'genius' of this version of Antiquity is repeatedly proclaimed with the objective of demonstrating that, uniquely amongst all ancient civilisations, it was White people's ancestors who were the most advanced and, it goes without saying, they remain so today.

This reminds me of the time I was invited to speak at a conference at Harvard. A Greek delegate, who seemed very proud of his origins, told us that his country had, 'a long time ago, invented democracy'. The high point of the celebrated Athenian democracy, which began in the sixth century BCE, came 100 years later in what has become known as the 'Age of Pericles'. But who enjoyed the benefits of this democracy? A handful of male citizens. Women and slaves were entirely excluded. In other words, most of the Greek population.

Recently, I read that slavery in Ancient Greece was widely accepted. And none of the great schools of philosophy, neither the Stoics nor the Platonists nor any great Athenian thinker declared that servitude was a vile practice. But history is always written based on the available sources. Let's be clear on this: nobody asked the slaves what they thought of slavery! But just because nobody in Antiquity thought to ask the slaves their opinion, we can't claim, over 2,000 years later, that they quietly accepted their fate! Every single day, the oppressed give voice to their oppression... it's just that the oppressor doesn't listen. And when the oppressed are given the choice, they don't hesitate for a second to free themselves from bondage.

We all know the saying: history is always written by the winners. This is a basic fact that we must never lose sight of when dealing with slavery and colonisation. In both cases, the dominant voice, the one that has survived down to today (from newspapers, intellectuals, institutions), gives the impression that these practices were never or hardly ever questioned. As for the opinions of the figure that the Indian intellectual Gayatri Chakravorty Spivak calls the 'subaltern',[1] she is at best ignored, but at worst crushed under the weight of the violence of the past.

For the free men of ancient Greece – just like for the average American or many Europeans today – there was no doubt about it: their country was the centre of the world. Maps, as ever, tell us a lot about perceptions at that time. Those from that era show Greece at the centre, positioned as a land of ideal climate: neither too hot nor too cold, neither too dry nor too wet. Aristotle wrote that: 'the Hellenic race, which is situated between [extremes], is likewise intermediate in character, being high-spirited and intelligent. Hence it continues free.'[2] Climate was a very important factor:

> Mostly, Greek scholars focused on climate to explain human difference. Humors arising from each climate's relative humidity or aridness explained a people's temperament.[3]
>
> For Hippocrates, topology and water determine body type, leading to differences between peoples of bracing, high terrain and those in low-lying meadows. Lowlanders he posited as broad, fleshy, and black haired [...] People living where the water stands stagnant 'must show protruding bellies and enlarged spleens'.[4]

There's an important point to highlight here. For most people today, slavery is something that affected Black people. But, in ancient times, slavery wasn't associated with a specific group. The very notion of 'race', Black or White, which still seems so obvious to those obsessed with skin colour, was meaningless during Antiquity. There were Black slaves in Athens, but as the philosopher and

1 Gayatri Chakravorty Spivak, 'Can the Subaltern Speak?', in *Marxism and the Interpretation of Culture*, ed. by Cary Nelson and Lawrence Grossberg (Urbana & Chicago: University of Illinois Press, 1988), pp. 271–313.

2 Aristotle, *Politics*, trans. by Benjamin Jowett (Kitchener, Ontario: Batoche Books, 1999), p. 162.

3 Painter, *The History of White People*, p. 5.

4 Painter, *The History of White People*, p. 9. This quote is from Hippocrates, 'Airs, Waters, Places', part 23, in *Hippocrates with an English Translation by W.H.S Jones*, vol. 1 (Cambridge, MA: Harvard University Press, 1923), p. 24.

historian Christian Delacampagne has argued: 'when they are judged by others, it is their social status, not the colour of their skin that is responsible. Indeed, neither the Greeks nor the Romans criticised Blacks because of their blackness.'[1] In Rome, mixed-race marriages were relatively common in fact. And let us not forget that Ancient Greece was home to major Black intellectuals, such as Aesop.

Aristotle wrote these telling words about skin colour: 'That is why, neither the whiteness of man nor his blackness constitute specific differences, and there is no specific difference between a black man and a white man, even if both were to be given different names [...] it is thus entirely by accident that man is white.'[2] Fine words but they didn't mean that Aristotle was against slavery, far from it indeed. For he considered slavery the most natural thing in the world, entirely justified by the very nature of the slaves themselves. As he wrote in his *Politics*: 'It is clear, then, that some men are by nature free, and others slaves, and that for the latter slavery is both expedient and right.'[3] As we shall see, this claim has been repeated down through history and it survives to this day. It casts oppression as natural, as the oppressed are deemed to be naturally inferior. In Greek ceramics, the slaves' inferiority is always made clearly visible. The message for the free men and women of Ancient Greece is clear: 'they are not like us'.

Distorting the vision of the Other made exploitation easier: they're strange, crazy, abject. From the fourth century BCE, the Greeks began to do this more systematically. Alexander the Great conquered Asia Minor, beginning with Anatolia (today's Turkey), then pushed into Syria, Egypt and Mesopotamia, driving all the way along the Indus River (into today's Pakistan and India). The Greeks imposed their culture on the cities they conquered, what they called *Hellenisation*. We duly learned all this in school. Alexander is one of these great triumphal figures on horseback onto whom all sorts of fantasies and desires are projected. What's never spoken about is what drove this 'conquest of Asia', which had been theorised well before Alexander. Economic factors provided the ulterior motive

1 Christian Delacampagne, *Une histoire du racisme* (Paris: Le Livre de Poche, 2000).

2 Delacampagne, *Une histoire du racisme*.

3 Aristotle, *Politics*, p. 9.

and propaganda provided the cover. Christian Delacampagne writes that, in the fourth century BCE:

> the truth of the matter is that Athens was, at that particular time, in a state of social gridlock: the middle classes were decimated [...] there was no more free land to distribute to the tens of thousands of mercenaries that the end of the war [the Peloponnesian War in the fifth century BCE] had made idle. This led to the idea of exporting the crisis by setting out to conquer Persia – an idea that was slowly made acceptable in speeches by orators who endeavoured to present Asia as not only different to Europe but inhabited by inferior beings.[1]

Delacampagne refers to this period as the era of 'contempt and hatred', which persuaded the Greek people that it was a good idea to go off and colonise their neighbours near and far. It'd be a good idea to teach this period to schoolchildren today so that they can learn just how dangerous and effective it is when groups are demonised. It's propaganda that provides the justification for violent attacks on other peoples.

In particular, we need schoolchildren to understand that it's thinking White in relation to Greek history that has led us to interpret this story in the ways we do. Political choices are recast as the advance of civilisation, which reinforces the idea of White superiority. This has been a constant throughout history. And, unfortunately, it remains the case today.

3. WHO DISCOVERED AMERICA?

Before you read any further, ask yourself this question: whenever Christopher Columbus's discovery of America is mentioned, do you imagine yourself on the boat with him or on the beach with the Amerindians?

We all learned the same thing in school: Christopher Columbus discovered America on 12 October 1492. And this 'discovery' leads

1 Delacampagne, *Une histoire du racisme*.

to the assumption that the history of this continent only began with the arrival of the White man. We don't tell schoolchildren that, before Columbus's arrival, the Americas were already inhabited by millions of people whose ancestors had been there for 15,000 years. We don't tell them that there existed in the Americas a mosaic of peoples, languages, cultures, empires and powerful cities, often richer and vaster than those in Europe. A melting pot of brilliant, sophisticated civilisations that were concerned about the environment, the Americas were not the undeveloped virgin continent that an official version of history has led us to believe.[1] And we definitely don't tell them that sixteenth-century Europeans automatically assumed themselves to be superior to the Amerindians. Certain Spanish theorists, such as Juan Ginés de Sepúlveda, argued that Spain had a legitimate right to invade the Americas.[2] Columbus arrived in the 'New World' and took possession of both the land and the people, as though they were just there for the taking.

The native population had limited use to him. At most, they could provide local information on where to find gold, precious stones and other natural resources, while, later on, they would become a source of free labour, exploited so that Europe could grow rich. But did these *natives* have a conscience or a soul? It would seem not. Columbus's journals reveal his complete inability to imagine that the Amerindians might have followed their own religion: 'I am of opinion that they would very readily become Christians, as they appear to have no religion.'[3] Christian Delacampagne rightly asks: 'As Columbus did not speak a word of any Amerindian language, how did he reach this conclusion so quickly?'[4] The answer is simple and it remains relevant today. White thinking – which enjoyed one of its high points during the long Catholic hegemony of the fifteenth and sixteenth centuries – takes itself for granted and makes other cultures simply vanish. It's what I call the 'culture of erasure'.

Now, some people will say, Columbus was a sailor, a man of the fifteenth and sixteenth centuries, and you can't criticise him

---

1 See Charles C. Mann, *1491: New Revelations of the Americas before Columbus* (NY: Vintage, 2006).

2 Delacampagne, *Une histoire du racisme*.

3 Christopher Columbus, *Journal*, 12 October 1492:
https://sourcebooks.fordham.edu/source/columbus1.asp.

4 Delacampagne, *Une histoire du racisme*.

for sharing the prejudices of his era. Well, I think you can criticise him because those prejudices weren't shared by everyone. In fact, the vast majority of Europeans would have known next to nothing about the 'New World'. But there were some who opposed the new racial hierarchies that were emerging. The Dominican missionary Bartolomé de Las Casas, a contemporary of Columbus, condemned the savagery unleashed on the Amerindians because he saw them primarily as human beings. Francisco de Vitoria, a professor at the University of Salamanca around the same time, wrote in his book, *Relectiones theologicae*, about the 'natural right' of Amerindians to live on their own land, a right far more important than the commercial imperatives of European merchants. And Francisco de Vitoria wasn't just opposed to the enslavement of the Amerindians; he argued that international relations as a whole should not be based solely on the use of force, but should be bound by moral considerations.[1]

If we're going to talk about anachronism, then I'd like to mention a book published in France, in 2011, by Marie-France Schmidt, a work of popular history that claims to be a 'biography' of Columbus. According to the author, Genoa's most famous son may have been a staunch advocate of colonisation and the enslavement of the Amerindian population; he may also have violently quelled Amerindian revolts. But what did that stuff matter when weighed against his amazing 'adventures'?[2] She calls Columbus 'the Discoverer' (yes, with a capital D), rendering the native populations all but invisible, and she spends over 300 pages praising his 'powerful and fierce willpower' and even his 'true genius'.

For Schmidt, the pre-existing civilisations in the Americas are totally unimportant: if Europe hadn't colonised the Americas, nothing important ever would have happened there. Detailing how Columbus unilaterally attributed new, Christianised names to the islands where he landed, she describes the process as 'moving, because it signifies the entry of these lands [...] into History and Geography'. When you think White, it's obvious that the Amerindians had yet to enter History. Whenever Columbus's men

---

1 Delacampagne, *Une histoire du racisme*.

2 Marie-France Schmidt, *Christophe Colomb* (Paris: Gallimard, 2011). The following quotes are all taken from this work.

imprison or kill Amerindians, it's described as an 'unfortunate incident'. When they kidnap indigenous women, they have just 'gone too far'. But when the Amerindians meet violence with violence, it's presented as a 'tragedy' or a 'massacre'. Because for Marie-France Schmidt, Columbus and his men are the good guys and the Amerindian rebels are the bad guys. She talks about 'Caonabo, the felon' (a 'felon' is no less than a traitor) or the terrible Quiban who dared to revolt against the Spanish and declares: 'Luckily, [the Amerindian] chief's plan was uncovered'.

It's perfectly understandable that the iron-willed Columbus was in favour of slavery: 'Columbus had noted that the Indians were physically robust and generally unarmed and he thus somewhat naively deduced that he could easily control and force them to work for him.' And what of Queen Isabella's opposition to slavery? Schmidt writes that: 'Columbus was on the ground and could see for himself that these Spanish lands would never prosper [...] without a servile workforce'. Equally, when she considers Las Casas's criticism of the violence committed against the Amerindians, she concludes that: 'Las Casas judges from afar, in the way of all those who like to lecture others, but Columbus is on the ground and his sole option is to quell all forms of opposition or else there would be anarchy'.

To further support her argument, she cites the change of heart by Diego and Fernando Columbus, who had accompanied their father on his expeditions. Initially, they 'adjudge their father too authoritarian [but] soon understand that he is right'. I just want to remind you here that this book was published in 2011 and not in the middle of the nineteenth century! If a French high-school student is asked to write an essay on the so-called discoverer of America, this is the type of narrative they're likely to encounter. It was all an exhilarating adventure, marred only by a few local rebellions that, of course, had to be put down. The most the author will admit is that Columbus was quite literally obsessed with gold and wealth, 'a character trait that makes him unsympathetic'.

As early as 1494, just two years after the first European encounter with these new lands, the Treaty of Tordesillas had awarded them to Spain and Portugal. When European colonisation began, the system of *encomienda* positioned the conquistadors as the obvious masters of the Amerindians. It was in the natural order of things.

In order to avoid criticism, colonisation needed a convincing story to tell about its actions. So the Amerindians were deemed inferior in order to make it easier to plunder them. Rosa Amelia Plumelle-Uribe writes that:

> [... T]he language of the group that rules as absolute master pitilessly heaps every failing upon those it annihilates. [...] There can be no question of crediting those you must crush or those you are already in the process of annihilating with the noblest qualities and the most highly developed intelligence. It is essential to do the reverse, for that is how relations of subordination are established.[1]

In particular, she cites the words of Thomas Ortiz, a sixteenth-century Dominican bishop who demonised Amerindians in a speech to the Council of the Indies:

> On the mainland they eat human flesh. They are more given to sodomy than any other nation. There is no justice among them. They go naked. They have no respect either for love or for virginity. They are stupid and silly. They have no respect for truth save when it is to their advantage. They are unstable [...] They are brutal [...] Punishments have no effect upon them [...] They eat fleas, spiders and worms raw [...] They exercise none of the human arts or industries [...] The older they get, the worse they become [...] I may therefore affirm that God has never created a race more full of vice and composed without the least mixture of kindness or culture.[2]

Culture played very little part in these developments. We need to remember that the colonisation of the Americas was primarily driven by economic greed. In 1537, Pope Paul III wrote in his

---

1 Plumelle-Uribe, *White Ferocity*, p. 21.

2 Plumelle-Uribe, *White Ferocity*, p. 22. Plumelle-Uribe's source is Tzvetan Todorov, *The Conquest of America: The Question of the Other* (Norman, OK: Oklahoma University Press, 1999), pp. 150–51.

papal bull, *Sublimis Deus*, that Amerindians were human, which meant they could not be enslaved but that did not prevent the colonisation of their lands. This didn't mean that the indigenous peoples of the Americas would be spared. Far from it indeed, as historians estimate that around 90% of them were exterminated within a century.[1] White thinking would lead us to believe that this was solely because of the flu, smallpox and other infections carried to the Americas by the conquistadors. And in the process make us forget about the inhuman treatment meted out to them. Is any schoolchild today taught the staggering fact that more than 10% of the world's population, more than 50 million human beings,[2] were exterminated by European colonisers at the beginning of this period that the White world calls the Renaissance?

Alongside this massacre, the conquistadors stole, destroyed, raped the cultures of the peoples they conquered: Aztecs, Mayans, Incas and many others. This is the culture of erasure at work. It's not enough to impose new norms and beliefs. It erases that which came before, as the old culture is ridiculed and made to appear backward, old-fashioned. The sense of feeling rooted in a culture is a powerful weapon that allows an oppressed people to stand tall, to maintain a sense of identity, to resist. If you attack that sense of belonging, then you can break a people, make them docile.

Serge Gruzinski is one of the leading French historians of the colonisation of the Americas. He has explained how the first colonisers in the sixteenth century were able to manipulate language in order to justify their project:

> In order to dominate these previously unknown societies, the Spanish did not limit themselves to military conquest. They also decided to invent the past of the indigenous population. They laid the foundations for their domination by writing

---

1 In March 2019, a study led by four scholars at University College London, Alexander Koch, Chris Brierly, Mark M. Maslin and Simon L. Lewis, estimated that the population of the Americas stood at 60 million in 1500. By 1600, this had fallen to 6 million. 'Earth system impacts of the European arrival and Great Dying in the Americas after 1492', *Quatenary Science Reviews*, 207 (1 March 2019), pp. 13–36.

2 The figures vary from one study to another: the world population in 1500 is estimated at somewhere between 425 million and 540 million.

the history of others. [...] This involved symbolic and intellectual violence of an extreme kind. The imposition of an entirely new conceptual framework by Europeans meant the permanent colonisation of these peoples. They abolished their whole world. From that moment on, these peoples could only perceive themselves through a mirror held up to them by the West: they were obliged to imitate Europe.[1]

Fifty-eight years after Columbus had arrived in the Americas, the Holy Roman Emperor and King of Spain, Charles V, organised what would come to be known as the Valladolid Debate. The aim of the debate was to determine whether it was legitimate to force the Amerindians to convert to Christianity and to make them carry out forced labour on behalf of the Spanish. They weren't there to decide if the Amerindians had a soul. As I've already mentioned, *Sublimis Deus*, the Papal bull of 2 June 1537, had settled this question: 'We [...] consider [...] that the Indians are truly men [...] capable of understanding the Christian faith [...] and [...] are by no means to be deprived of their liberty'.[2] The 'Indians' had a soul but they would have to be baptised in order to 'save' them. Even that wouldn't prevent the conquistadors from mercilessly exploiting them.

The debate lasted for two and a half months (1550–51). The key figures were Juan Ginés de Sepúlveda and Bartolomé de Las Casas. Sepúlveda was in favour of the Spanish conquest. He claimed the Amerindians were cruel beings that engaged in human sacrifice. Only their conquest by the Spanish could save them from eternal damnation and spare the lives of their victims. But Las Casas drew the assembly's attention to the violence meted out to the Amerindians by the Spanish. And he explained that the practice of human sacrifice was part of a religious ritual. Charles V was receptive to the position defended by Las Casas, and he tried to bring an end to the violence against the Amerindians. In the midst of these debates, the conquistadors alighted on a suggestion that had

---

1 'L'Europe a construit sa domination en écrivant l'histoire des autres', *BibliObs*, 22 December 2017.

2 https://www.papalencyclicals.net/Paul03/p3subli.htm.

been made by Las Casas: the 'Indians' of the high plains weren't built for hard labour on the plantations, and he suggested the use of Africans instead. So it was that Europe increasingly turned to another continent and another 'human reservoir'. European exploration meant that the contours of Africa had by then become familiar. This would allow European merchants to continue to plunder the riches of the Americas, developing their predatory economic model. And thus a new and lucrative stage was reached in the evolution of White thinking: the African slave trade.

4. THE SLAVE TRADE

In the period from the fifteenth to the nineteenth century, 'between 12 and 13 million Africans were led on to European slave ships, heading for various destinations, and the average rate of death on board was around 15%. The number of victims in Africa is estimated at between four and five times the number of captives shipped across the Atlantic.'[1] That amounts to somewhere between 50 million and 65 million people. In 1500, Africa was home to 17% of the world's population. By 1900, that figure had fallen to 7%.[2] Such devastation. But it has been almost completely ignored. White thinking prefers to highlight its humanism. The 'triangular' trade (between Africa, the Americas and Europe) began around 1530. I won't try to summarise that vast human tragedy here, but later on I will talk about the *Code Noir*, the 'Black Code' that regulated slavery in the French colonies until its final abolition (for the second time!) in 1848.

I want to start by pointing out just how insistently White thinking associates 'slavery' with Black people. As though White people had never been forced into slavery. As though no one would have dared to insult them in this way. As though only Black people were capable of allowing such a fate to befall them. White slavery existed

1 Marcel Dorigny and Bernard Gainot, *Atlas des esclavages: de l'Antiquité à nos jours* (Paris: Autrement, 2013), p. 20; see also Olivier Pétré-Grenouilleau, *Les Traites négrières* (Paris: Gallimard, 2004).

2 Jean-Pierre Guengant, John F. May, 'L'Afrique subsaharienne dans la démographie mondiale', *Etudes: Revue de culture contemporaine*, 415.10 (2011), pp. 305–16.

until the nineteenth century, but there is no collective memory of this fact. Why is that so? It's strange, as the very word 'slave' is derived from 'Slav', for the peoples of Eastern Europe were often victims of slavery.

Nell Irvin Painter has reminded us that 'over more than a millennium, the vast story of Western slavery was primarily a white story':[1] 'If we are to understand the peopling of Europe with its great mixing of folk, we must take Vikings – those great movers of people – into account.'[2] Of course, they were displaced after they had been enslaved. Between the fifth and the ninth century, thousands of White Northern Europeans and Russians were kidnapped and traded by other White people. In the eleventh century, Dublin, the capital of Ireland, was home to a huge slave market. Ancient texts from both England and Iceland mention *wealh* and *thralls*, those White slaves from the northern lands. A similar story was traced in the Ottoman Empire, where the White slave trade shaped the history of the Mediterranean for centuries (although it should not be forgotten that the Ottomans also enslaved Black Africans).

Many people are unaware that St Patrick, Ireland's patron saint, was enslaved by the Vikings. Just as the great Spanish author Cervantes, author of *Don Quixote* (1605), was captured by the Ottomans. In the world of fiction, it's often forgotten that Daniel Defoe's famous hero, Robinson Crusoe, was a slave trader who was himself enslaved by the Moroccans. White slavery is a historical fact that has been rendered invisible. The patriotic song 'Rule, Britannia' states that 'Britons never, never, never shall be slaves' precisely because all the peoples of the United Kingdom had previously been victims of slavery![3]

America too was partly populated by White slaves. It's not well known but, in 1620, there were White slaves amongst the passengers aboard the *Mayflower*, the most mythologised of the ships that brought early European settlers to the American continent. Somewhere between 300,000 and 400,000 White people – English, Scots and Irish – were sent to the British colonies in the New World to work the fields and the plantations. A sizeable

---

1 Painter, *The History of White People*, p. 38.

2 Painter, *The History of White People*, p. 35.

3 These facts are drawn from Painter, *The History of White People*, pp. 37–38.

number of those sent to the Americas were vagrant children, men and women living in extreme poverty, prisoners and prostitutes who became 'indentured servants'. A terrible fate awaited them and life expectancy was short. The first US census in 1800 detailed the number of 'free white males', which just goes to show that not all of them were free.[1]

As for the French colonies in the Caribbean, they were home to what were called the 'thirty-six monthers', White Europeans who wanted to emigrate to the New World but were unable to pay for the voyage. They (essentially) sold themselves to American plantation owners, usually for a period of three years – hence their name – and were freed at the end of their contract. Black and White slaves may have enjoyed a certain sense of solidarity but they can't really be compared, as the Black slaves had almost no chance of being freed. It's worth pointing out that these poor, mistreated Whites went on to settle lands where their descendants saw themselves as superior to non-Whites. Superior because they were White.

The history of slavery demonstrates that White thinking doesn't really care about the colour of those it exploits when it's in need of labour. We shouldn't forget that serfdom lasted until the nineteenth century in Europe. It's also useful to be reminded of the 70 million White Europeans who left Europe in the course of the nineteenth century to settle in the United States, Australia, the Maghreb, South Africa, South America and Canada. Do European schools have much to say about these emigrants? White people, too, are exploited by White thinking.

5. CHRISTIANITY

In 1494, Pope Alexander VI used the Treaty of Tordesillas to divide the 'New World', including lands yet to be discovered, between Portugal and Spain.

There are always good reasons to invade foreign lands, to exploit their women, their men and their children, and to pillage their resources. And the most important of these is commercial. But it's not easy to construct a system built on the subjugation

---

1 Painter, *The History of White People*, pp. 40–42.

of millions of human beings and to keep it going for centuries, in some cases right up to today, solely on the basis of a single-minded commercial cynicism. More often than not, you also need to tell a story that makes it seem legitimate. The kings and queens of Europe, working on behalf of their merchants and traders, did what they've always done best, namely finding convincing ways to justify slavery and exploitation. In other words, they enlisted the services of their kingdom's intellectuals to explain away these acts. Religion provided the best cover for such domination as its authority couldn't be challenged. Religion transformed the brutal violence of the merchants into virtue. It gave everyone an excuse to say nothing or at least to temper any criticisms. Who would dare to contradict the Word of God?

It was quickly made to seem 'obvious' that, through the colonisation of the Americas, Europeans were in effect carrying out God's will on earth. Serge Gruzinski has stated that:

> One of these Spanish historians, a missionary named Motolinia, established numerous parallels between the plagues of Egypt and the conquest of the New World, or between the destruction of the holy city of Jerusalem, and the destruction of Mexico City, in order to situate the Conquest within the grand Biblical narrative. [...] This alignment of the colonised territories and European Christianity would later be pursued by the other colonial powers in other territories, and it eventually spread across the entire planet.[1]

For example, Gonzalo Fernández de Oviedo y Valdés, a sixteenth-century Spanish scientist and man of letters, wrote that: 'God will soon destroy them. [...] Who can deny that to use gunpowder against the pagans is an offering of incense unto Our Lord?'[2] And what about when an African was kidnapped, mistreated, enslaved, all to satisfy the greed of the merchant classes and to ensure the material comfort of Europe? Christian Delacampagne argues that:

---

1 Serge Gruzinski, 'L'Europe a construit sa domination'.

2 Cited in Plumelle-Uribe, *White Ferocity*, p. 22; again, her source is Todorov, *The Conquest of America*, p. 151.

'European merchants [...] salved their consciences by declaring that the Black would, in any case, be happier as the slave of a Christian rather the slave of a Muslim or a "pagan"'.[1]

The Bible was widely drawn upon to support this process. But, needless to say, the following passage from Exodus 21:16, and its outright denunciation of slavery, was quickly glossed over: 'And he that stealeth a man, and selleth him [...], he shall surely be put to death'. Glossed over precisely because it was necessary for Black people to be considered inferior to White people. So, instead, it was a specific episode from the Book of Genesis, the story of Ham, which was highlighted. Ham was the son of Noah – the one with the Ark – and, in Genesis 9:20–27, the Bible story tells us that he stumbled upon his father who was drunk and naked. Noah was so furious at Ham's 'crime' that he cursed Ham's son, Canaan: 'Cursed be Canaan; a servant shall he be unto his brethren.' Canaan was thus doomed to the fate of becoming the slave of his uncles, Japheth and Shem.

From the Middle Ages onwards, this Bible story began to take on a new set of meanings. Then, in the seventeenth century, a Swiss pastor named Johann Heinrich Heidegger decided to embellish the story. Aimé Césaire sardonically recounts Heidegger's version as follows: at the very moment that Noah pronounced his curse, 'Canaan's hair twisted [...], his face blackened, which naturally meant that all Negroes were Canaan's sons and they should eternally remain as slaves.'[2] Ham was thus cast as the father of the Black peoples of Africa (the Hamites), Japheth became the father of White Europeans (the Japhethites) and Shem was cited as the origin of the inhabitants of North Africa (the Semites).

Let's get things straight. Nowhere in the Bible does it say that Canaan was Black or that Japheth was White. Nor that White people should dominate Black people. But, as is so often the case, the powerful simply appropriated and reinterpreted religion to legitimise their violent acts. This was the case with the Crusades, the slave trade, colonisation. And still it goes on today.

---

1 Delacampagne, *Une histoire du racisme*.

2 Aimé Césaire, 'Introduction à Victor Schœlcher', in Victor Schœlcher, *Esclavage et colonisation* (Paris: PUF, 1948).

While we're talking about religion, let me ask you a question: how many White people are capable of imagining that God is Black? If the origin of mankind lies in Africa, then why wouldn't God be Black? Often, when I ask Black children how they imagine God, they tell me that he's got a long white beard and white hair. When I ask him what colour he is, they all say he's White. Typically, I say to them: 'It's often said that God made Man in his own image. Why then would a little "brown" girl or boy like you imagine that God is White?' They always seem really surprised at my question. To them, it's just a basic fact that God is White; it's not something that changes depending on our point of view. Isn't that clear evidence of the ways in which our thinking has been Whitened?

6. THE ENLIGHTENMENT

A few years ago, I was called upon to testify to a commission on human rights. At one point, I mentioned the *Code Noir* and I'll never forget the response: 'We had no idea. This is all news to us.' These weren't people who just walked in off the street. I imagine that many of them had attended elite French universities, and they were supposed to be experts on racism. But apparently they knew nothing about the *Code Noir*, a text from 1685 that provided the legal framework governing the lives of slaves in the French colonial territories. And it still forms the basis of anti-Black racism in France today. Was this just intellectual laziness on their part?

In 1987, the historian Louis Sala-Molins published the first edition of his book, *Le Code Noir ou le calvaire de Canaan* (*The Code Noir or Canaan's Calvary*). At that time, very few people had a deep knowledge of what he called 'the most monstrous legal text of the modern era'.[1] He did come across a schoolbook from the early 1980s but it claimed the Code was the 'slaves' primary means of protection'. This is a shameful travesty of the reality, which underscores the profound hypocrisy of White thinking. Just imagine a group of slaves gathered glumly together, until one of

---

1 *Le Code Noir ou le calvaire de Canaan*, p. xviii.

them suddenly announces the good news: 'We should be happy, we are protected by a code!' In fact, the *Code Noir* did the very opposite. It legalised slavery in the French colonial empire.

Why have so few historians researched a text that governed the lives of enslaved Black people in the French colonial territories for over 160 years (1685–1848)? A text that helped to enrich a greedy minority. There have been some books and articles, but they have not been widely read and they're now largely forgotten: for example, Lucien Peyraud's *L'Esclavage aux Antilles françaises avant 1789* (*Slavery in the French Caribbean before 1789*), which was published in the late nineteenth century and which greatly influenced the work of Louis Sala-Molins.[1] Isn't it troubling also that the average French person has never come across a book – whether essay, novel or graphic novel – focused on slavery in the French Caribbean? Or that the same average French person hasn't seen a single film on a topic that France has considered to be a 'crime against humanity' since a law passed in 2001? There have been few feature or documentary films about François-Dominique Toussaint, better known as Toussaint Louverture, or the maroons, those fugitive slaves who fled the plantations for a free life in the mountains and the forests of the Caribbean islands. Toussaint Louverture fought against the army sent by Napoleon Bonaparte, who wished to reinstate slavery in Haiti. He should be celebrated today as a hero of the fight against the domination of White thinking. Toussaint used to say: 'In overthrowing me, you have cut down in San Domingo only the trunk of the tree of liberty. It will spring up again by the roots for they are numerous and deep.'[2]

The economist Thomas Piketty underlines the injustice of Haiti's fate after independence:

> The most extreme injustice is undoubtedly the case
> of Saint-Domingue, the jewel of the French slave
> islands in the 18th century, before their insurrection
> in 1791 and their proclamation of independence
> in 1804 under the name of Haiti. In 1825, the
> French state imposed a considerable debt on the

[1] It also influenced foundational texts such as the doctoral thesis completed by Paul Trayer in 1887.

[2] C.L.R. James, *The Black Jacobins: Toussaint L'Ouverture and the San Domingo Revolution* (Allison & Busby, 1980 [1938]), p. 334.

country (300% of the Haitian GDP at the time) to compensate the French owners for their loss of slave property. Threatened with invasion, the island had no other choice but to comply and to repay this debt which the country dragged like a millstone until 1950, after multiple refinancing and interest paid to French and American bankers. Haiti is now requesting that France refund this iniquitous tribute (30 billion Euros today, which does not include the interest) and it is difficult not to agree with them. [1]

What lies behind this pretty implausible forgetfulness about a tragic chapter of French history? A chapter that might have enlightened generations of schoolchildren and adults about the lengths to which people can go in the name of greed. I'm not trying to claim there's been a 'plot' on the part of editors, producers and authors to ignore Haiti. Nor do I believe this to be some incredible expression of contempt towards Black people. Instead, I see this as a 'White out'. White thinking views history through the prism of the myths that it constructs, and it always casts itself as the good guy. It leaves out vast swathes of history so as to draw a veil over its institutional violence, its disrespect for human rights and the humanist principles it claims to defend.

But not all of this history is unknown to us. Many French people would be familiar with Jean-Baptiste Colbert, who oversaw the drafting of the *Code Noir*. Colbert was the General Inspector of Finances for King Louis XIV and he's still considered one of the greatest managers of state finances, as well as one of the most important historical figures of the seventeenth century. He even gave his name to the practice of *colbertisme*, or state intervention in industrial projects, something that still finds favour with French elites today. But Colbert's links to slavery and his role in the creation of the *Code Noir* are largely unknown. Or rarely mentioned by those who do know. In 2017, France's Representative Council for Black Associations (CRAN) launched a campaign to rename all streets and high schools named after Colbert (and there are lots of them) in an attempt to raise awareness of the *Code Noir*. The campaign was met

1 Thomas Piketty, 'Confronting racism, repairing history', *Le Monde*, 16 June 2020, blogpost: www.lemonde.fr/blog/piketty/page/2/.

with contempt, as though it was in bad taste to even ask the question. I can only imagine that the violence Black people have suffered and continue to suffer is irrelevant to some people in France.

In general, what do French people remember about the history of pre-Revolutionary France? A key place is occupied by the likes of Voltaire, Montesquieu, Rousseau and other philosophers of the Enlightenment, these incredible thinkers we still admire for their humanism and their foresight. A recent high-school textbook on approaches to teaching the history of colonisation states that: 'the issue of colonial violence [was] denounced at the time by the philosophers of the Enlightenment'.[1] This book fabricates an idealised history in which the myths of the Enlightenment and the French Republic are preserved intact. These myths explain that there was always at least some opposition to the oppression of non-Whites. It's a comforting idea, but the sad reality is that the vast majority of Enlightenment philosophers did not condemn the ferocious violence of the slave trade. Nor did they condemn the idea that Black people were inferior, ape-like creatures. Admittedly, Voltaire denounced the vile treatment of Black slaves in his famous text, *Candide* (1759). But the principle that Black people should be enslaved in no way shocked him. In another of his well-known texts, he even wrote that: 'One could say that if their intelligence is not of another species than ours, then it is greatly inferior. They are not capable of paying much attention; they mingle very little, and they do not appear to be made either for the advantages or the abuses of our philosophy.'[2] Another philosopher, Fontenelle, made fun of a marquise who had received two birthday presents: a 'pickaninny' – a little Black boy – and a monkey: 'Africa has spared no efforts on your behalf, Madam, she has sent you the two most hideous creatures that she has produced'.[3] My comments here are valid for most European countries, although some criticisms associated with the so-called abolitionist movement did begin to be heard in the English-speaking world. In 1787, the first autobiographical slave narrative was published in London. The former slave Ottobah

1 Sophie Dulucq, David Lambert, Marie-Albane de Suremain, *Enseigner les colonisations et les décolonisations* (Paris: Canopé Editions, 2016).

2 Voltaire, *An Essay on Universal History, the Manners, and Spirit of Nations* (Charleston, SC: Nabu Press, 2011 [1755]).

3 Bernard le Bovier de Fontenelle, 'Lettres galantes de M. le chevalier d'Her***' (1683), in *Œuvres diverses*, 8 vols (Paris: [no pub] 1715), pp. 130–31.

Cugoano stated firmly that a refusal to oppose the slave trade made all Europeans complicit in the oppression of enslaved Africans.[1]

As for Montesquieu, he borrowed an idea from ancient Greece, claiming that climate played a key role in the differences in 'temperament' between peoples. Of course, the climate in Europe didn't predispose its inhabitants to be enslaved, but the climate elsewhere did. As he wrote in *The Spirit of Laws* (1748): 'Asia has properly no temperate zone [...]. [T]here reigns in Asia a servile spirit, which they have never been able to shake off; and it is impossible to find, in all the histories of that country, a single passage which discovers a freedom of spirit.'[2] He added that: 'slavery must be accounted unnatural, though in some countries, it be founded on natural reason'.[3] Jean-Jacques Rousseau used the strategy that had been elaborated for the plantation owners in the colonies. A slave can only be enslaved in the colonies. As soon as a slave sets foot in the imperial centre, their status is the same as any other subject of the kings and princes of the realm. Rousseau stood against the principle of slavery, but said nothing about the reality of slavery in the French Caribbean, where actual slaves where starved, beaten, mutilated, raped, killed. Even the famous *Encyclopedia* (1765), edited by Diderot and d'Alembert, had this to say about Black people in the entry written by Louis de Jaucourt: 'Characteristics of the Negro in general – Although one might by chance meet honest men amongst the Negroes of Guinea (the greater number is wicked), they are mostly inclined to debauchery, vengeance, rape and lies.'[4] Is it really the case that White people don't display any of these characteristics?

Some people will say, it's sad, but things were like that back then. I think this lets them off too easily because, as early as the sixteenth century, there were many enlightened figures who condemned the Atlantic slave trade. The Dominican theologian Domingo de Soto, the Spanish soldier and explorer Martín de Ledesma Valderrama, the Portuguese navigator and grammarian Fernão de Oliveira, the

1 Ottobah Cugoano, *Thoughts and Sentiments on the Evil of Slavery* (London: Penguin, 2007 [1787]).

2 Montesquieu, *The Spirit of Laws*, in *The Complete Works of M. de Montesquieu* (London: T. Evans, 1777 [1748]), pp. 351, 356–57.

3 Montesquieu, *The Spirit of Laws*, p. 317.

4 Elsa Dorlin, *La Matrice de la race: généalogie sexuelle coloniale de la nation française* (Paris: La Découverte, 2009).

Spanish historian Bartolomé de Albornoz, among others. Two centuries before Voltaire and Montesquieu, these figures didn't see the slave trade as inevitable. But, today, the names of these earlier humanists are barely known.

Another humanist who deserves a mention in this context is the Jesuit priest Guillaume-Thomas Raynal, better known as Abbé Raynal. In 1770, he published an enormously successful but scandalous book, *Histoire des deux Indes* (*A History of the Two Indies*), which he co-authored with Diderot. The book fell foul of the state censors due to its criticism of French colonialism, and copies were publicly burned in 1781. Raynal wrote the following lines about the enslavement of Black people:

> But the Negroes are a human species born for slavery. They are stubborn, deceitful, wicked: they acknowledge themselves the superiority of our intelligence and almost recognise the justice of our empire.
>
> The Negroes are stubborn, because slavery breaks the last resorts of the soul. They are wicked, but not as much as you deserve. They are deceitful because one does not owe the truth to tyrants. They recognise the superiority of our minds because we have perpetuated their ignorance; the justice of our empire because we have abused their weakness. Faced with the impossibility of maintaining our superiority through the use of force, a criminal policy based in deception was crafted. You have almost persuaded them that they are a singular species, born for abjection and dependence, for work and punishment. You have gone to great lengths to degrade these poor unfortunates, and then you reproach them for being vile.[1]

This text proves to us that, thankfully, there always have and always will be free spirits who do not allow their minds to be twisted by the lies involved in thinking White. Raynal denounces 'Barbarous

---

1 Abbé Raynal, *Histoire des deux Indes* (Amsterdam: [no pub], 1770), p. 131.

Europeans! The splendour of your businesses does not blind me. Their success does not conceal the injustice.' He goes on to describe 'swarms of cruel and hungry vultures with as little morality and conscience as these birds of prey'.[1]

Now, let's get back to the *Code Noir*, the most important text of the period. Although it was the text that provided the legal framework governing the lives of Black people in the French territories, the Enlightenment philosophers had little to say about it, contemporary historians rarely study it and the media seem completely unaware of it. The Code was drawn up at Colbert's initiative, signed off by Louis XIV and promulgated in 1685, the same year as the revocation of the Edict of Nantes, which deprived French Protestants of religious and civil liberties. This was disastrous for Protestants, but at least this tragic act has not been forgotten. The sixty articles of the *Code Noir* would not be abolished until 1848, sixty years before the birth of my grandfather. Yes, that's right, slavery is a family affair. That goes for you too, whether you like it or not. The Code stated that slaves were 'chattels' (art. 44), which meant that these human beings could be bought, sold and inherited, like any other object. All newborn slaves belonged to the masters of the slave women (art. 12) – in legal terms, their biological fathers didn't exist – and they could be sold off at the master's whim. Slaves weren't entitled to possessions and could leave nothing to their children (art. 28), as they did not even have legal names. They could be whipped or even killed if they attempted to congregate (art. 16), were punishable by death if they hit their master, even if in self-defence (art. 28). If they attempted to escape, they could be mutilated (ears amputated, tendons severed), branded (the royal *fleur de lis* stamped on their shoulders with a red hot iron) or put to death (art. 38). These savage punishments existed because slaves never believed, as Aristotle did, that slavery was 'both expedient and right',[2] and the desire to be free never left them.

At the heart of thinking White lies a profound desire for reassurance, the need to convince itself that it's always been on the side of the *good guys*. That's what has led some, mostly White people, to claim that Colbert's *Code Noir* offered at least some

1 Cited in Claude Liauzu, *Race et civilisation*, p. 181.
2 Aristotle, *Politics*, p. 8.

protection to slaves. To support these claims, they cite certain articles that give a semblance of rights. Article 12 stipulates that, in certain cases, a child cannot be simply taken from its mother: 'The children who will be born of marriage between slaves will be slaves and will belong to the master of the women slaves, and not to those of their husband, if the husband and the wife have different masters'.[1] Article 22 obliges masters to feed their slaves: every week, slaves should be given 'two and a half jars […] of cassava flour […], two pounds of salted beef or three pounds of fish […] and to children […] half of the above supplies'. Article 25 obliges them to clothe their slaves: 'two outfits of canvas or four aulnes [roughly one square metre] of canvas'. The master must continue to feed his slaves when they are old, sick or infirm (art. 27). A slave can be chained and whipped but not mutilated or killed (art. 42). The slave can even, where necessary, call on the public prosecutor to act if he believes that his rights have been abused (food, clothes, upkeep: art. 26).

The only trouble is that two other articles effectively rule out any legal recourse. Indeed, article 30 stipulates that: 'Slaves will not be allowed to be given offices or commissions with any public function, nor to be named agent by any other than their masters to act or administer any trade or judgement in loss or witnesses, either in civil or criminal matters; and in cases where they will be heard as witnesses, their dispositions will only serve as memorandum to aid the judges in the investigation, without being the source of any presumption, conjecture or proof.' While article 31 goes on to declare that: 'Nor can slaves be party, neither in judgement, nor in civil suits, either as plaintiff or defendant, neither in civil or criminal suits, excepting where their masters act and take civil action or pursue a criminal action for reparations for affronts and excesses committed against their slaves.'

In these circumstances, how exactly were slaves supposed to claim their rights? It will come as no surprise then that such cases were extremely rare. I know of a case from Anse-Bernard, in the north of Guadeloupe where I was born and spent my early years as a boy. A slave named Lucille took her master, Jean-Baptiste

---

1 This and all further quotes are drawn from the English translation of the *Code Noir* by John Garrigus, a historian of the Haitian Revolution. See:
http://www2.latech.edu/~bmagee/louisiana_anthology/texts/louis_xiv/louis_xiv--code_noir_english.html. Note that article 31 is not translated in full by Garrigus.

Douillard Mahaudière, to court there in 1840, just eight years before the second abolition of slavery. Lucille had been accused of poisoning livestock and was thrown into a cell with her legs in irons, and she languished there for almost two years. The ample evidence of her mistreatment should have been more than enough to see Douillard Mahaudière convicted, but pressure from the White people on the island led to his acquittal.[1] What a surprise.

The historical record tells us that, in many contexts where slavery was practised, slaves made up 80–95% of the population. Living in fear of revolt, the slave masters maintained a constant reign of terror. Black people were starved, mistreated, the women raped, and children could be torn from their parents and sold at any point. When slaves became infirm and thus unproductive, masters would accuse them of acts of violence, which gave them an excuse to have them put to death, rather than have to continue feeding them. The regulations stated that any slave killed gave rise to a reimbursement (in 1756, the rate stood at 1,600 pounds for a man and 1,000 pounds for a woman). As for the possibility of fining those masters who were excessively cruel towards their 'chattels', it was effectively rendered null and void by article 43 of the *Code Noir*: 'We enjoin our officers to criminally prosecute the masters, or their foreman, who have a killed a slave under their auspices or control, and to punish the master according to the circumstances of the atrocity. In the case where there is absolution, we allow our officers to return the absolved master or foreman, without them needing our pardon.'

The *Code Noir* appeared to place at least some limits on violence towards slaves, but in reality it sanctioned the most appalling and shameful treatment. In France, we imagine the era of Republican government as having introduced a more enlightened system. The Third Republic (1870–1940) was inspired by the French Revolution's Declaration of the Rights of Man and the Citizen (1789). While the Fourth Republic (1946–58) contributed greatly to the drafting of the 1948 Universal Declaration of Human Rights. However, both Republics permitted barbaric acts to be committed in the name of France in the colonies. They did so because they knew that you can only dominate another people if you can terrorise

---

1 See the radio series, 'Les Antilles françaises enchaînées à l'esclavage' (1/4), *France Culture*, 6 May 2019: www.franceculture.fr/emissions/series/les-antilles-francaises-enchainees-a-lesclavage.

them. And they knew that blind, brute force was the only way to maintain a system built on injustice.

Why did the French accept the extreme violence of the *Code Noir*? Today, in France, we still allow things to happen that demonstrate a refusal to recognise the humanity of certain people within our society. How can we be sure that, over the centuries, force of habit hasn't made us just as blind to injustice as our ancestors?

7. RACE SCIENCE

Beginning in the eighteenth century and especially from the nineteenth century, science began to liberate humanity from the stranglehold of religion. But a form of pseudoscience was at the heart of the new discourse of White domination. Slavery and then colonisation would have to be made to seem normal so as to give legitimacy to economic and commercial conquests. Slavery had been abolished by the French revolutionaries in 1794, not solely for humanist and political reasons, but also because they were under pressure from the growing number of slave revolts in the colonies. Equally, Napoleon Bonaparte restored slavery in 1802 for primarily economic reasons, as the plantation owners were a central pillar of the French economy and steadfast supporters of the Emperor. Lobbying wasn't the term used back then but that, essentially, is what led to the shameful restoration of slavery. That's why it's misleading to think of slavery as a confrontation between Black people and White people. Nowadays, lobbyists use biased scientific studies to manipulate public opinion and the political classes on a range of issues from the dangers of electromagnetic waves to the use of chemical pesticides. And, from the eighteenth century onwards, the vast business of exploiting men and women who were considered inferior leaned on science to disarm critics. Of course, the slave trade existed before its 'scientific' justification, but race science retrospectively justified the status of the enslaved and gave weight to the superiority of White people, henceforth seen as an irrefutable fact.

Louis Sala-Molins writes that: 'White science did whatever it took. Essentially, it cobbled together a set of ideas that would allow it to remain within its ideological comfort zone, convinced of its watertight rationality, to enable it to enslave those it needed to grow sugar cane and then grind it, or to cultivate coffee plants then pick the beans.'[1] Moreover, it's possible that the word 'race' derives from the Italian word *razza*, whose origin is the Latin term, *ratio*, meaning reason. So, it seems that reason and race are inextricably linked! And, really, this is no surprise, as the eighteenth century witnessed a mania for the scientific classification of almost everything, including humankind.

Do I need to remind you here that the notion of separate human races has no scientific validity at all? My good friend, the paleoanthropologist Yves Coppens, explains that, since the birth of *Homo sapiens* in Africa, around 300,000 years ago, we have all been of the same race. To borrow an expression from the great African American writer Toni Morrison, talking about so-called human races is a product of the 'genetic imagination'.[2] The classification of humankind into a hierarchy of different races served only one purpose: to justify White supremacy, which made White people the norm against which all others would be judged.

This classification is not that old. In the eighteenth century, the English anatomist Edward Tyson was one of the first to demonstrate the physical 'similarities' between humans and monkeys. He was soon followed in the 1740s by the Swede, Carl Linnaeus (later Carl von Linné after his ennoblement), who placed humans with monkeys in his classification of the primates. Then came Buffon, a Frenchman who, around 1750, noted a resemblance between primates and the 'Hottentots' of South Africa, who were seen as the 'missing link'. The next generation of scholars introduced a hierarchy into these classifications. Using various measures and building on a range of studies, the English physician Charles White noted a gradation between Europeans, Asians, Amerindians, 'Negroes' and monkeys.

In 1795, the 'cranial angle' was deemed an indicator of cerebral development. The Frenchmen Georges Cuvier and Étienne Geoffroy Saint-Hilaire could thus demonstrate that the greater this angle, the more space the brain had to develop, and the more intelligent the subject.

In the nineteenth century, Julien-Joseph Virey brought these controversial debates about the hierarchy of humankind

1 *Le Code Noir ou le calvaire de Canaan*, p. 28.

2 Toni Morrison, *The Origin of Others* (Cambridge, MA: Harvard University Press, 2017), p. 15.

to a wider audience, presenting his findings on the supposed anatomical superiority of White people: greater cranial capacity, a larger brain, more voluminous cerebral hemispheres, a far more developed cerebral cortex, a less active nervous system, and so on. The phrenologist Franz Joseph Gall helped to established what came to be known as cerebral determinism. He defended the thesis that there was a direct correlation between the form of the brain and the capacity for thought, and argued that the brain was also the site in which moral and intellectual 'inclinations' were located. In his justifications for slavery in the southern states of the US, Josiah Clark Nott enlisted the findings of Samuel George Morton, who had sought to prove the cranial superiority of White people.

Paul Broca maintained that not all of the 'human races' were equally perfectible, for he was convinced that each so-called race had its specific intellectual abilities, and that these were hereditary. As a result, he was deeply pessimistic about the possibility of primitive peoples becoming 'civilised'. Broca and his followers aligned themselves with Darwin's theory of evolution, and believed that 'primitive peoples' were the 'missing link' between apes and civilised man.

The notion of a 'superior race' was increasingly being asserted, and the most sustained exploration of the concept, in French, was to be found in a voluminous text, *The Inequality of Human Races*, by Arthur de Gobineau, which was published in stages between 1853 and 1855. This type of racial anthropology may have remained marginal, but its ideas have often resurfaced in the political sphere. Gobineau began publishing his text just five short years after the abolition of slavery, and his goal was to maintain the hierarchy of the races. Gobineau stood out from his contemporaries in his firm conviction that contemporary societies were destined to go into a decline that was rooted in the mixing of what were originally 'pure' races, such as the Arians, a group he traces back to central Asia. For Gobineau, the inexorable growth of racial mixing was fatally undermining this purity.

Paul Broca provided 'proof' of the inherent inferiority of colonised peoples. He founded the 'science' of anthropology, which still exists today, but has thankfully rid itself of his false and dangerous ideas. But, back in the mid-nineteenth century, Broca was claiming that:

> On average, the mass of the encephalon [the brain] is more substantial [...] in great men than in mediocre men, and in the superior races than in the inferior races. [I'm surprised he didn't add 'greater in men than in women'!] Thus, the slant and the protrusion of the face [the form of the skull] [...], the degree of blackness of the skin, the woollen condition of the hair, are frequently associated with intellectual and social inferiority, while a lighter skin, straight hair [...] are the everyday prerogative of the most elevated peoples of the human species.[1]

His followers, Hovelacque and Hervé in particular, set about inventing a way of calculating the 'cranial capacity' of the Black peoples of West Africa, claiming that it was inferior to that of White Europeans by 'roughly 100 cm^3'. Indeed, all the colonised or native peoples, whether sub-Saharan Africans, Amerindians or Australian Aboriginals, were deemed to have a lower cerebral capacity than White people. Not just that though. The angle of their skulls and their jaws, the shape of their pelvises, the proportions of their limbs were all proof of their inferiority to White people.[2] The geographer Elisée Reclus wrote that: 'according to physiologists, the blood of Black people is thicker, less red than that of White people; it coagulates faster and flows more slowly. The Black man, just like the Yellow man of Asia [...] suffers far less during surgery and traumatic fevers are less harmful to him.'[3]

Around the same time, an American doctor, Samuel Cartwright, went so far as to invent a condition, *dysaesthesia aethiopica*, to identify the 'innate' inertia of Black people:

> From their natural indolence, unless under the stimulus of compulsion, they doze away their lives

1 Quoted in Liauzu, *Race et civilisation*, pp. 95–96.

2 These ideas taken from Liauzu, *Race et civilisation*.

3 Elisée Reclus, *Les Grands Textes*, edited by Christophe Brun (Paris: Flammarion, 2014).

with the capacity of their lungs for atmospheric air
only half expanded, from the want of exercise…
The black blood distributed to the brain chains the
mind to ignorance, superstition and barbarism.[1]

He went on to claim it was lucky that slavery provided 'forced exercise, so beneficial to the Negro'! If it was so beneficial, then why did so many slaves try to escape? Dr Cartwright had the answer to this too. It was due to 'drapetomania, or the disease causing slaves to run away'![2]

In 1871, 'science' was used to legitimise colonisation. The French historian and philosopher Ernest Renan, still celebrated today as a major political theorist, wrote that nature had given different abilities to each race:

We aspire not to equality but to domination. The
country of a foreign race must become once again a
country of serfs […]. It is not a question of eliminating
the inequalities among men but rather of widening
them and making them into a law. […] Nature has
made a race of workers, the Chinese race; […] a race
of tillers of the soil, the Negro; […] a race of masters
and soldiers, the European race. […] Let each one do
what he is made for, and all will be well.[3]

A Haitian anthropologist, Joseph Anténor Firmin, stood in opposition to his European colleagues and asserted that there was only one human race. He became a member of the Anthropological Society of Paris but could not convince the other members to change their mind. So, in 1885, he published *The Equality of the Human Races*, as a direct and powerful response to Gobineau who had claimed that 'all civilizations derive from the white race'.[4] Firmin considered the idea of racial

---

1 Cited in Morrison, *The Origin of Others*, p. 4.

2 Cited in Morrison, *The Origin of Others*, p. 4.

3 Cited in Plumelle-Uribe, *White Ferocity*, p. 106.

4 Arthur de Gobineau, *The Inequality of Human Races*, trans. by Adrian Collins (London: Heinemann, 1915), p. 230. Joseph Anténor Firmin, *The Equality of the Human Races*, trans. by Asselin Charles (NY & London: Garland, 2000).

purity highly debatable, for human history had been consistently marked by the mixing of different peoples. Moreover, he argued that the very notion of race served primarily to create divisions between people.

White supremacy eventually contaminated the entire world during the era of European colonialism, and human zoos played a key role in this process.[1] From the mid-nineteenth century to the end of the 1930s, millions in the West paid the price of a ticket to discover non-Whites, called 'natives' or 'savages', in shows that gradually became widespread. Eventually, they established themselves as the 'prime venue in which the encounter with the "Other" took place'.[2] Between 1880 and the First World War, there were about 30 of these events held every year in France. Then, in the interwar period, it was the great colonial exhibitions that took centre stage as a genuine mass cultural phenomenon. Finally, in the 1930s, they gradually began to fade away.[3] What had made them successful was the Western fascination with exoticism. But, fundamentally, these exhibitions were a device for disseminating the idea of racial hierarchy.

Moreover, until the early twentieth century, the 'specimens' exhibited in these 'human zoos' were studied by anthropologists as part of their anthropometric research. Pascal Blanchard succinctly summarises the nature of these practices as follows:

> Colonial discourse, scholarly works and popular performance of the 'savage' (including on the stages of theatres and music halls) all came together in a complex and haphazard fashion that sketched the contours of a way of thinking in which the racial and cultural superiority of the West legitimised colonial domination – and possibly even made it seem necessary.[4]

1 Pascal Blanchard, et al. (eds), *Human Zoos: Science and Spectacle in the Age of Empire* (Liverpool: Liverpool University Press, 2008).

2 Pascal Blanchard, 'Décolonisons nos mentalités', *Revue internationale et stratégique*, 73 (2009), p. 122.

3 Pascal Blanchard, Gilles Boëtsch, Nanette Jacominjn Snoep, *Human Zoos: The Invention of the Savage*, Exhibition Catalogue (Paris: Musée du Quai Branly/Actes Sud, 2012).

4 Blanchard, 'Décolonisons nos mentalités', p. 122.

These shows played a significant role in the construction of a White identity. In France, a widespread propaganda extolled the French Empire and justified its colonial conquests (as was also the case in the other imperial powers). However, human zoos have been purged from the collective memory, even though they contributed to all aspects of colonial culture.[1]

In 1877, the first edition was published of what would become a famous French schoolbook, *Le Tour de France par deux enfants* (*The Tour of France by Two Children*). The idea of White superiority was so widespread and seemed so self-evident at that time that this book referred to 'the white race, the most perfect of [all] the human races'.[2] What is most shocking is that this book was reprinted annually almost unchanged right up until 1977.

Powerful echoes of this thinking still shape beliefs today. It's easier for White people to attain certain positions of responsibility right across society, and that's because a whole swathe of public opinion is still firmly convinced that only White people are capable of fulfilling these roles. Let's be honest about it: dance, sport, music, these are the areas where we expect Black people to excel. Although even that depends on the type of dance, sport or music we're talking about. It's rarely stated openly but often implied that when it comes to intellectual matters, politics, law, medicine, engineering, then White people are entirely at home.

Right up until the second half of the twentieth century, there were no limits to the cruelty perpetrated by the White people in the United States and the various colonial empires. They were within their rights to use physical violence against Black people under the slightest pretext. Let me give you an example: in the colonies, under the rules of the forced labour regime, it was permitted to abuse Black bodies without restriction, including murder.[3] In the United States, White people could freely murder Black people however they chose to: by hanging, with guns or by burning them alive. In 1857, the US Supreme Court ruled that 'Blacks are excluded from the national community by

1 Pascal Blanchard, et al. (eds), *Colonial Culture in France since the Revolution* (Bloomington, IN: Indiana University Press, 2013).

2 G. Bruno, *Le Tour de France par deux enfants*, p. 188.

3 See Pascal Blanchard, et al. *Sexe, race et colonies* (Paris: La Découverte, 2018).

the Constitution itself'.[1] African Americans only gained the nationwide right to vote in 1965 and the right to marry a White man or woman in 1967! My mother was twenty years old at that time. Black people were deemed inferior, subservient to the dominant race. Even a man as great as Thomas Jefferson, one of the leading lights of the abolitionist movement, wasn't genuinely interested in the fate of Black people. The issue that really outraged him about slavery was that it legally permitted White people to give free rein to their worst impulses: rape, summary execution, cruelty.[2] The hell that Black people were living through was incidental. What Jefferson truly feared was the inhumanity of White people, and the abolition of slavery would save them from their worst selves.

It wasn't just biology that was enlisted to legitimise White violence. The new science of psychology had been invented in the late nineteenth century, in particular to measure diverse forms of intelligence using James McKeen Cattell's 'mental tests', which would later become the IQ tests devised by William Stern. These IQ tests, which were devised by and for elite White men, determined non-Whites in the colonies, as well as women in general, to be intellectually deficient. In 1894, the French sociologist Gustave Le Bon wrote that:

> This abyss between the mental constitution of the different races explains how it is that the superior peoples have never been able to impose their civilisation on inferior peoples. [...] A negro [...] may easily take a university degree or become a lawyer; the sort of varnish he thus acquires is however quite superficial, and has no influence on his mental constitution. [...] Our negro [...] may accumulate all possible certificates without ever attaining to the level of the average European.[3]

Thirty years later, the influential French philosopher Alfred

1 Cited in Plumelle-Uribe, *White Ferocity*, p. 153.

2 Achille Mbembe, *Necropolitics*, trans. by Steven Corcoran (Durham, NC & London: Duke University Press, 2019).

3 Gustave Le Bon, *The Psychology of Peoples* (New York: Macmillan, 1898), p. 37.

Fouillée explained that the White man was the pinnacle of human evolution:

> The common characteristics of the savage today can permit us to understand the [white] man of the past. Absentmindedness, weakness of will and of thought, daydreaming, fixed ideas, an excess of everyday emotions and the impossibility of experiencing new emotions, instability and contradiction [...] this is what all observers find, to different degrees, amongst both children and savages.[1]

In 1899, the former French naval officer Léopold de Saussure wrote that: 'One must recognise the dominant feature of the negro's character, a vanity that is extraordinary, grotesque, incredible, something that one can only satisfactorily define by a particular adjective: simian'.[2] If we want to talk about vanity in this period, then surely it was a White trait. Who was it that constructed an ideology placing White men above women and all people of other 'races'? This way of thinking wasn't simply tolerated in this era, it was widely recognised and even lauded as revealing a profound truth about humankind. Indeed, we are still convinced today that the predominantly White societies of the West are more sophisticated than all the others. But what does it really mean to be 'sophisticated'?

8. COLONISATION

As far as I'm aware, the history of colonialism and its psychological legacies are not taught in any great depth in schools in France, the UK or indeed any of the former colonial powers. Are we conscious that this history lives on within us? Let's just consider some of the basic facts. At its height, in the early 1930s, the French Empire covered 12,347,000 km^2, or if you prefer 22 times the landmass of mainland France. In total, France colonised around 50 countries or territories around the world. Slavery may have been recognised

1 Cited in Liauzu, *Race et civilisation*, p. 116.

2 Léopold de Saussure, *Psychologie de la colonisation française dans ses rapports avec les sociétés indigenes* (Paris: Félix Alcan, 1899), p. 210.

by the French state in 2001 as a 'crime against humanity', but the criminal enterprise otherwise known as colonisation still occupies an ambiguous position within France's collective memory. Of course, most French people know full well that colonisation was in reality nothing but a massive land grab. But too little is known about the brutal realities of colonisation, the predatory exploitation of people and resources, for there to be unanimity about this subject. France may well be the land of museums but there isn't a single one devoted to telling the history of colonisation, even though many historians have been calling, for many years now, for the creation of such an institution.[1] And this absence means that, still today, a section of public opinion feels able to claim that we need to weigh up the 'pros' and 'cons' of colonialism, for colonialism was a complex 'adventure' that gave as much as it took, so it can't be dismissed out of hand.

Was it this ignorance of the realities of colonialism that led French parliamentarians, with the support of President Jacques Chirac's government, to insert two contentious articles into a law published on 23 February 2005, which declared that: 'school programmes should recognise, in particular, the positive role of the French presence overseas, especially in North Africa'.[2] Under pressure from public opinion and criticisms from historians, Chirac finally withdrew the offending articles a year later. But this whole episode is revealing about the fear that stalks White thinking. In 2018, a right-wing magazine, *Valeurs actuelles* (*Contemporary Values*), felt justified in publishing a special issue openly celebrating colonisation and its millions of victims. The front cover read: 'The true history of the colonies: the epic tale of four centuries of colonialism, for which France should show no remorse.' This illustrates that some White people still don't understand that no one is asking them to show remorse or to beat

1 See Pascal Blanchard, 'Un musée sur l'histoire coloniale: il est temps', *Libération*, 29 May 2019; Pascal Blanchard, Nicolas Bancel, 'Pour un musée des colonisations et de l'esclavage!', *Le Monde*, May 2016; 'Manifeste pour un musée des histoires coloniales', *Libération*, 8 May 2015 (chosen for the symbolism of VE Day); 'Faire de l'hôtel de la Marine un musée de l'esclavage', *Le Monde*, 18 January 2011; Robert Aldrich, 'Le musée colonial impossible', in Nicolas Bancel, Pascal Blanchard, Sandrine Lemaire (eds), *Culture post-coloniale 1961–2006* (Paris: Autrement, 2006).

2 Article 4, paragraph 2, of the law offering the recognition and support of the nation for those French repatriated (from Algeria).

themselves up but rather to acknowledge the violence and the blind greed that was at the heart of the colonial system.

Is it possible to be human first and White second? I'm not so sure, as I often get the impression that their collective unconscious pushes White people to do whatever it takes to present a consistently positive vision of White identity. This is the mindset that underpinned an infamous speech delivered by another French president, Nicolas Sarkozy, in Dakar, Senegal, in 2007: 'The coloniser took, but I want to say with respect, that he also gave. He built bridges, roads, hospitals, dispensaries and schools. He turned virgin soil fertile. He gave of his effort, his work, his know-how.'[1] So, if European states colonised all over the world, it was because they were driven by good intentions:

> I want to say it here, not all the colonialists were thieves or exploiters. There were among them evil men but there were also men of good will. People who believed they were fulfilling a civilising mission, people who believed they were doing good. They were wrong, but some were sincere.[2]

I'm sure there were men 'of good will', men who were 'sincere', but that's not the point. It's the colonial system as a whole that we need to analyse. Do you want to know the reality of French colonialism? Then take the time to read the report written by the Franco-Italian explorer and colonial administrator Pierre Savorgnon de Brazza in 1905, a report that was covered up by the French Ministry for the Colonies as soon as it was published. It's all in there: the collection of arbitrary 'taxes', hostage-taking, summary execution, the physical abuse of 'natives' for the 'crime' of failing to salute White people, confessions made under torture and punished by a whipping that would often end with the death of the victim.[3] The objective of all colonisation was the enrichment

1 Nicolas Sarkozy's Dakar Speech, https://www.africaresource.com/essays-a-reviews/essays-a-discussions/437-the-unofficial-english-translation-of-sarkozys-speech?start=1.

2 'Le discours de Dakar de Nicolas Sarkozy'. For an African response to Sarkozy's speech, see *L'Afrique répond à Sarkozy: Contre le discours de Dakar*, edited by Makhily Gassama (Paris: Philippe Rey, 2008).

3 Pierre Savorgnon de Brazza, *Le Rapport Brazza, Mission d'enquête au Congo: rapports et documents* (Paris: Le Passager clandestin, 2018).

of the imperial homeland. The colonisation of the Americas, then Africa, Oceania and Asia was nothing more than economically driven pillage. As I've already mentioned, Columbus was obsessed with the boundless riches of India, which he thought he had reached. This rule that colonisation must always enrich the homeland was central to the conquest of Africa. And it's no doubt this rule that leads some to still claim today that colonisation had its 'good points'. Indeed, colonialism was extremely lucrative, but the profits all flowed one way.

More than anything else, it was this economic greed that informed the debate at the Berlin Conference (1885). Have you heard of this event? It's only recently been included in French school textbooks. This conference should be one of our historical landmarks, as it powerfully demonstrates the relationship between politics and finance.[1] Indeed, it was at the Berlin Conference that the European colonial powers (Great Britain, France, Germany, Portugal and Belgium) shared Africa between them, as though they were slicing up a birthday cake.[2] In short, the politicians of the 'White continent' had sent their troops to invade the 'Black continent' in a haphazard fashion all through the nineteenth century. The agreement reached in Berlin would allow them to officially sanction their existing colonial possessions. At the time the conference took place, much of the territory they were sharing out had not even been explored by Europeans: Europe designated the ownership of this land without knowing the slightest thing about it.

The Berlin Conference symbolises the extraordinary contempt for the peoples of Africa displayed by the White powers of the time (not to be confused with the people of Europe more widely). These White powers gave themselves *carte blanche* to occupy and pillage an entire continent, as though it were an empty wasteland and not home to an estimated population of 140 million Africans. Europe was free to impose borders of its choosing, drawn in straight lines, as though holding a ruler to a map. These arbitrary, absurd borders gave no consideration to the peoples who lived there, and it is Africans who still pay the price today in the form of the numerous conflicts

---

1 On this topic, see the remarkable documentary film, *Berlin 1885, la ruée sur l'Afrique*, by Joël Calamettes (2011).

2 I borrow this image from the historian, Henri Brunschwig, and his book *Partage de l'Afrique noire* (Paris: Flammarion, 1971).

they have given rise to. But Berlin also demonstrated that commercial interests took precedence over diplomatic and political concerns. As Henri Brunschwig reminds us, the main aim of the Berlin Conference was to allow the European powers to monopolise trade and to line their pockets by cashing in on Africa's natural resources.[1] The first sentence of the first article of the General Act published at the end of the conference stated unambiguously that: 'The trade of all nations [who have signed this act] shall enjoy complete freedom.'[2] And the entire Act is devoted to the nature of the merchandise, to commercial routes and the postal service, except for article 6, which proclaims the curious alibi that the European powers 'bind themselves to watch over the preservation of the native tribes, and to care for the improvement of the conditions of their moral and material well-being'.[3] These were fine words, but as the following decades would illustrate, they were just words. For example, all of the European powers solemnly swore that they wanted to end slavery in Africa, but it was allowed to continue long after its formal abolition (1848, for France; 1833, for the UK). Although obviously this was only done out of respect for 'African traditions'. You've got to admire their nerve, and it was such a good lie that it was regularly trotted out. Take, for example, Admiral de Jauréguiberry, the Minister for the Marine and the Colonies who claimed in 1880 that:

> In the case of all of these annexations [by France], we have formally undertaken to respect [...] the traditions of all of the tribes concerned and, within these traditions, slavery plays a central role, but, to be a bit more precise, it is merely a form of hereditary serfdom.[4]

At the end of the 1920s, the campaigning journalist Albert Londres noted that slavery still hadn't disappeared from the colonies. But who in France recalls that now, as we are called upon to celebrate

---

1 Brunschwig, *Partage de l'Afrique noire*.

2 The General Act of the Berlin Conference on West Africa, 26 February 1885: https://loveman.sdsu.edu/docs/1885GeneralActBerlinConference.pdf.

3 General Act of the Berlin Conference on West Africa, 26 February 1885.

4 Quoted in Olivier Le Cour Grandmaison, 'Après l'abolition de l'esclavage... l'esclavage toujours', *Mediapart*, 9 May 2013.

the 1848 abolition with such fanfare? White thinking has always been good at forgetting inconvenient facts.

What do French people today, young people in particular, know about the realities of daily life in the colonies? What do they know of the institutionalised violence that was perpetrated in the Empire? Not much. Are French people aware that their cherished image of France as home of the Rights of Man never extended to the colonies? Basically, French law distinguished between the right of citizens (i.e. White people) living in the Empire and subjects (Africans, Malagasy, Indochinese, Kanaks, Antilleans, Melanesians). The former enjoyed all the rights bestowed upon them by the laws of the imperial homeland. The latter were subjected to 'special' laws: they were deprived of most of their freedoms and political rights; in terms of their civil rights, they were only allowed to retain a limited personal status, linked to their religious or customary origins. We'd be entitled to label this as segregation or apartheid: French legislators referred to it as 'distinction' or sometimes 'double legislation'. This legislation officially established, within the colonies, the existence of two races that would be treated differently. Despite this, many French people are convinced that only the United States and South Africa have practised segregation.

Article 109 of the Constitution of France's Second Republic (1848) stipulated that the nation's overseas possessions were governed 'by their separate laws until a special law shall place them under the provisions of the present Constitution'.[1] This Republic didn't last very long, but the principle of 'special laws' was maintained in different forms right up until the era of decolonisation, over a century later. This clearly demonstrates that the gains of the Declaration of the Rights of Man of 1789 simply did not apply in the colonies. The text that really allows us to understand this opposition between France and its colonies is the *Code de l'indigénat* (*Native Code*). Unfortunately, hardly anyone knows about it, even though it played an essential part in the creation of France's White imagination. Apart from the occasional researcher, such as the political scientist Olivier Le Cour Grandmaison, few historians have closely examined this penal code, which was drafted

1 Cited in Olivier Le Cour Grandmaison, *De l'indigénat* (Paris: La Découverte, 2010), pp. 12–13.

in 1875 initially to govern Algeria but subsequently exported to all of France's colonies.

This Code gave licence to the worst excesses of the colonial regime. Take 'forced labour', for example, which was authorised until 1946, that is to say almost a decade after the Geneva Convention (23 April 1938) had outlawed all forms of forced labour. 'Forced labour' is just another way of describing slave labour. Unpaid work carried out in unspeakable conditions. In French Indochina, vast swathes of land were handed over to colonisers to grow profitable crops (e.g. rice, coffee, tea, tropical wood). And the colonial authorities had the right to requisition 'natives' to construct hospitals for the White people, to forge tracks, build roads and railway lines, all so that these raw materials could be sent to the ports and onwards to the imperial homeland. A classic example of this process is the construction of the 318-mile Congo-Ocean railway line linking the cities of Pointe-Noire and Brazzaville, via the highlands of the Mayombe Forest, in what is today the Republic of the Congo. We need to recall the resistance met by this project powered by forced labour, the desertions, the uprisings all across French Equatorial Africa. We mustn't forget that 'native workers' were crowded into camps, badly fed, worked to the bone and died in their thousands. Indeed, it's estimated that the railway line cost the lives of 20,000 workers. In fact, French newspapers of the time were outraged, headlines referring to 'black death on the sleepers' (sleepers being the wooden beams between the rails). A few years ago, Olivier Le Cour Grandmaison and the former Malian Minister for Culture, Aminata Traoré, published an opinion piece in the French daily newspaper, *Le Monde*, calling for forced labour in the colonies to be commemorated and recognised as a crime against humanity.[1] I couldn't agree more. White thinking forgets that each of these deaths demands that justice be served.

Justice in the colonies was entirely arbitrary. In place of an actual court with actual judges, the governor could simply announce an 'administrative internment', which meant that any non-White could be imprisoned for any reason and for any length of time. Any subject who refused to obey the demands of the colonial

1 Olivier Le Cour Grandmaison and Aminata Traoré, 'Le travail forcé dans l'empire français doit être reconnu comme un crime contre l'humanité', *Le Monde*, 13 April 2019.

regime could thus find themselves under arrest and locked away just like that, with no grounds for appeal. In the courts, the rule of law as practised in France did not really exist, as judges were legally permitted to do whatever they pleased. The Native Code included the idea of 'collective responsibility'. In other words, if an individual did something that displeased the colonial authorities, then the whole community could be held responsible. Everyone would be punished. For example, the colonial authorities might send a military expedition to burn the village to the ground. The Code also provided for the possibility of 'sequestration', which effectively meant that, if a community was accused of a 'hostile act' towards White people, then its land could be confiscated. The 'hostile act' might have been an uprising or it might have been a suspicious gunshot. In this way, thousands of acres of land were stolen from their rightful owners and given to colonial settlers. Some would say that this notion of collective responsibility is still at work in the former colonies today.

When a colonial subject was brought before the courts, judges were under orders to hand out the harshest sentences possible. If there wasn't enough proof to support a conviction, they were entitled to rely on their 'personal conviction'. In other words, they could do whatever they pleased with no concern for legal niceties such as the presumption of innocence. A legal expert of the time justified these practices in these terms:

> the interests of public order and security [...] must take precedence over the rights of the individual [...]. That is why [...] judicial procedures must be simplified and time limits restricted so as to produce a vigorous and, in particular, a prompt repression, which should be summary if required.[1]

Another wrote that this cruelty could only be deemed abusive if it were applied to White people, as these punishments fitted naturally with the 'native temperament':

> This principle sits perfectly with the primitive mentality of the primitive races. If well-meaning

1 Albert Billiard, cited in Le Cour Grandmaison, *De l'indigénat*, p. 69.

magistrates were to hesitate in punishing a guilty party, the latter would assume that this decision was driven by fear or weakness. [...] To safeguard the prestige of White people, one is often obliged to punish a violation with greater severity [...]. Our egalitarian ideas are understandably shaken by such anomalies, but it is a question of colonial legislation.[1]

In other words, White prestige had to be maintained at all costs.

In terms of punishment, imprisonment was only one possible outcome. Unsurprisingly, colonial justice authorised the death penalty, a sentence that could not be commuted, again the strict opposite of practice in France. It also authorised 'transportation' (to a penal institution in a faraway country, often the imperial homeland itself) and even physical punishments (caning and whipping, penalties outlawed in France). In 1905, a legal scholar wrote that:

It has repeatedly been stated that the natives are big children [...]. Well, the child, whose character has yet to be shaped, is broadly analogous to the animal; both remember a good thrashing, and will think twice about committing an act for which they have previously been chastised. [2]

Needless to say, segregation was also central to the electoral process in the colonies. For example, the right to 'universal' suffrage was denied to Algerians until 1946. Even after that date, Algerians were only given partial democratic rights, electing 'Muslims' to their own specific electoral college. The colonial system couldn't imagine natives as capable of electing their own representatives. A former governor of Algeria, Maurice Viollette, claimed that: 'The vast majority of these miserable people live in such complete poverty that a ballot paper means nothing to them; the first troublemaker to come along would be able to exploit

---

1 Jules Verrier de Byans, cited in Le Cour Grandmaison, *De l'indigénat*, p. 70.

2 Cited in Le Cour Grandmaison, *De l'indigénat*, p. 72.

them'.[1] The true meaning of this doublespeak? There are just so many of these Algerians, way more than the French settlers. If we let them vote, they'll elect a load of nationalists who'll try to take back the country.

Let's give credit where it's due, though. In 1936, Viollette did try, in a very limited way, to extend the franchise to a handful of 'advanced natives', essentially those who'd received a French education or military honours. It's estimated there were about 21,000 of them in Algeria. In the long term, this might have undermined the French domination of Algeria. So, at a congress in Algiers on 14 January 1937, the 300 mayors representing French Algeria unanimously declared their opposition to this draft bill. In France, the right, the far-right and parts of the left joined forces to kill this reform bill. And kill it they did.

Less than a decade later, attitudes had evolved. Well, a little bit. The 1946 Lamine Guèye Law (named after Amadou Lamine Guèye, mayor of Dakar and deputy for Senegal in the French parliament) proclaimed that all inhabitants of French colonial possessions would henceforth become citizens. Did that put an end to the existence of colonial subjects? Not really, as the old colony of Senegal, with its long history of representation in the French parliament, remained an exception. The practical implementation of this newly declared equality showed that White people weren't ready to give up their privileged position. For example, in Algeria, a 1947 statute declared 'genuine equality between all French citizens' in terms of access to public and electoral office. But, in reality, there was a 'twin-track' electoral college with 500,000 White voters given the same weight as three million 'native' voters.[2] If the aim was to show that Whites were at least six times more important than non-Whites, then they went the right way about it.[3]

Is it possible to speak about colonisation without mentioning the key role played by sex in establishing White domination? The

1 Cited in Le Cour Grandmaison, *De l'indigénat*, p. 63.

2 Le Cour Grandmaison, *De l'indigénat*, p. 63.

3 Pascal Blanchard, Nicolas Bancel, Sandrine Lemaire, *Décolonisations françaises: la chute d'un empire* (Paris: La Martinière, 2020).

first colonisers to reach the Americas (they actually thought they were in the East Indies) were astonished to encounter naked men who 'made no effort to hide their shameful parts'.[1] In Europe, the naked body was associated with original sin, which meant that men and women had a duty to hide their nudity. The fascination with the 'noble savage' grew as Europeans discovered people with bodies that were waxed, tattooed, adorned with feathers and jewellery. People with loose morals and multiple sexual partners in what seemed a semi-Edenic world. In order to counter the sensual appeal of these men and women, Europeans transformed them into demons, thereby hiding their own attraction to them behind moral principles. These principles gave Europeans the right to kill and rape and to brand them as their own property, a practice that would become systematic with the advent of the transatlantic slave trade.

The right to control the native's body, in particular women's bodies, seemed self-evident. This body can be an object of contempt or desire, a disposable object to be used, then discarded. The control of the native woman's body is the point where sexism and racism meet, sexuality acting as a field of domination. As Françoise Héritier has argued, the oldest form of domination is that of men over women: 'Man is the only species where the males kill the females.'[2] The White man played a central role in the racist practice of colonial domination. Yes, that's right: White thinking is above all else masculine. We can see this at work in the multiple forms of domination that developed during the colonial period. Just think about the thousands of images on postcards, advertising posters, paintings, photographs, films that staged the inferiority of non-Whites, reducing them to vile and degrading sexual fantasies. These images are analysed brilliantly in the volume *Sexe, race et colonies* [*Sex, Race and the Colonies*].[3]

In the heart of Paris, there's a museum dedicated to the work of the famous artist Eugène Delacroix. I've studied the

1 Letter from Pêro Vaz de Caminha to King Manuel I of Portugal in 1500, cited in Blanchard, Bancel, et al., *Sexe, race et colonies*.

2 Françoise Héritier 'L'Homme est la seule espèce dont les males tuent les femelles', *Sciences et avenir*, 169 (2012): https://www.sciencesetavenir.fr/fondamental/francoise-heritier-l-homme-est-la-seule-espece-dont-les-males-tuent-les-femelles_7660.

3 Blanchard, et al. *Sexe, race et colonies*.

Orientalist paintings there and they've allowed me to understand how, all through the nineteenth century, White thinking created an idea of the Orient that reinforced White identity. I began to understand how sexual domination forged the image of the 'Oriental' woman as a lecherous temptress. It also cast the non-White man as the source of a primitive savagery, a pure, threatening force of nature. Racial domination has such deep historical roots that it would be naive and deceitful to claim that such prejudices no longer exist today.

Who can forget?
That Black people were never called Sir *or* Madam…
Not because they were spoken to like friends
It was just that Sir *and* Madam *were reserved for White people.*

Who can forget?

They told me
You're a wog! A monkey! A cockroach!
You're dirty! Dirty wog!
Your mother slept with a Nigger, you're a bastard!
They told me
You should go back where you came from! Back to the jungle!
Back to your hut!
You should climb back up your tree! Swing from your vine! Get your bananas!
You should thank Belgium for taking you in!
Even if you were born here…

Who can forget?
That Black people were never called Sir *or* Madam…

You will have to learn to keep on the move…
It's already been rented! The vacancy's already been filled! We're full up!
You will have to learn to justify yourself…
I'm Belgian! I've got a degree! I've got qualifications!
You will have to learn another history too…

Africa! Savages! The under-developed!
Integrate. Assimilate.
Cage yourself. Limit yourself.
Doubt yourself. Be afraid.
Feel ashamed of your colour.
Forget about your brothers and sisters.
You, the little exotic bird, like Josephine Baker,
Gazelle, tigress, what a butt, what an ass!

Who can forget?
That Black people were never called Sir *or* Madam…
That Arabs were never called Sir *or* Madam…
That the Roma were never called Sir *or* Madam…
You, my father, were never called Sir…
You weren't spoken to like a friend
It was just that Sir *and* Madam *were reserved for White people.*

Who can forget?

Lisette Lombé, 'Who can forget?'[1]

9. A CIVILISING MISSION

To justify its existence, colonisation liked to present itself as a civilising mission.[2] Colonisation was a project designed to raise 'savages' to the same level as White people. The French Romantic author Chateaubriand claimed that this meant the non-White world needed 'White chiefs' if it wanted to raise itself up: 'When they [the Orientals] go a long time without seeing a conquering hero delivering the justice of the heavens, they appear like soldiers without a leader, citizens without a legislator and a family without a father.'[3] Taking charge of their affairs was thus doing them a favour. In fact, it was a moral obligation that flowed directly from the natural superiority of White people. You can see this type of propaganda everywhere. Take for example, Daniel Defoe's famous

1 Lisette Lombé, 'Qui oubliera?', in *Black Words* (Amay: L'Arbre à paroles, 2018).

2 See Pascal Blanchard, Françoise Vergès, Nicolas Bancel, *La Colonisation* (Paris: Milan, 2012).

3 Cited in Liauzu, *Race et civilisation*, p. 169.

novel, *Robinson Crusoe* (1719). The castaway Robinson describes his first encounter with the 'Indian' Friday in revealing terms: 'at length, he came close to me, and then he kneeled down again, kissed the ground and laid his head upon the ground, and taking me by the foot, set my foot upon his head: this, it seems, was in token of swearing to be my slave forever'.[1]

At the end of the nineteenth century, Paul Leroy-Beaulieu, a Professor at the prestigious Collège de France, didn't beat about the bush in expressing his belief in White superiority:

> It is neither natural nor just that the civilised peoples
> of the West should leave perhaps half the world
> in the hands of small groups of ignorant, impotent
> men, truly simple-minded children sprinkled across
> an incommensurable vastness, or leave them to
> decrepit peoples with no energy or direction.[2]

Around the same time, Pierre Larousse, the famous lexicographer, claimed that Europe was interested only in helping the colonised. In his *Universal Dictionary of the Nineteenth Century*, Larousse wrote of the 'Negro': 'Their intellectual inferiority, far from conferring upon us the right to prey on their weakness, imposes a duty upon us to aid and protect them.' The violence of these words hits me like a punch in the stomach. But, when you think about it, many people today still think that Black people are inferior, don't they? By the 1930s, the discourse on Black inferiority had evolved a bit. But not much. The Minister for the Colonies, Albert Sarraut, could bring himself to admit that Europe had initially established control over the colonies through the use of violence. But now they were just there to help: 'Our actions in the colonies [...] are no longer, as they were in the early days, guided by the law that "might makes right" but by the law that "it's right for the strong

---

1 Daniel Defoe, *Robinson Crusoe* (London: Penguin, 1994 [1719]), p. 200.

2 Paul Leroy-Beaulieu, *L'Etat moderne et ses fonctions* (Paris: Guillaumin & Cie, 1900 [1890]), p. 451.

to aid the weak", which truly appears to be the most noble and elevated law of all'.[1]

If we return to the late nineteenth century, we can cite the example of Jules Ferry, a politician primarily remembered in France as a leading figure of the Third Republic and the victory of progress and modernity over religion and tradition. That same Jules Ferry gave a speech in parliament on 28 July 1885, where he explained in no uncertain terms what colonisation truly meant:

> The policy of colonial expansion is part of a political and economic system; I have already stated that one can relate this system to three types of ideas; economic ideas, civilisational ideas of the greatest significance, and political and patriotic ideas.
>
> If we examine the economic question, I have chosen to lay before you, supported by some facts and figures, those considerations that justify the policy of colonial expansion in terms of that need, experienced with ever greater urgency by the industrial populations of Europe, and, particularly, in our rich, industrious country of France: the need for new economic outlets.[2]

White thinking is always on the lookout for new markets.

And Ferry went on to present a prime characteristic of White thinking: the pursuit of economic gain disguised as a civilising mission:

> Why? Because just next door, Germany is putting up trade barriers, because on the other side of the ocean, the United States of America has now opted for a protectionist policy, and it is protectionism pushed to new extremes; because not only are the big markets, I would not say closing, but shrinking, becoming more and more difficult to access with our industrial goods; because these great states are beginning to

1 Albert Sarraut, *Grandeur et servitude coloniales* (Paris: L'Harmattan, 2012), p. 74.

2 Jean Garrigues, *Les Grands Discours parlementaires: de Mirabeau à nos jours* (Paris: Armand Colin, 2017).

flood our own markets with previously unseen products. This holds true not only for agriculture, which has cruelly suffered and for which competition is no longer limited to the circle of great European states largely in relation to which the old economic theories had been established; today, as you are fully aware, competition, the law of supply and demand, free trade, the role of financial speculation, all of these things have an influence that extends to the ends of the earth. This greatly complicates things, creating economic difficulties [...]. It's an extremely serious problem.

Gentlemen, it is so serious, so exhilarating, that the short-sighted are obliged to envisage, to prepare for and to provide for an era in which the great market of South America, which belonged to us, so to speak, almost since time immemorial, will be fought over, and perhaps taken from us by products from North America. There is nothing more grave, no social problem more serious; in this context, our programme is inextricably linked to colonial policy.[1]

As for the 'humanitarian and civilisational aspects of the question':

Gentlemen, we must loudly proclaim the whole truth. We must openly proclaim that the superior races do indeed hold a right over the inferior races [...]. I repeat that the superior races hold a right because they also have an obligation towards [the inferior races] [...]. When we landed in Algiers [in 1830] to destroy piracy and ensure freedom of trade in the Mediterranean, were we acting like bandits, conquerors, destroyers? [...] Who would deny that it is the good fortune of these unfortunate peoples of Equatorial Africa to fall under the protection of the French nation or the English nation? Is it not our

1 Garrigues, *Les Grands Discours parlementaires*.

primary duty [...] to fight the trading of Negroes, this vile trafficking, and slavery, this infamy?[1]

Never underestimate the potential for hypocrisy of politicians serving the interests of a greedy minority.

Some people will no doubt say, 'OK, so Ferry was a colonialist, but who wasn't back then?' Well, as a matter of fact, there wasn't unanimous support for Ferry's speech. Far from it, indeed. His opponents weren't fooled by his unbearable cynicism. Take, for example, Camille Pelletan, the member of parliament for the Bouches-du-Rhône region in southern France, who denounced these attempts to hide the ferocious violence of colonialism behind a mask of civilisation. Jules Maigne, who represented the Auvergne region, challenged Ferry directly, telling him that his speech, delivered in the parliament of the country where the rights of man had been proclaimed, was quite frankly embarrassing.[2] To which Ferry replied that the Declaration of the Rights of Man hadn't been written 'for the Blacks of Equatorial Africa'. I suppose at least he was being honest.

The most famous French opponent of White thinking at that time was Georges Clemenceau, who in 1885 was a member of parliament for Paris. He didn't mince his words in denouncing Ferry's hypocrisy:

> No, there is no such thing as the rights of so-called superior nations over so-called inferior nations; there is the struggle to exist, a fatal necessity which, the greater our degree of civilisation, the greater the need to contain this struggle within the limits of justice and the law; but, let us not attempt to dress up violence with the hypocritical name of civilisation; let us not speak of rights and obligations! [...] It is not a right; it is its very negation. To speak about civilisation in this context is to add hypocrisy to violence.[3]

---

1 Cited in Liauzu, *Race et civilisation*, pp. 190–191.

2 See Blanchard et al., *Culture coloniale en France*.

3 Speech in the Chambre of Deputies, 30 July 1885.

But very few people were willing to listen because what he said ran counter to the economic interests of the period. The perverse but all-too-common idea expressed by Ferry – we've colonised these peoples out of a sense of obligation and they should thank us for it – was the subject of a wide consensus. It was taught to all French schoolchildren of the Third Republic. Just take a look at Ernest Lavisse's famous history textbook, which was first published in 1913. This is how it describes Pierre Savorgnan de Brazza, one of the adventurers who helped to colonise central Africa:

> Brazza was a remarkable man. He travelled across a vast country in Africa, called the Congo. He did not harm the inhabitants. He spoke to them kindly and asked them to obey France. Once they had done so, he planted a tall pole in the earth on which the French flag was raised. This meant that the area in question belonged to France. One day, as the flag was being raised next to a village in the Congo, a group of slaves was passing. Brazza halted them and said: 'Wherever the French flag is found, there must be no slaves.' And you can see here [in the photo accompanying the text] that the collar that imprisons their necks and the ropes that bind their legs are removed. Two of these poor creatures who have just been freed are so joyous that they are capering about. This proves once again that France is kind and generous to the people it has subjugated.[1]

Too many White people want to believe that, although Europe's role in 'pacifying' the colonies was clumsy and incomplete, deep down, it was guided by a genuine desire to do good in Africa, Asia and the rest of the world. I'm sure that must feel reassuring. And that's why I want to close this chapter by citing two examples. The first relates to France's Black African troops, the famous *tirailleurs sénégalais* who fought with the French against Nazism

---

1 Ernest Lavisse, *Histoire de France, cours élémentaire* (Paris: Armand Colin, 1913), pp. 168–69.

in May–June 1940. Several thousand were slaughtered by the Germans.[1] Others were imprisoned for the next four years. When they were liberated, they demanded to be paid the back pay due to them. They were sent back to Senegal and other parts of Africa. When a contingent arrived at the demobilisation camp in Thiaroye, just outside Dakar, in November 1944, the army refused to pay them. The soldiers protested and, in response, on 1 December, many of them were gunned down in cold blood. An official narrative was promoted in order to disguise both the theft and the murders.[2] Even today, we still don't know exactly how many men were killed.

The second example relates to General Lothar von Trotha, commander of Germany's colonial forces who oversaw the massacre of the Herero people in Namibia. In 1904, he claimed that:

> I am fairly familiar with tribes in Africa. They are all alike in thinking that they will surrender only to force. Indeed, my policy has always been to exert such force by brutally instilling terror, and sometimes by cruelty. I annihilate the insurgent tribes in streams of blood because this is the only seed that will grow into something new and stable.[3]

In just a few years, the violence advocated by von Trotha led to the genocide of three quarters of the Herero (and vast numbers of the Nama people): men, women and children. Admittedly, taken as a whole, colonisation was not primarily driven by genocidal intent. It was, however, a component of colonisation, and it would be negligent of us to forget it. Colonisation never has been and never will be achieved without criminal acts. Every revolt, every act of resistance

---

1 Raffael Scheck, *Une saison noire: les massacres de tirailleurs sénégalais* (Paris: Tallandier, 2007).

2 Armelle Mabon, *Prisonniers de guerre "indigènes": visages oubliés de la France occupée* (Paris: La Découverte, 2019); Julien Fargettas, 'La révolte des tirailleurs sénégalais de Tiaroye: entre reconstructions mémorielles et histoire', *Vingtième siècle, revue d'histoire*, 92 (2006), pp. 117–30.

3 Quoted in Plumelle-Uribe, *White Ferocity*, p. 92.

was met with fierce, bloody repression[1] Neither colonial conquest nor decolonisation is ever achieved without mass murder.[2]

10. IS COLONISATION REALLY OVER?

I come from one of the richest countries on the planet. Yet the people of my country are among the poorest of the world.

The troubling reality is that the abundance of our natural resources – gold, coltan, cobalt and other strategic minerals – is the root cause of war, extreme violence and abject poverty.

We love nice cars, jewellery and gadgets. I have a smartphone myself. These items contain minerals found in our country. Often mined in inhuman conditions by young children, victims of intimidation and sexual violence.

When you drive your electric car, when you use your smartphone or admire your jewellery, take a minute to reflect on the human cost of manufacturing these objects.

As consumers, let us at least insist that these products are manufactured with respect for human dignity.

Turning a blind eye to this tragedy is being complicit.

It's not just perpetrators of violence who are responsible for their crimes, it is also those who choose to look the other way.

My country is being systematically looted with the complicity of people claiming to be our leaders. Looted for their power, their wealth and their glory. Looted at the expense of millions of innocent men, women and children abandoned in extreme poverty.

---

1 See Bancel, et al. *The Colonial Legacy in France.*

2 Yves Bénot, *Massacres coloniaux, 1944–50: la IVᵉ République et la mise au pas des colonies françaises* (Paris: La Découverte, 1994); Marc Ferro (ed.), *Le Livre noir du colonialisme, XVIᵉ-XXIᵉ siècle: de l'extermination à la repentance* (Paris: Hachette, 2004).

While the profits from our minerals end up in the
pockets of a predatory oligarchy.[1]

Nobel Lecture by Denis Mukwege
Gynaecologist and human rights activist
Nobel Peace Prize Winner 2018

Is colonisation really over? The official history tells us that
decolonisation had been completed in most French colonies by
the early 1960s. It's forgotten that Djibouti was only decolonised
in 1977, five years after I was born. Does decolonisation mean
that these newly independent states gained genuine sovereignty?
Sovereignty involves the freedom to take your own decisions on
strategic, diplomatic, economic and military issues. But almost
all of the West's former colonial possessions live under a system
imposed by White thinking. Their political decisions continue to
be shaped by powerful external forces, and their governing elites
act primarily to preserve their own interests. In France, the secret
deals – forged through pressure, threats and corruption – between
Paris and the capitals of the former colonies are collectively
known by the term *la Françafrique*. It's often claimed that this
system was put in place by General de Gaulle in 1959–60. But
in reality he was just continuing the exploitation of Africa in a
neo-colonial form.

The previous chapters have shown that greed usually lies
behind religious, scientific and political justifications for
exploitation. *La Françafrique* is no different. Its very existence
is predicated on economic imperatives and the desire to
protect France's strategic interests on the African continent.
Decolonisation happened as a result of revolts, wars and the will
of the colonised peoples to bring an end to colonialism, and this
obliged France to give up direct control of vast territories that
it had been pillaging for a very long time. The loss of access to
these raw materials and, in particular, these sources of energy
(Algeria's oil and gas) could not be tolerated. France had to
guarantee its supplies and maintain its independence from the

---

1 www.nobelprize.org/prizes/peace/2018/mukwege/55721-denis-mukwege-
nobel-lecture-2/.

great global powers, especially the United States. Thus, a neo-colonial politics was born.

For instance, the French state may have seemed ready to admit as early as 1959 that Algerian independence was inevitable but, at the same time, it wanted nothing to change, at least when it came to its economic interests. The Algerian example is particularly telling: General de Gaulle came to power in France in 1958, at a time when all of the conditions necessary for peace were already in place but it took four long years until Algeria was granted its independence. Why? It wasn't simply because Algeria was a beloved territory, dear to France. Vast reserves of oil had been discovered under the Saharan desert in the 1950s. And the Algerian Sahara was also the site of the nuclear tests that France had been preparing for years, the first bomb detonated in 1960 (after Algerian independence, they were moved to French Polynesia, in 1966; the Sahara was also the site of the French space programme, which would later be transferred to French Guyana). To relinquish control of French Algeria was difficult, but to abandon this massive oil wealth, as well as France's status as a nuclear power was unthinkable. As early as 1957, the French government in Paris worked to create a Communal Organisation of Saharan Regions (OCRS), which centred on two Algerian departments with the largest oil deposits. A decree issued on 22 November 1958 created the oil code, a suite of regulations that gave French companies the exclusive rights to manage and prospect for this black gold. The objective was clear: to maintain a stranglehold on these lands even if Algeria were to become independent. It was no surprise then that the Evian Accords (1962), which brought the war to a close, recognised the oil code and left real control of the nation's oil deposits in the hands of the former coloniser, even though they officially belonged to the Algerian people. These economic rewards came at the cost of four more years of war and tens of thousands of lives. For France, this was a price worth paying to allow it to get its own way when negotiating Algerian independence.

What happened in Algeria allows us to understand that the former colonisers were not willing to simply abandon the resources that once belonged to them in these newly decolonised countries. Just look at the African franc (CFA), which has been used since 1945 in most of France's former African colonies. This currency is tied to the euro and is still used today by over 150 million Africans. It was never intended to promote the economic development of these countries but rather to maintain their dependence on France.[1] The abbreviation 'CFA' today refers to the 'African Financial Community' in West Africa and to 'African Financial Cooperation' in Central Africa. But for many years it meant 'French Colonies of Africa'. I will acknowledge that the CFA franc has provided a certain monetary stability during often troubled periods on the continent. I am also happy to accept that it has prevented currency speculation by the financial markets on countries weakened by political crises.[2] But the example of Guinea in 1958 shows us the dark side of the CFA franc. Much to the annoyance of General de Gaulle, Guinea had gained its independence through a referendum in 1958, and when the country tried to launch its own currency, Paris immediately sought to undermine it. Operation Persil was launched and, in the words of Maurice Robert, a diplomat and former head of the intelligence service, it involved 'introducing a large number of counterfeit Guinean banknotes into the country with the aim of destabilising the economy'. The operation was just another front in De Gaulle's efforts to overthrow the Guinean president Sékou Touré:

> We wanted to undermine Sékou Touré, make him vulnerable, unpopular and make it easier for the opposition to take power. [...] An operation on this scale has to be carried out in stages: the collection and analysis of intelligence, developing a plan of action on the basis of this intelligence, considering the logistical requirements and putting them in place, taking all necessary measures to bring the plan to fruition [...] With the aid of Guinean refugees in Senegal, we also formed guerrilla groups in the Fouta-Djalon region. They

1 See Fanny Pigeaud, Ndongo Samba Sylla, *L'Arme invisible de la Françafrique: une histoire du franc CFA* (Paris: La Découverte, 2018).

2 On this topic, see Kako Nubukpo, Martial Ze Belinga, Bruno Tinel, Demba Moussa Dembelé (eds), *Sortir l'Afrique de la servitude monétaire: à qui profite le franc CFA?* (Paris: La Dispute, 2017). See also Kako Nubukpo, *Urgence africaine* (Paris: Odile Jacob, 2019).

were trained by French experts operating in secret. We armed and trained these Guinean opposition figures, many of whom were Fulani, in order to create a climate of fear in Guinea and, if possible, to overthrow Sékou Touré.[1]

So, after Guinea became independent, the aim of the French government was to undermine the country. The choice was clear: opt for the CFA or face a permanent monetary crisis.

Even though France's former African colonies have all gained their independence, they continue to suffer economic domination by their former coloniser, in particular the imposition of the CFA currency and the limits this places on their economic freedom. Would the French accept it if their currency was tied to a foreign currency, printed in a foreign country and if their economic policy was decided by a former colonial power? Well, that's what's happened to France's former colonies in Africa. When decolonisation was being negotiated, the currency issue became a way of ensuring that these countries would remain within the former coloniser's sphere of influence. The benefits of this shared currency were highlighted. It would stabilise exchange rates and prevent high rates of inflation that might have followed the launch of a new, independent currency. This state of dependency has led, however, to an overvalued currency, which is helpful when you want to bring in imports but is deeply harmful to exports. This hampers the development of domestic industry and leads these countries to buy products on the world market (and in particular from France) that they could make themselves at a fraction of the cost of these imports. But it's the symbolic importance of the CFA franc that has attracted the most criticism. For many critics, it is an attack on the sovereignty of the two central banks in Francophone Africa. The Togolese economist Kako Nubukpo has argued that it's even worse than that:

> we suffer [from] chronic bad governance [and] we need to escape the 'protection' offered by the CFA franc. It works like an anaesthetic because

1 Maurice Robert, *'Ministre' de l'Afrique*, interviews with André Renault (Paris: Seuil, 2004).

even when they govern the economy badly, these rulers are reassured that Paris will always be there to cover for their mistakes [...]. As there are no limits to the sums that can be converted into other currencies, the local elites can freely deposit their money in foreign bank accounts or buy themselves an apartment in Paris. That's the key point.[1]

In December 2019, Emmanuel Macron, the French president, made a statement that finally seemed to respond to the demands of African citizens and break with this neo-colonial system. A collective of African intellectuals summed up Macron's statement in the following terms:

The predicted reforms are as follows: the CFA franc in West Africa will be renamed ECO; the Central Bank of the West African States (BCEAO) will no longer have to deposit its currency reserves with the French Treasury; France will no longer have representatives on the management bodies of the BCEAO.[2]

Will that really be enough? Because France will remain the guarantor of this new currency, and now the EU and the European Central Bank will be able to exercise control over the monetary policy of the member states of the West African Economic and Monetary Union.

But *la Françafrique* is also a political, diplomatic and military reality. During the Cold War, its role was to prevent former African colonies from falling into the Soviet 'camp'. Indeed, that was pretty much the mission assigned to France by NATO. The role of Paris was to install regimes friendly towards France, keep them in power, and to sideline all genuine and potential opponents. How many military coups? How much repression? How many opposition figures

1 Interview with Laurence Caramel, 'Il faut sortir de l'omerta sur le franc CFA', *Le Monde Afrique*, 30 September 2016.

2 'Déclaration des intellectuels d'Afrique et de la diaspora sur les réformes du franc CFA', Dakar, January 2020: https://blogs.mediapart.fr/fanny-pigeaud/blog/070120/declaration-dintellectuels-africains-sur-les-reformes-du-franc-cfa.

imprisoned or summarily executed? And all instigated, supported and financed by the Fifth Republic.[1] So many leaders marginalised or eliminated because they were adjudged to be 'incompatible' with Western interests: Sékou Touré in Guinea, Thomas Sankara in Burkina Faso, Sylvanus Olympio in Togo, Patrice Lumumba in the Congo (today's Democratic Republic of the Congo), Salvador Allende in Chile. Are the hierarchies of the past not still with us? But on this point, like on so many others, White thinking prefers to look the other way. How many Westerners are aware of just how much they owe the former colonies? Are you aware?

At the heart of *la Françafrique* was Jacques Foccart, General de Gaulle's *Monsieur Afrique*. President Jacques Chirac, who brought Foccart back in from the cold in the 1990s, was fond of saying: 'Much of the money in our coffers was obtained through centuries of exploitation in Africa.' In January 2001 at the France-Africa summit in Yaoundé in Cameroon, Chirac reacted with rare honesty to a statement released that very day by the French episcopate calling for France to distance itself from authoritarian African regimes. Speaking off the record with journalists, he stated that:

> We bled Africa dry over four and half centuries. Then we pillaged its natural resources; then we said [Africans] are good for nothing. In the name of religion, we destroyed their culture and, now, as we're supposed to be more refined, we steal their best minds with scholarships. Then we observe that poor old Africa is in a terrible state, that it is incapable of producing its own elites. We got rich at Africans' expense and now we lecture them.[2]

How long would the French economy survive if it were deprived of the uranium that supplies our nuclear reactors (France derives about 70% of its electricity from nuclear energy)? And this uranium, this fuel for our reactors, where does it come from? The major deposits of uranium from which France draws its supplies are to be found in Australia, the United States, Canada, South

---

1 See Jean-Pierre Bat, *La Fabrique des 'barbouzes': histoire des réseaux Foccart en Afrique* (Paris: Nouveau Monde Éditions, 2015).

2 Remarks reported in *Le Monde*, 15 February 2007.

Africa, Russia. And a third of it comes from Niger, an African country that is twice the size of France but extremely poor. Its sales of uranium to France earn the country $140 million a year or, in other words, one tenth of the earnings made in France for producing almost three quarters of our electricity! It was estimated that, in 2020, Niger would supply half of the nuclear fuel imported by France.[1]

Many people believe that France intervened in the military conflict in Mali in 2013–14 because it was next door to Niger and the uranium mines in Arlit and Akokan that belong to the French nuclear energy company Areva (now known as Orano). Indeed, if the mines in Niger were to shut down, it would be catastrophic for French industry and our whole way of life. I acknowledge that this military intervention is, on the one hand, a war against Islamic extremism that has ravaged this region of the Sahel. But it is also (and we could say the same for military interventions elsewhere in Africa and around the world), a symbol of the power struggles that exist between global economic powerhouses to gain control of natural resources. During the colonial era and still today, the White world always uses its military might to defend its strategic interests and maintain its standard of living. That's no doubt why there was such a wide consensus in France in support of the military intervention in Mali.

During the colonial era, Niger's role was to supply the imperial centre. Even though Niger has been independent since 1960, has that really changed today? This country, which is the fourth-largest producer of uranium in the world, is depleting its own natural resources for the benefit of the world's leading economic powers. Yet it still endures desperate levels of poverty. It suffers from chronic food insecurity and recurring natural disasters (drought, floods, plagues of locusts). Niger is one of the poorest nations on earth: the average income is just $420 a year. In 2018, the country was bottom of the 189 countries listed on the UN's

---

1 'Mines d'uranium: "La France n'a pas d'intérêt à ce que le conflit malien s'étende au Niger"'. Interview with Emmanuel Grégoire, Director of Research at Institut de Recherche pour le Développement, by Angela Bolis, *Le Monde*, 31 January 2013.

Human Development Index.[1] For its part, Amnesty International stated in a 2017–18 report that 82% of the population lives in 'extreme poverty': 'Women were particularly affected by food insecurity in rural areas, a fact linked to, among other things, their socioeconomic status and the impact of climate change and extractive industries [i.e. primarily uranium]'.[2] The World Bank explains that the country is 'confronted by significant macroeconomic risks [...] [due to] the persistent weakness in the price of raw materials'.

Do you think the price of uranium is set by Niger? Well, think again. Niger's natural resources are bought for miserly prices based on decisions informed by White thinking. The value of raw materials is set by the stock market, using mechanisms dominated by financiers of various kinds: pension funds, banks, various international investors, capitalists guided by White economic thinking. All of these different players act in the interests of the wealthy, and their trade dealings make the rich richer while poor countries grow ever poorer, for they have no control over these markets. That's why the president of Niger has called for a 'rebalancing' of the partnership with France. He has complained that his country does not earn enough from its wealth of natural resources. There have long been calls for greater financial transparency in the energy sector. Thankfully, in the wake of an EU directive, French law has since 2014 required companies in the mining sector (gas, oil, metals, uranium) to publish an annual list of payments made to the countries in which they operate. It has thus been established that Paris pays ten times as much money to Kazakhstan as it does to Niger, even though the former provides less uranium to France.[3] Are we in the West not ashamed of a system that keeps down the price of raw materials and leaves the

---

1 Human Development Indices and Indicators, Statistical Update 2018. Report produced by the United Nations Development Programme:
http://hdr.undp.org/sites/default/files/2018_human_development_statistical_update.pdf.

2 Amnesty International, Report on Niger 2017/18: https://www.amnesty.org/en/countries/africa/niger/report-niger/.

3 See the report published on 13 April 2017 by a group of NGOs (One, Sherpa & Oxfam): 'Beyond Transparency: Investigating the New Extractive Industry Disclosures': https://www.oxfamfrance.org/wp-content/uploads/2017/09/file_attachments_beyondtransparency.pdf.

inhabitants of these countries in poverty, all so that we can live in comfort? Is it not time to take a stand against this?

White thinking prefers to develop a form of propaganda that leads us to believe that Niger, like many other countries, is solely responsible for its own poverty. There is continuity between the reality of the world as it is today and as it was in the past. Countries get rich through predatory behaviour that allows them to gain control of natural resources in other countries. In the past, they used violence (i.e. colonisation), while today they adopt a neo-colonial system. In many countries, local politicians work hand in hand with the former colonial powers to exploit their own peoples. Co-opting local elites remains the norm.

This predatory behaviour doesn't stop at raw materials. It extends to the domination of the bodies of women and children. White thinking dictates who is allowed to have children and who isn't. In July 2017, the French President, Emmanuel Macron, claimed: 'When there are countries today where women still have seven or eight children, then you can decide to spend billions of euros, but you won't stabilise the situation at all.'[1] Macron's vision of African women is an old refrain that was immediately denounced by the political commentator Françoise Vergès: 'Third World women are made responsible for under-development. In effect, this reverses the causality: most studies prove that today it's under-development that leads to over-population. The theory of over-population also avoids any questioning of the role of colonialism and imperialism in the creation of poverty.'[2]

We should not forget that the reach of White thinking in France extended as far as policies designed to limit birth rates in its overseas departments and territories (DOM-TOM). These policies led to a scandal in the French department of Réunion (in the Indian Ocean) in 1970 when it was revealed that thousands of non-White women had undergone forced sterilisation. In mainland France, abortion was still a crime (under the Vichy law of 1942, which led to the execution a year later of Marie-Louise Giraud for carrying out abortions) and forms of birth control were

1 Émilie Tôn (and Geoffroy Bonnefoy), 'G20: les propos de Macron sur les "7 à 8 enfants" par Africaine passent mal', *L'Express*, 11 July 2017.

2 Cited in Balla Fofana, 'M. Macron, laissez tranquille le ventre des Africaines', *Libération*, 11 July 2017.

limited to the 'natural' methods promoted by the Catholic Church. However, in the post-war period, this did not prevent a vast system of contraception, abortion and sterilisation being implemented for non-White women in the overseas departments, using an 1893 law offering free medical assistance to the poor (AMG), which was extended to overseas France in 1946. In particular, the cost of surgery was reimbursed by the welfare system. The AMG law was implemented by town halls and doctors, and became part of government policy: divorced from its original purpose of aiding the destitute, it became a way of rewarding or punishing families, who were left dependent on the state.[1] Abortions were carried out against the will of pregnant women, often in late-stage pregnancy, and afterwards their tubes were tied. One woman underwent an operation while three months' pregnant and, when she woke up, was told that she had suffered appendicitis. But in reality the surgeons had tied her tubes and killed the child she was carrying. A journalist for the French news magazine *Le Nouvel Observateur* wrote: 'If the operation went wrong [...], women didn't have the right to a blood transfusion, as the vials of blood were reserved for insured or paying patients.'[2] The Saint-Benoît clinic, run by Dr David Moreau, was the leading player in this system.

What's more, doctors profited from the system by embezzling public monies, sometimes even submitting claims for surgery that never took place. This allowed doctors to accumulate AMG vouchers with which they could systematically claim reimbursement from the social welfare system. In Réunion alone, it is estimated that thousands of abortions were performed. According to the *Nouvel Observateur* reporter: 'It was said that, at that rhythm, doctors shouldn't have any trouble paying for their villas, their yachts and their travel.'[3]

Similar practices occurred in the French Caribbean – members of my own family endured them – but this is less well known than the situation in Réunion, which culminated in a trial. The charges that led to that trial were as much to do with fraud as they were with

1 See Françoise Vergès, *The Wombs of Women: Race, Capital, Feminism*, trans. by Kaiama L. Glover (Durham, NC & London: Duke University Press, 2020), p. 13.

2 Cited in Vergès, *The Wombs of Women*, p. 21.

3 Vergès, *The Wombs of Women* p. 21.

forced sterilisation, and those who were eventually sentenced were largely bit-part players. Dr Moreau 'was declared civilly responsible but received no punishment'.[1] Writing in *Politique Hebdo*, Claude Angeli has argued that Moreau's almost total impunity and the lack of publicity to which the trial gave rise can be explained by the role of White, male thinking:

> It's also a mock trial [*procès blanc*] that the Courts have covered over with their fake marble. The judges, the prosecutor, the deputy prosecutor, the majority of lawyers, and four of the five defendants had fair skin. A trial rigged for men, in the end. Men judged other men and made dozens of worried, uncomfortable women parade before them, like so many pieces of evidence. With irony, awkwardness, clumsiness or imbecility, these men talked about these women's genitalia, their periods, their tubes, and their female 'mechanics'.[2]

If we are to truly understand such a case, we have to go all the way back to slavery and the way in which the French state treated the bodies of Black women. It begins with the decision to opt for a slavery based on the capture of ever more slaves rather than one based on reproduction of existing slaves. Slave women were not captured with an eye on their capacity to produce a future generation of slaves (even though the Code Noir declared that any child born of a slave was the property of the master), but rather for their physical strength, just like their male counterparts. The French colonists in the slave plantations calculated the cost of a slave based on physical reproduction and decided that it was better to replenish their stock through 'commercial reproduction'. In the era of the slave trade, therefore, there was a systematic choice to purchase more men than women, which led to a profound gender imbalance in these colonies. This imbalance persisted after the abolition of slavery and continued to scar these territories long after they were supposedly integrated into the French state. From 1920 onwards, this male surplus had finally disappeared and the

1 Vergès, *The Wombs of Women*, p. 19.

2 Cited in Vergès, *The Wombs of Women*, pp. 21–22.

population began to grow, no longer via 'immigration' but via the birth rate. Unaware of this evolution, the French government began to develop a discourse very similar to that promoted by various international organisations, which claims that the development of the so-called 'Third World' was hindered by the fact that women in these countries have 'too many children': '[D]emographics in the Third World [we]re [...] a threat to global security. [...] Third World women's fertility was practically equated with a terrorist threat.'[1]

'It was a question of convincing the thousands of young women and men arriving on the "job market" in the DOM that there were no prospects where they were and that only the metropole would save them from poverty and a dead-end future.'[2] In the early 1960s, the French state created a public body, BUMIDOM, whose mission was to promote and facilitate migration from the overseas departments (DOMs or *départements d'outre-mer*) to mainland France, promising that 'the future is elsewhere'. At the same time, the government was encouraging inhabitants of mainland France to move in the other direction and relocate to the overseas territories, which led to a new form of racism as the 'zoreys' sought to distinguish themselves from the local White people. 'Between 1967 and 1974, Guadeloupe and Martinique lost thirty-nine thousand and forty thousand inhabitants, respectively, or 12% of their population.'[3] In France, Caribbean women largely worked in the service industries (carers, nursery assistants) but also as cleaners. Indeed, a training centre was opened in the greater Paris region to ensure a steady supply of 'good cleaners'. The French state also ensured that these migrants were closely monitored.

In 1962, a finishing touch was applied to this system of domination designed to 'civilise' the non-White working classes:

> [T]he director of the Departmental Direction of Sanitary and Social Affairs (DDASS) proposed taking poor Reunionese children from their families and integrating them into select French

1 *The Wombs of Women*, pp. 59–60.

2 *The Wombs of Women*, p. 75.

3 *The Wombs of Women*, p. 79.

families in underpopulated areas of France. Between 1963 and 1982, 2,150 children — this is the final number given by the governmental commission created in 2016 [...] — between the ages of eight months and twelve years were thus ripped from their families by the DDASS and sent to deserted regions of [France].[1]

These 'welfare' kids were put to work from an early age in terrible conditions often scarred by racism and violence. The French state acknowledged moral responsibility for its actions in 2014, thanks in large part to the testimony of one of these children, Jean-Jacques Martial, who told his story in his book, *Une enfance volée* (*A Stolen Childhood*): 'We were like the slaves, our forebears: suffering in silence, swallowing our pain and showing no reaction'.[2] His case reminds me of a grim incident in Chad that took place in 2007 when L'Arche de Zoé (Zoe's Ark), a charitable organisation, undertook a mission whose alleged purpose was to help orphaned children and deliver humanitarian aid. In fact, the organisers were found guilty of trafficking children.

These personal testimonies as well as studies carried out by researchers have shone a light on these predatory and exclusionary policies. But White thinking still manages to conjure up phantom enemies. These are mostly to be found in the former colonies, in regions that are largely non-White. In France, this phenomenon extends to the perception of the *banlieues*, the high-rise complexes on the edge of many French cities, where there are large non-White populations.

Predatory behaviour extends into the world of the intangible, the symbolic. Writing about the plunder of African works of art during the colonial period, Felwine Sarr and Bénédicte Savoy state that 'it's not simply objects that were taken, but reserves of energy, creative resources, reservoirs of potentials, forces

---

1 *The Wombs of Women*, p. 80.

2 Jean-Jacques Martial, *Une enfance volée* (Paris: Les quatre chemins, 2003), p. 13.

engendering alternative figures and forms of the real, forces of germination'.[1] Indeed, 90–95% of the cultural and artistic heritage of certain sub-Saharan African countries is today held in collections outside of Africa. If we take the example of France alone, it is in possession of over 88,000 works of art. Sarr and Savoy were tasked by President Macron with tracing the broad outlines of a policy of restitution for this plunder. In their report, they argue that it is beyond question that the absence of these works from the continent has done terrible damage, hampering the cultural and aesthetic development of African civil society, undermining its cultural sensibility and its identity.

A debate now rages as to whether these works should be partially or fully returned to their countries of origin. These masks, statues and other objects in Western collections, which were torn from the cultures of Africa, Asia, the Americas and Oceania, are loaded with history and meaning. White thinking often reduces them to their commercial value as works of art. But that misses the point. These objects are laden with a ritual power, with a sensibility particular to the place in which they were created. Isn't it time for White thinking to gain some wisdom and learn to listen to this energy that has sought so long to be liberated? These objects are watching us and are waiting for us to act. These spirits are trapped in a land far from their own and this situation is beneficial to no one. White thinking must seize this opportunity to relieve itself of a great burden. Isn't it time for healing and humility? Time to listen?

Breaths

Listen more often
To things than to creatures,
The voice of the fire can be heard,
Listen to the voice of the water.
Listen to the wind,
To the sobbing of the bushes:
'Tis the breath of the ancestors.

---

1 Felwine Sarr and Bénédicte Savoy, *Restituer le patrimoine africain* (Paris: Philippe Rey/Seuil, 2018), p. 69. An English-language version is available online at: http://restitutionreport2018.com/sarr_savoy_en.pdf.

Those who have died have not departed
They are in the shadow that lightens
They are in the shadow that deepens,
The dead are not beneath the ground:
They are in the tree that quivers,
They are in the moaning forest,
They are in the flowing water,
They are in the sleeping water,
They are in the dwelling, they are in the crowd
The dead are not dead.
[…]
Those who have died have never departed:
They are in the breasts of a woman,
They are in the wailing infant
And in the freshly blazing firebrand.
The dead are not beneath the ground,
They are in the dying embers,
They are in the echoing rock-face,
They are in the weeping grasses,
They are in the forest, they are in the dwelling,
The dead are not dead.
[…]

[Listen] to the sobbing of the bushes:
'Tis the breath of the ancestors.
It repeats each day the pact which binds,
Which binds our fate to the law
[…]

Birago Diop
'Breaths'[1]

1 Translators' note: The poem was initially published in French as part of the story 'Sarzan' in Diop's short story collection, Les Contes d'Amadou Koumba (before appearing in Léopold Senghor's famous anthology of black poetry, 1948). The version here was translated by Dorothy S. Blair for the 1965 Longman translation of Les Contes d'Amadou Koumba. Birago Diop, The Tales of Amadou Koumba (London: Longman, 1965).

Marcel Antoine Verdier, *Beating at Four Stakes in the Colonies*, 1849
© The Menil Collection, Houston

2

BEING WHITE

Look at this 1843 painting by French artist Marcel Antoine Verdier called *Beating at Four Stakes in the Colonies*. I'd like to know what you see in it. I'm guessing your attention is focused on the tragic spectacle of the slave lying flat on the ground, his limbs pulled apart and tied to the stakes. I'm guessing you're distressed as you imagine the sharp lash inflicted on the slave's bare back by the firmly held whip of his tormentor.

Maybe you've noted in passing that the man administering the punishment is also Black. That's how it was in the colonies: White people ordered the punishment of slaves, but other slaves, or drivers, frequently carried it out. Maybe you see the terrified expression of the slave in the background, looking on with dread at the punishment that awaits him as soon as the driver is finished with the task at hand.

Beating at Four Stakes in the Colonies was shown in an exhibition called *Le Modèle noir* [*The Black Model*] organised by the Musée d'Orsay in Paris in 2019. My own involvement in this exhibition meant I had the chance to take people, notably groups of schoolchildren, to visit it. When one of the organisers said to me, 'This painting is too violent, don't show it to children,' I insisted: 'If there's one painting that must be seen, it's this one!' Because for me, Verdier's painting exposes the absolute brutality and subjugation inflicted on Black people and makes real something that might otherwise seem abstract for twenty-first-century schoolchildren. But more than anything, I insisted the painting be shown because there is *something* to be seen here that we haven't spoken about yet. This *something* is what I see when I first look at the painting and which you may not have noticed: the White family on the left-hand side.

What are they doing, this father, mother and their child who, we can imagine, are the owners of the tortured slave as well as the man whipping him? They are watching the scene in the shade of a cabin. The father seems quite calm, as though used to these ordinary scenes of slave society. The mother is holding her child close to her: we don't know what she thinks of the principle of this barbarous punishment – it's possible that, like everybody else, she believes there's nothing unusual about meting out such treatment to an insubordinate slave. She seems to be getting used to the spectacle. Her child, who she's holding tightly, seems absolutely terrified and shocked by what's happening before them. Just imagine the dreadful sound of the whip lashing the skin, the cries for mercy, the smell of blood in the air mixed with the sweat of the driver.

The child is young and not yet conditioned to the violence of the society in which they live. They want to get away; they're a long way from accepting it. In other words, they're not yet White; they're becoming White. And the more of these scenes they witness, the more certain it is they will become White. They will learn that they are the ones who know, who speak, who judge, and who, because of the colour of their skin, will never find themselves in the position of this tortured Black man. So, for now, what they see is a brutalised human being who society is treating worse than an animal. And they don't like it. Let's look more closely. Look at the Black woman who is turned towards the child, reassuring them. The oppressed must contribute to the smooth running of this unequal system. I can imagine her saying: 'Don't be frightened, don't worry – this is perfectly normal.' With time, the child will be persuaded that the injustices perpetrated against Black people *are normal*.

The White people in this painting are passive observers at the same time as they are the beneficiaries of the social order being confirmed before their eyes. Everyone is in their place. But did the abolition of slavery really mean the end of White thinking's belief in its own racial supremacy? Did you see in the bottom left-hand corner of the painting, positioned at the same level as the dog, a Black baby nobody is comforting?

Is it not the case that, for hundreds of years, White children have been raised from a young age, younger than we might think, to develop a civilisational superiority complex? Over centuries, White thinking has constructed a mythology that White identity is based on still today. I can see clearly the demands this system makes of Black people like me. First, don't upset White people; second, reassure them; third, admire them. It's exactly what men demand of women, isn't it?

It's possible to be indifferent to or even genuinely appalled by all forms of racist prejudice and still participate in supporting a society that, objectively, is racist. Participating means contributing to White domination through one's attitudes, gestures and thoughts – and even by doing nothing.

Not all of the men, who, for hundreds of years, participated, and continue to participate, sometimes unconsciously, in male domination, are anywhere close to being vile misogynists who hate women. They are individuals locked within a system of thought. In the same way, White people – apart from those who, for centuries, agreed to decentre their gaze and deracialise their imagination – are stakeholders in an entire set of beliefs and 'self-evident facts' that extol their virtues and lead them to underestimate non-White people. They've been raised according to a myth of superiority that reminds me of Plato's allegory of the cave. The Greek philosopher asks us to imagine people who have spent their entire lives imprisoned in a cave, chained and facing a wall, unable to turn around. Behind them is a fire with a raised walkway above it where people are circulating, carrying objects that cast shadows on the wall. As they look at the shadows in front of them, the prisoners believe they are perceiving reality. To put it more simply, the prisoners have mistaken a world of appearances for reality, and have succumbed to its authority. But what if somebody took them by the arm and led them outside to daylight? Plato says they would be horribly blinded at first and want to rush back inside to their own beliefs.

Two recent examples seem to illustrate this blindness for me. The first is the spring 2019 cover of a popular French weekly magazine with the simple headline 'When Europe ruled the world' and a subheading that explains 'why it has not yet had its final say'.[1] Underneath, there's an image of a group of scientists and monarchs that includes Marie Curie, Robert Koch and Queen Victoria. The other example is the widely broadcast ire of a French writer in response to several big wine-producing châteaux in Bordeaux changing their names to suit the whims of their new Chinese owners. So, for example, Château Clos Bel-Air became Château Great Antelope and Château Senilhac was changed to Château Tibetan Antelope, causing the incensed writer to ask, 'Is there no way to reattribute this wine to its legitimate, centuries-old place of production?'[2]

It's safe to say a lot of readers will quietly share this view. Ah yes, it's true that Europe once ruled the world and, my word, weren't those 'the good old days' of great scholars, internationally renowned writers!… In fact, those days were so good that saying they 'haven't had their final say' is tempting them back. But how many people realise they are nostalgic for a time of blatant inequality and the absence of any human rights? What is it they really miss – the principle of absolute superiority? And among the readers indignant at those shameless Chinese disrespecting the names of our châteaux, how many recall that White Europe completely renamed the lands it conquered, from America (named after the navigator Amerigo Vespucci) to Congo-Brazzaville (now Republic of the Congo and originally named after the explorer Pierre Savorgnan de Brazza)? How many are aware that White colonisers systematically gave Christian first names to the subjugated women, men and children they baptised? Relatively

---

1 *Le Point*, 23 May 2019.

2 I'm referring here to the writer Philippe Sollers, 'Château lapin impérial ou antelope tibétaine… Ces domaines viticoles rebaptisés à la chinoise,' *Le Figaro*, 26 February 2019. [Available: https://www.lefigaro.fr/conjoncture/2019/02/26/20002-20190226ARTFIG00002-chateau-lapin-imperial-ou-antilope-tibetaine-ces-domaines-viticoles-renommes-a-la-chinoise.php]

few I suspect. Yet it happened to Nelson Mandela, whose first name Rolihlahla was changed when he went to school.

These two examples show just how much White thinking fears being downgraded, as though Whites alone have the right to name the world.

1. TERRITORIES

In 2019 I went to a private viewing of work by artist Joan Miró at the Grand Palais in Paris. My partner and I wandered around the beautiful exhibition in awe and admiration at the subtlety of the works displayed. All of a sudden it struck me that among the almost one hundred invited guests we were the only Black visitors. There were other Black people there, but they were all working in security.

More than anything I wondered whether we were the only ones among all those present who noticed the line dividing us. It's highly likely that the other guests, lost in Miró's work, hadn't noticed the existence of this border that was in fact staring them in the face. And if I had taken each one of them aside and asked them about this distribution based on skin colour in a multicultural city such as Paris at the end of the second decade of the new millennium, what would they have said? Many might have shrugged their shoulders, unable to explain its deeper meaning. Others would have suggested that it's normal for the guests to be on one side and security on the other; and very often one group is White and the other Black. It's just a question of social class.

DEFENDING YOUR TERRITORY

There are many different territories within any given society. The more privileged territories are, the more White people we find there; they are spaces of power for which people of all colours work. Maybe that's putting it too crudely. It's true that our society has tempered its language and goes all out to hide the coarse nature of reality. Only a small minority of bona fide racists still speak behind closed doors about 'niggers', 'Pakis', 'slopes', 'kikes' and 'races' that really shouldn't be allowed to mix. However, such mixing happens only rarely; places are allocated. We live in a world where men often learn to dominate women from an early age, just as many White people learn to dominate Black people.

Strangely, only a few elected representatives evoke the reality of this discrimination in all its violence. I'm thinking of the wall former US president Donald Trump started to build between the United States and Mexico. This wall betrays a vision: one of a 'them' and an 'us'. 'They' are on the other side of the wall, with their barbarous way of life, their strange customs, their weird language, and 'we' must absolutely protect ourselves from being contaminated. They want their impure blood to flow and mix with ours. This is also what Brazilian president Jair Bolsonaro said during his election campaign: 'There will not be a centimetre demarcated for indigenous reservations.'[1] Bolsonaro is symbolically refusing to cede any territory associated with power to Brazil's indigenous populations, who he can't exactly accuse of having invaded Brazilian lands. There's no way the Other can be allowed to set foot in our space or mix with us. It's the same with the 'Great Replacement' conspiracy theory and its paranoid allegation of a plot by Western elites to allow as many non-White people as possible to come and replace Whites with hordes of Muslims, Asians and Blacks. Analysing these ideas is interesting because they reveal the deep-rooted feelings of certain White people. They are afraid. But of what exactly? Losing power? Disappearing as a 'race'?

The Cameroonian philosopher Achille Mbembe writes that our society is experiencing a troubling 'desire for apartheid':

> The Other's burden having become too overwhelming, would it not be better for my life to stop being linked to its presence, as much as its to mine? [...] Today, manifestly, little interest is shown in making the circle more inclusive. Rather, the idea is to make borders as the primitive form of keeping at

---

1 Somini Sengupta, 'What Jair Bolsonaro's victory could mean for the Amazon, and the planet', *New York Times*, 17 October 2018. Available: https://www.nytimes.com/2018/10/17/climate/brazil-election-amazon-environment.html

bay enemies, intruders and strangers – all those who are not one of us.[1]

In a few words, Mbembe describes the violence of the White Western unconscious:

> Histories about foreigners and about hordes of migrants in whose faces our doors must be slammed shut; about the barbed wire that we must hastily erect lest we get swamped by a tide of savages; about the borders that must be reestablished as if they had never disappeared; about nationals, including those from very old colonies, who still need to be labelled as immigrants; about intruders […], histories about […] soil, fatherland, traditions, identity, pseudo-civilisations besieged by barbarous hordes, about national security […], endless histories that are continuously recycled in the hope of pulling the wool over the eyes of the most gullible.[2]

Yes, there is a border between people of different skin colour. Its walls are made of glass, but it ensures that positions of power are allocated according to a certain order. These borders appear very early on in our lives but often in a hushed and subtle way. I spent part of my childhood in the Fougères housing estate in Avon, south-east of Paris in the department of Seine-et-Marne. It was a working-class neighbourhood with a large multicultural population. I still remember the extraordinary diversity of backgrounds I encountered in school and among my friends: French people of different origins, Portuguese, Spanish, Pakistani, Algerian, Congolese, Vietnamese. I wasn't conscious of it, of course, but, thanks to them and their parents, I encountered languages, food and ways of thinking from different continents. And I remember these encounters as easy-going, calm, natural. There was no need for big words such as 'diversity' or 'cultural melting pot' in order to experience this as the opportunity for

---

1 Mbembe, *Necropolitics*, p. 3.

2 Mbembe, *Necropolitics*, p. 61.

cultural enrichment that it was. The great joy for me, and children like me who grow up in multicultural neighbourhoods, was that I didn't see White people or Black people or any other kind of people. I just had my friends with all their qualities and all their faults, no more, no less.

A few years later I played for a team in Fontainebleau, and I hung out with a more White, more middle-class crowd. There were no problems. Sometimes I slept over at a friend's house and was surprised to see how people lived in those wealthier suburbs where children have their own room and a ping-pong table in the garden. For me, living in a flat with my mother and four siblings, this all seemed so 'exotic'. But the most interesting thing were the conversations I had. I remember one day that some of them spoke to me about the more 'diverse' Portugais de Fontainebleau football club where I had started my playing days: 'You guys always seemed like thugs to us.' These boys were talking about a reality they didn't know. Intrigued, I observed how strongly we can be conditioned to think in a certain way about things we've never seen. Naturally, I didn't conceptualise any of this, but I started a small exercise that has obsessed me ever since: understanding the position from which you speak.

These boys were speaking from the comfortable White world that I perceived to be theirs. It seemed to me that they drew a line through space, like an invisible wall separating humans into two categories that were of great importance for them: them and us; us and them. Them, you and us. Us, you and them. I had the impression, for example, that for many of my new friends, the dutiful White French were on one side, and foreigners and thugs on the other. It was all a little puzzling to me, but in a vague way I understood that drawing these dividing lines gave them something important to defend in their lives: a territory, an identity, a hierarchy. Nothing they said was angry, hateful or racist. All of that comes later in life; but the seeds were there. They all believed firmly in what they said and in their own position, and this gave them a form of superiority. The wealthy are superior to others, White people are superior to non-White people, rich White people are superior to poor White people or those of immigrant origin. I've since come to know this system well. It's about marking off a distance and demonstrating through your beliefs and attitudes that there are borders that can't be breached. Our society is constructed on a caste system where everybody is assigned a clearly delineated place based on their skin colour. But our castes are not official, they're not acknowledged; they're simultaneously visible and invisible, and our own Brahmin elite and untouchables are not referred to in those terms.

At this point in my life I still knew nothing about the pernicious politics of segregation that had torn apart the United States until 1964. But if I'd heard about what are called the 'Jim Crow laws' I think I'd have recognised them because they represent, in a systematic and perfectly brazen way, the border that White thinking traces between White and non-White people. The Jim Crow laws said that under no circumstances should Black and White people mix. They could live in the same spaces – because there was no choice – but they didn't have the right to mix in schools, factories, hospitals, on public transport, in restaurants, not even in public toilets or prisons. Even pavements were subtly segregated in ways that made Black people step aside for White people. Needless to say, in the majority of states any type of interracial marriage or cohabitation was forbidden and punishable by prison. Segregation functioned as though Whites possessed a purity that could not be sullied.

The racial meaning of the term 'White' emerged in the French language in a context of colonial separation. According to the historian Frédéric Régent, the very first time it was used was not in a philosophical or a scientific text, but in the 1673 document of a French Caribbean company expressly forbidding White people to have children with Black people.[1] A decade later, the French philosopher, doctor and traveller François Bernier first used the term 'race' for classifying humanity.[2] Albert Einstein noted in 1946 that 'separation is not a disease of coloured people. It is a disease of white people.'[3] When I was a child, it was a

---

1 'La Fabrication des Blancs dans les colonies françaises', in Sylvie Laurent and Thierry Leclère, *De quelle couleur sont les Blancs?* (Paris: La Découverte, 2013).

2 'Nouvelle division de la Terre, par les différentes Espèces ou Races d'hommes qui l'habitent, envoyée par un fameux Voyageur à M. l'Abbé de la *** à peu près en ces termes'. Article published in *Journal des sçavans*, Paris 1684.

3 Cited by Mathew Francis in 'How Albert Einstein Used His Fame to Denounce American Racism', *Smithsonian Magazine*, 3 March 2017. Available online: https://www.smithsonianmag.com/science-nature/how-celebrity-scientist-albert-einstein-used-fame-denounce-american-racism-180962356/.

disease that infected another country I knew almost nothing about: South Africa. The system of apartheid (meaning 'separation' in Afrikaans) was enforced there and gave Whites priority in all areas of life. As African American writer Toni Morrison observed, one is racist first in order to situate one's self. We are 'us' because there's a 'them'. As Morrison explains:

> One purpose of scientific racism is to identify an outsider in order to define one's self. [...] The danger of sympathizing with the stranger is the possibility of becoming the stranger. To lose one's racialized rank is to lose one's own valued and enshrined difference.[1]

The law of the oppressor endlessly creates hermetically sealed compartments closing them (non-Whites) off from Whites, them (women) from men, them (Jews and Muslims) from Christians, them (homosexual people) from heterosexuals. Perhaps this obsession says a lot about the conditioning of White people and especially, as Toni Morrison says, about the fear of fading away and no longer being somebody.

In *The History of White People*, Nell Irvin Painter gives a perfect account of how, from the nineteenth century to the Second World War, the great thinkers of her country constructed White identity through exclusion. Being a 'true' White American was first and foremost defined by what you were *not*. But at that time, being White did not have the same meaning it has today: 'No consensus has ever formed [in the history of the United States] on the number of human races or even on the number of White races. Criteria constantly shift according to individual taste and political need.'[2] According to many English-language intellectuals, a lot of White 'races' arrived on American soil, but they weren't all equal. There were the proud and intelligent superior Whites referred to as 'Anglo-Saxons' or 'Teutons' whose origins were English and Germanic. There were 'Alpine' and 'Mediterranean' races that grouped together Italians and Greeks. The latter were considered biologically, intellectually and morally inferior, and some people

---

1 Toni Morrison, *The Origin of Others*, p. 6, p. 30.

2 Nell Irvin Painter, *The History of White People*, p. 383.

believed that the particular shape of their skulls was proof of their inadequacy. Russian, Polish and Hungarian Jews, Slavs, Italians had to wait until the end of the nineteenth century – and the Irish a few decades more – before being considered worthy Whites and no longer obliged, as they had been previously, to educate their children in schools with a majority of Black pupils.

Something similar happened with nineteenth and twentieth-century immigrants to France from Eastern Europe and the Baltic nations, especially Poles, Yugoslavs and Romanians, but also Italians, Belgians, Spanish and Portuguese. Nowadays, their descendants consider themselves to be White and possibly don't even think to question this aspect of their identity. However, their ancestors were judged to be 'dirty foreigners'. The hostile reception they received has all but been forgotten, even though in 1893 it led to the infamous massacre of Italian immigrant labourers in the Mediterranean town of Aigues-Mortes. Similarly, in the French Caribbean, locals see the Lebanese diaspora as White, but I'm not sure this would be the case in metropolitan France. Being White is relative. It just highlights that you're lighter-skinned than others. In fact, nobody is White, because it's a political and economic construct. In *The History of White People*, Nell Irvin Painter explains that the term 'Caucasian', still used officially in the United States to refer to White people, came from late-eighteenth-century writings by the German anthropologist Johann Friedrich Blumenbach, who thought women from the Caucasus region were very beautiful. At the time, however, Caucasians were said by Russians to have Black skin!

Irvin Painter highlights what she terms a 'white neurosis', the age-old obsession with protecting 'pure' blood, the fear of such apparent purity being stained or tarnished by mixing skin colours, the absolute precedence given to preserving purity at all costs by declaring a great biological 'clean-up'.

In Nazi Germany, 'White neurosis' led to the murder of millions of Jews, Roma, disabled people and homosexual people as well as the social isolation and forced sterilisation of Black people and those of mixed race. It's why the Nazis refused to detain African prisoners of war on German soil between 1940 and 1944, instead forcing the French authorities to hold them in camps, known as *Frontstalags*, throughout occupied France. In the United States, 'White neurosis' had such a profound impact on thinking that it gave rise not just to the politics of racial segregation but also led many states to order the sterilisation of so-called biologically degenerate women to prevent them having children – in reality, these women were psychologically vulnerable or simply poor. The policy, known as eugenics, from the Greek *eugenes* meaning 'well-born', was aimed at supporting a 'biological improvement of the human race'. Not many people know about it, even though the courts ordered the compulsory sterilisation of thousands of American women between the beginning of the twentieth century and the early 1970s.[1] A similar policy was implemented in certain Scandinavian countries, as well as in Switzerland and Nazi Germany.

I believe that something of this neurosis concerning racial contamination is still present in the white subconscious. Century after century, the White Western 'community' has constructed itself by excluding those it didn't want to recognise as its own, branding them first as different and then as inferior. There is no history of White identity without a history of the labelling of non-White people and their relegation to an inferior status. There is no White identity without the refusal to accord non-Whites an identity that is equal in the eyes of the law and in terms of human dignity. The American sociologist Margaret A. Hagerman has carefully examined the way White families, particularly from wealthy backgrounds, develop ideas about race, and she argues that the understanding of their identity begins at a very early age indeed, almost in the cradle. 'The decisions parents make about their children's lifestyle influence their understanding of race a lot more than angry speeches or silences on the matter [...]. Even at this age, children develop an understanding of what privilege is every day.'[2] Hagerman explains that 'children also develop their ideas about race through interaction with their peers: they know who is invited to sleepovers and who isn't; they see that it's better to admire some celebrities more than others'. In particular, she cites the example of a young girl who really wants Rihanna to be 'a white woman with fake

---

1 See Nell Irvin Painter, *The History of White People*, pp. 273–77.

2 Laure Andrillon's interview with Margaret A. Hagerman, author of *White Kids: Growing Up with Privilege in a Racially Divided America* (New York: NYU Press, 2018). *Libération*, 2 January 2019.

tan' rather than black.[1] Nonetheless, according to Hagerman, most families never speak about race in the home:

> They believe in a 'post-racial' society where skin colour does not dictate individual opportunities and experiences. In their view, talking about race is itself racist and bringing up the subject would only make their children focus on something that makes no difference. But even if these families say they don't talk about [race], they do it all the time in coded ways or on the edges of conversations.[2]

For Hagerman, when people talk about 'not feeling safe' or about 'poverty' on certain streets or in certain neighbourhoods, it means 'children observe and register racial dynamics constantly, whether adults show it to them or not'.[3]

I've spoken a lot with White friends about these things and I know that these truths aren't always well received. I can't help noticing that most intellectual resistance comes from the men I speak to, whereas White women, in general, are a little more disposed to believing there's some foundation to them. The reason why is clear: for thousands of years women have also experienced a form of subjugation that's not too far removed from what I've been talking about in this book. Speak to a woman about the feeling of hitting a glass ceiling and she'll immediately know what you mean. The glass ceiling is the barrier that society erects above certain people, preventing them from doing what they want when they want. It's there to remind them that there are limits on what they can do with their lives.

Needless to say, people are born free and equal. But this is only in theory, because in reality women and non-Whites can't occupy all the roles they would like. Except in exceptional circumstances, becoming a CEO of a large company, prime minister, a renowned researcher, a big-name soprano or tenor, a university vice chancellor, a high-profile surgeon or a conductor is not for them. They are

---

1 Ibid.

2 Ibid.

3 Ibid.

destined for other roles. The Black man is 'naturally' suited to being a cleaner, a security guard, a rapper, a comic actor or a champion in certain sports. A woman, even when she is well qualified, is still paid less today than men and is often limited to certain 'female' jobs such as teacher, nurse, health and social care worker, receptionist, 'weather girl'; in other words, roles designed to support others or that depend purely on physical appearance.

Above all, lots of women understand how easy it is to make a link between the idea of 'natural White superiority' and 'natural male superiority'. For thousands of years women had to listen to self-important arguments that justified fencing them in, mistreating them, limiting their ambitions, considering them unreasonable and consequently denying them the right to vote. A woman who wanted freedom was condemned as a witch.[1] And even if things have improved a lot, women continue to be dished up this discourse that endorses the arbitrary domination of one half of humanity by the other.

This social order persists, unchanged, until those who are discriminated against rise up and seize the rights they are entitled to. There's no point in requesting politely; justice must be demanded. In the eighteenth century, when Black people tried to gain some of the advantages enjoyed by the White community, repression by the authorities was swift and bloody. A ruling by the Governor General of Martinique on 25 November 1783 provides a clear explanation of this refusal:

> It is important so as to maintain law and order that the state of humiliation attached to the [black] species be cultivated in all respects; previous determination that is of special use, because it is found in the very hearts of Blacks and contributes importantly to the very peace of the colonies.[2]

It's easy to understand the 'special use' of prejudices for maintaining 'peace' and therefore social order. It suggests why most White people, still today, fail to act when non-Whites are humiliated.

---

1 See Mona Chollet, *Sorcières, la puissance invaincue des femmes* (Paris: La Découverte, 2018).

2 Cited in Plumelle-Uribe, *White Ferocity*, p. 55.

CONTROL

Control depends on force of habit. From a young age, there are things that non-Whites are not allowed to dream of. Opportunities are already limited because White thinking guides them. Of course, this is never said out loud or written anywhere. But these social and cultural rules are still deeply rooted and fully internalised in my homeland, this so-called country of equal opportunities.

One day my friend André and his business partners went to a meeting with clients. Greetings were exchanged and negotiations began. After an hour, during which nobody had asked André any questions, my friend said something along the lines of: 'No, we're not doing this deal. We're not going to do it this way.' He was met with complete silence as the surprised clients turned and looked at him as if to say, 'Why is *he* speaking?'

In order to understand what was happening, let me make clear that André is Black and all his business partners are White. The clients' surprise came from the fact that none of them had even imagined the boss could be Black. I don't think they were racists. They simply believed that Black people are naturally incapable of running a business or managing a team. In fact, most Black people would have been just as surprised. This general surprise stems from the fact that a Black 'manager' is not in the natural order of things, even when it comes to team sports or leading sporting organisations. And yet the first Olympic gold medal won by a Black athlete was in Paris in 1900! Black people in the West can be found in all areas of life, but never at the very top, or at least rarely so. This is why White people find it so hard to appoint a Black person to a leadership role, even when they have the necessary skills and experience.

I remember an interview with the great Guadeloupean writer Maryse Condé, winner of the 2018 alternative Nobel Literature prize in Stockholm. She's also a journalist and emeritus professor at New York's University of Columbia. Despite this, she admits to having taken several decades to overcome society's negative view of her: '[I've made it here] even though I was told as a young girl that people like me couldn't become writers. I was a twelve-year-old in Pointe-à-Pitre when a friend of my mother's offered me an unusual gift.' That gift was Emily Brontë's novel *Wuthering Heights*. 'The very next day I ran over to thank the woman. And I told her: "One day I'll write books as beautiful as Emily Brontë's." She looked at me in a sort of scandalised astonishment: "You're crazy. People like us don't write!" What did she mean "like us"? Women? Black people? People from a small island like Guadeloupe? It didn't matter. I was crushed by her reaction and told myself that the world and the profession I dreamed of were forbidden to me; it was the wrong path, sacrilegious even. If she hadn't had such a reaction, I wouldn't have waited forty-two years before publishing my first book.' And in summing up her literary life, Condé says: 'For my entire life I never stopped doubting and being afraid.'[1]

If you want to control somebody you have to control their imagination. Just read Article 2 of the Code Noir: 'All the slaves who will be in our Islands will be baptised and instructed in the Catholic, Apostolic and Roman religion.'[2]

As I said earlier, if you ask a Black child what God looks like, there's a strong possibility they'll say He's a White man. It's obvious: God is White. Maryse Condé's Guadeloupe is a very Christian society whose inhabitants are regular worshippers. If you happen to visit a church there, take a good look and you'll notice the same thing I once did: the churches are filled with Black people, including the priests, but a multitude of White figures loom over them: Jesus, Mary, the apostles, the saints and all those represented in the stained-glass windows, sculptures and paintings.

There were almost certainly non-White people in Judea and Samaria when Jesus was alive, but you have to wonder why this is never represented in religious imagery. It's always a slim, bearded, light-skinned, blond or brown-haired man. Why should God be a White man? I'm certain it's because White people couldn't identify with a Black Jesus; the churches would empty out. And yet, throughout the world, Black people fill churches and pray to a pale-skinned Jesus, a White Mary and White apostles, which naturally has an effect – White people are venerated everywhere. The Christian God is without doubt the greatest invention of White thinking. It leaves no room for doubt that History has been whitewashed.

1 See Annick Cojean, 'La négritude de Césaire n'est qu'un beau rêve', *Le Monde*, 9 December 2018.

2 From the Garrigus translation of the *Code Noir*, op. cit.

One day a man recognised me in a street in Ouagadougou, Burkina Faso, and wanted to take a selfie with me. I agreed and noticed that his screensaver was an image of a White Jesus. I teased him a little by asking whether he really believed that Jesus was White. He replied, very seriously: 'You know, White people come second only to God.' I laughed, certain he was joking. But no, he nodded his head and continued to explain that I just needed to open my eyes and see what had happened in his country to realise that, well, after God come White people. Flabbergasted, I repeated to a passer-by what the man had just said: 'Well yes. He's right' was the reaction.

This is how White thinking takes possession of the imagination of too many non-White people from childhood. The idea that White people are more powerful and more intelligent than them is so firmly enshrined there seems something 'natural' about it. A few years later I told the above story to the mayor of Ouagadougou, who replied: 'It's not surprising. We have a saying here: "God is great but the White man is not small."' I've even had a Black man tell me that Black people are cursed and God doesn't love us. Did he know that he had internalised the Old Testament story of the curse of Ham which was invented to justify the enslavement of Black people? Why else did so many Black people hold on to religious beliefs that were forcibly imposed on their ancestors through enslavement and colonisation? Why do they worship a White God? Could White people worship a Black God?

Sometimes this feeling of inferiority is embedded in everyday expressions. When you scold a child in Cameroon you tell them, 'Your heart is as black as your skin.' And the supreme compliment is to be told, 'You're like a real White person.' One of my relatives said to me once, 'White people are so intelligent.' I frowned and asked, 'So intelligent compared to?...' She hesitated, as though embarrassed by what had sounded like an admission: 'I didn't mean to suggest...' No, of course she didn't mean to say that White people are so intelligent compared to us, Black people. But she had said it nonetheless in her own way. Very often White people figure in conversation as an implicit presence, something unsaid, that is still highly revealing. It can be surprising to see that Black people have internalised an inferiority complex in relation to White people. But it's natural, because non-White people, who have been conditioned by White thinking for centuries, end up believing that Whiteness is the ultimate standard. And given that it was the most powerful and most widespread system of thought over centuries, White thinking has become global. We know that 'Black people can demonstrate racist bias against their own group, a fact that underlines the considerable impact of racist stereotypes in society and the consequences for all members of the population'.[1] It shows the tremendous danger of White thinking for non-White people. Can you imagine White people being racially prejudiced against themselves?

How can you build a peaceful, confident future for yourself if you have such self-destructive beliefs about who you are? The African American writer James Baldwin describes the reality of it here:

> What this [discrimination] does to the subjugated is to destroy his sense of reality. [...] It comes as a great shock, around the age of five, or six, or seven, to discover, Gary Cooper killing off the Indians, when you were rooting for Gary Cooper, that the Indians were you. It comes as a great shock to discover the country, which is your birthplace, and to which you owe your life and your identity, has not, in its whole system of reality, evolved any place for you.[2]

When White thinking declares that Black people are 'better at sport' or 'better at dancing', it's implied, never said explicitly, that they are better than White people. In what activities, then, are White people better than Black people? This isn't said, because there's no need to. It goes without saying that they are believed to be more intelligent, more learned, better read. And often more beautiful. And beauty, like other value judgements, is deeply

---

1 See Julie Grèzes and Lou Safra, 'L'Origine de l'expression des émotions', *Nuit des sciences et lettres*, ENS, 7 June 2019.

2 Cited in Raoul Peck's 2016 documentary, *I am not your Negro*. Baldwin is here speaking at the infamous 1965 University of Cambridge debate.

inscribed within a cultural subconscious that dates back to the beginnings of White domination.

In the French Caribbean, where I come from, beauty is easy to define: the more light-skinned a person is, the more successful they are in other people's eyes. As it happens, the contestants who represent the French Caribbean islands in the Miss France beauty pageant are never very dark-skinned. The concept of colourism clearly frames this definition of beauty just as it continues to construct discourses, standards and the erotic imagination. This idea people have of a skin-tone spectrum is extremely harmful. The lighter a person's skin tone, the more they're considered to have been 'saved'. A society that was born out of enslavement and has a majority so-called 'Black' population should, above all else, have rejected this way of seeing things. And yet it remains imprisoned by it. When my mother was young she was led to understand it was better to have children with a light-skinned man so their skin would be *chappée*, a Creole term that derives from the French adjective *échappé* meaning 'escaped'. Escaped from what? From Black skin, of course, from the Black 'condition'. Even to this day, in the French Caribbean, just as in the White world, you're likely to have a better future if you're White. If you don't believe me, go there and you'll see that all the high-level senior government positions are occupied by White people, even though most of the population is non-White. Can you think of one country outside sub-Saharan Africa where Black people are welcome?

Throughout the world, in African countries, the Middle East, India, the Far East, 'pale skin' is synonymous with 'beauty'. The colour white may *transfix* the world, but the West *transforms* it. Everywhere, the onslaught of videos, ads and films from the global North established White as the colour of success and desirability and, therefore, of beauty. This fact would eventually become deeply embedded in people's minds. In the 1940s, psychologists Kenneth and Mamie Clark developed the 'doll test' to demonstrate the dreadful alienation that African American children endured from their earliest years. The two scientists showed some dolls – perfectly identical other than the fact that some were Black and some were White – to children aged three to seven. The children were asked which doll was the most beautiful, the naughtiest, the kindest, the ugliest. It's no surprise to learn that everything positive was associated with the White dolls, whereas the Black dolls were said to be naughty and ugly.[1] This experiment has been conducted several times since and filmed, including quite recently, and the results haven't changed: a majority of children, regardless of whether they're White or Black, associate notably more positive qualities with White dolls. A story American lawyer Kimberlé Crenshaw recounts from her childhood demonstrates this really well. 'In kindergarten we used to play a game where we took it in turns to become different characters, with the most coveted one being the princess. Despite my best efforts, my turn never came. I didn't have the words for it, but I understood that I would never be Snow White or Cinderella. A lot of little Black girls who live in societies where beauty is associated with an image of something other than themselves share this feeling.'[2]

In professional football, a world I know well, I saw certain behaviours that were informed by the same kind of logic. Countless times I heard Black players in the dressing room showers boasting and saying: 'Look how Black you are! I'm lighter-skinned!' In other words: 'I'm better-looking.' The players who laughed when they said this weren't aware of the subtext, but it's easy to understand the real meaning.

When I was in AS Monaco's youth academy, Sandra, who would become the mother of my two sons, came to visit. My friends, who didn't know her, came with me to the airport to pick her up. When they saw her, several of them expressed surprise: 'Erm… your girlfriend is Black?' I'll confess at eighteen years of age I was caught unawares by their surprise and thought, 'So what if Sandra's Black?' I didn't know where they were coming from and, more than anything, I didn't understand the force of what they were saying. That weekend a number of them said things to me like 'She looks like she's your sister'…

I encountered this behaviour throughout my playing career. People would say, jokingly, that 'Lilian is into Black women'. They would ask, 'Don't you like White women? Are you racist?' – as

<hr />

1 See Gerald Markowitz, David Rosner, *Children, Race and Power* (London: Routledge, 2000).

2 In Coumba Kane, 'Kimberlé Crenshaw: "La lutte contre le racisme doit inclure le combat contre le sexisme"'. *Le Monde*, 7 March 2019.

if I should feel guilty about something! This ribbing revealed a staggering contempt for Black women. And where did the surprised amusement of my friends come from? From the fact that I was earning a good salary and, as I could have attracted a White woman, therefore I should have done so. When you have money, a big house, a big car and a big gold watch, you marry a White woman. As Fanon says, the White woman becomes a trophy and is part of the 'whitening' process; she is the White mask worn by successful Black men who are considered to be exceptions to their condition. Does this explain why most non-White men 'who succeed' often marry White women? The man who doesn't conform to these models of success seems to be going against the fate he's said to deserve, almost provocatively so. Would a successful White man be *guilty* of having a White partner? How many successful White men are married to non-White women? Must a successful Black man feel guilty for not choosing a White partner? Should you apologise as though it were a form of racism? The comments I've received just because my partners have been Black have made me stop and think. Very often people choose partners who share the same language, religion, skin colour and social class, that unremarkable tradition of marrying within your group. Anthropologists refer to it as 'endogamy'. Yet although this unexceptional endogamy describes my own situation, I'm made to believe that living with people who supposedly have the same skin colour as me makes me unusual. I've understood for a long time that, as Black men, our erotic imagination and our desire are completely conditioned by White thinking and that we also make Black women carry the weight of this whitening to a significant extent. To be considered beautiful and desirable to men, especially Black men, Black women must whiten themselves. To understand why most successful non-White people have a White partner we need to go back to history and understand the 'White bias' that controls the choices of White and non-White people, including emotional choices – we've already seen how children, girls and boys, preferred White dolls.

Let's go back to this system we could call non-White self-loathing. In order to understand it, I think it's useful to look at the experiment conducted by Jane Elliott in the late 1960s. One day this Iowa schoolteacher decided to do an exercise with her pupils called 'blue eyes, brown eyes'. She announced that all the pupils with blue eyes would be in 'the superior group'. She tied a sort of brown collar around the neck of the other children as a clear way to stigmatise them. Then she sat them at the back of the class and scolded them louder and more frequently when they got things wrong. Worse, she gave the blue-eyed children certain perks such as second helpings in the school canteen, longer breaks, games that the brown-eyed children couldn't have, and so on. The blue-eyed children were told to play within their own group and to ignore their brown-eyed peers.

But the exercise went further than just bullying. Like the discourse I describe in the first part of this book, Elliott invented a pseudo-scientific 'blueist' discourse claiming the blue-eyed children were more intelligent than the others. And what happened? The children who had been selected as 'superior' eventually became more arrogant and nastier towards the other children. Proud of their new status, they even improved their performance in class tests! The brown-eyed children, in contrast, lost confidence and, overall, their results showed a dip.[1] The following week, Elliott inverted the roles. However, the exercise turned out to be less conclusive this time – as soon as the experience of being discriminated against has been internalised by the group who dominates it doesn't disappear so easily.

Some people might think that conducting an exercise like this on children as young as eight or nine years old is a little harsh, and Elliott was heavily criticised for it. But what one section of American society didn't like was that she had imposed this treatment on children who were White. Few people at the time understood that her aim was first to make people feel concerned for the welfare of Black children. One woman sent her a furious letter: 'Black children grow up accustomed to such behaviour, but White children, there's no way they could possibly understand it. It's cruel to White children and will cause them great psychological

---

1 Stephen G. Bloom, 'Lesson of a Lifetime', *Smithsonian Magazine*, September 2005. Available:
https://www.smithsonianmag.com/science-nature/lesson-of-a-lifetime-72754306/

damage.'[1] Yes, she's right: there is indeed a great risk that these children might want to make society more just!

DISCRIMINATION

There's no easy answer to the question of whether White people who don't experience racism really know what non-White people put up with. It's both yes and no. Yes, because when I go to schools, universities and conferences to talk about racism and ask who would like to be treated the way society treats Black people, you won't be surprised to learn that nobody raises their hand. Everybody knows that everywhere society subjects Black people to negative treatment. From that I can only conclude that this inferior position is so well established and so widespread that the collective unconscious has normalised it. If everybody knows that Black people are the subject of discriminatory treatment and violence, why do so few of us denounce it? It's because this disdain is part of a dominant discourse that makes most people accept it by hiding behind a sort of fatalistic 'That's just the way it is'.

So, for me, the answer to the question 'Are White people aware of what non-White people experience?' must be 'yes', even if, no, I don't believe White people can fully understand the burden of being non-White. Deep down, White people know the reality, but they don't go far enough in their thinking to really grasp what it means to be treated as non-White. Nobody is really capable of imagining discrimination that doesn't directly affect them. We saw this with the rise of #MeToo following the Weinstein revelations. Lots of men – me first and foremost – were shocked to learn that women are forced to endure harassment and prejudice on a daily basis. Their wives, sisters, colleagues and female friends told them about the everyday nature of offensive behaviour that most men used to think was quite rare. What is the responsibility of the person who doesn't know the reality or doesn't know it well? Are they innocent or responsible for not having made the effort to get to know it? In which case, are they complicit? Just as antiracist organisations have done, feminists have long denounced discrimination. It has been said that women finally felt free to speak. But, in fact, they forced people to listen. Women had always spoken about their experiences of gender-based violence

1 Ibid.

and sexual predators, but the problem wasn't so much ignorance, it was that nobody listened. Men didn't want to know.[1]

I have no definitive answer for why most White people are so deaf to the demands of non-White people. But I know that all too often people who know nothing pretend to know everything. And it needs to be recognised: #MeToo was also a moment when women's revelations about the abuse they put up with caused certain men to raise an eyebrow sceptically. 'Really?' some of them asked. 'Isn't all this talk a bit over the top, always playing the victim card?' As for me, I still all too often encounter dubious reactions when I talk about the things non-White people put up with in our society. 'Oh, come on,' some White people seem to say, 'things have improved. The situation isn't that bad.' They just don't get how much their scepticism feels like a slap, a spit in the face, for people who experience discrimination.

When a woman swears that she experiences different forms of sexual harassment every day, nobody is obliged to believe her. But when ten, a hundred, a thousand, tens of thousands of women confirm what she's saying, a person would really need to be disingenuous – or biased – not to believe there's every chance she's telling the truth. In any case, you can't be a man and claim you think women have equality if what they say is considered at best a slightly paranoid exaggeration, at worst a pack of lies. Similarly, you can't be White and claim to support the idea that, regardless of the colour of their skin, everybody should be treated with dignity and given the same opportunities and then shrug your shoulders when somebody non-White denounces the racism directed at them. The Sioux have a saying: 'Oh great spirit, keep me from ever judging a man until I have walked in his moccasins.' And nobody knows better than the victim the reality of being discriminated against.

If we are all equal, then the very least thing you can do when a non-White person talks to you about racism is put your White bias aside and listen to them. Take the time to listen to what they have to say and to think about the arguments they're making. Maybe they're a bit over the top, maybe they've got a persecution complex. Or maybe they don't. And if what they're saying is corroborated by

1 See Elsa Dorlin, 'Manifeste d'autodéfense féminine', *Le Nouveau Magazine littéraire*, February 2018.

a large number of witnesses and supported by a lot of sociological studies then they are surely right.

The first strategy of avoidance is to ask the person complaining: aren't you in some way responsible for the behaviour you're criticising? Does your attitude towards the police, the way you dress, the way you walk on the pavement explain, at least in part, their behaviour towards you? Feminist organisations are very familiar with the so-called 'short-skirt' argument that implies a woman who's been harassed, attacked or raped by a man may have been dressed too provocatively. It would explain behaviour which, naturally, is otherwise to be deplored, right?

This insidious explanation enables the person who doesn't want to be confronted by the reality of their dominant position to turn the tables completely so the victim of violence is almost made to feel like they're the guilty party. The victim is made to look within first, at their behaviour, their choices, to find explanations for the discrimination they endure. This process hides where real responsibility lies, and this is extremely serious. At times, when I was still a footballer, I witnessed shocking, shameful scenes you could scarcely believe, but which in fact aren't that rare. For example, a footballer is subjected to racist insults from the fans (monkey noises especially) that hurt and of course inflict emotional trauma on him. He goes to complain a first time to the White referee who, generally, says nothing. If he goes back a second or third time, he's shown a yellow card!

At a more political level but still informed by the same psychological ideas, let's take another look at the comments made by the French president, Emmanuel Macron, in Africa in 2018 that I quoted earlier. 'When there are countries today where women still have seven or eight children, then you can decide to spend billions of euros, but you won't stabilise the situation at all.' What Macron is really doing with this statement is identifying the person responsible for a continent's woes: the African woman. But plenty of studies prove that it's poverty that leads to unchecked population growth, not the other way round. Poverty in Africa doesn't come from a woman's womb; it comes from a calamitous social and economic situation inherited from colonisation and from the prevailing rules of contemporary global market competition, rules that, behind a liberal façade, benefit the wealthiest countries, including France.

But, of course, a French president can't say that. It's much easier to flip the blame. White thinking sees White Western children as a boon and African children as a misfortune. Just think how many Europeans believe Africa is overpopulated.

The other way of avoiding the truth is to look for more 'plausible' explanations than those offered by the victim. All too often we hear that racism is natural, that it's innate. It's as much part of human nature as the instinct to reproduce and, as a result, it will never be fully eradicated. There's nothing we can do about it. It's mostly White people who think this; but sometimes non-White people too. White thinking wants us to believe racism is natural even though it's an ideological invention of White men. And because White men benefit from racism and they don't accept they're responsible for it, they make everyone believe it's part of human nature. Black people know perfectly well racism isn't natural. They know it's a cultural construct because in their day-to-day lives they see how racism allows White people to dominate them. Moreover, if everybody was naturally racist, Black people would have had to construct their theory about everybody else's inferiority. Has there ever been a Black scientist who developed theories of Black superiority in order to exploit White people and their resources? Instead, what might be considered anti-White racism among Black people is a feeling of anger, the expression of powerlessness and a weariness at being held in contempt by White people who barely recognise them.

Some Black people have been treated badly so often in their lives they've given up hope of things changing. My mother's answer to my question 'How come Black people are treated like that?' was: 'That's the way things are and they'll never change: people are racist.' By 'people' she meant 'White people' of course. Hearing that 'things will never change' is extremely distressing for a nine-year-old child. All the same, I'm convinced mentalities evolve and ideas that seemed to be 'common sense' gradually become outdated. It takes time and energy, but things do change. Racism isn't an inevitability. It doesn't exist in some pure natural form: it's ingrained in our minds by dominant social forces.

In a similar vein, how many times have I heard that racism is a minor detail and that in actual fact the only question that matters is that of social inequality? It's an argument mainly put forward by White people. They say that if non-White people are the targets of constant police monitoring it's often because they belong to the poorer social classes, and the State crushes the poor because it invariably suspects them of wanting to revolt. This is clearly a way of saying that the argument about 'skin colour' is baseless and therefore denouncing systemic racism isn't really justified.

Clearly, I'm not denying that there are poor White people nor that they're also the victims of discrimination. Of course the social argument matters. But I want to stress that racist habits exist, and this explains why poor White people, no matter how badly they're treated, can be racist towards non-Whites. Indeed, their worst nightmare is to be treated like non-Whites. Their professional outlook and experiences may be limited, but not as much as non-Whites in the same social class. Indeed, racism serves the interests of a quite obvious but rarely discussed strategy of pitting the poor against each other and preventing them from joining forces. This is the strategy that was used during slavery and colonisation, and is still used today. The poor tear each other apart and fail to understand that, whatever their colour, it's in their interests to unite to defend themselves against their exploiters. Instead, poor White people forget to fight the real oppressor because this racism would have them believe it's better to preserve their advantages and reject any alliance with those who are presented above all as enemies. Racism has always been the project of a certain elite and it has become systemic.

2. SYSTEMIC RACISM

UNACKNOWLEDGED RACISM

For a long time, the historian Pascal Blanchard and myself have been calling for a major exhibition on Black France. A while ago we met several influential people from the world of culture to explain our project. Some of them really seemed very interested, but not by everything we were proposing. Our idea was to organise an exhibition in two parts: the first would present the all-too-little-known history of Black people in France (reaching back approximately four centuries in France itself and connecting with the colonial past); the second part would establish links between the treatment inflicted on them in the past and that imposed on them today. Because, even if the forms have changed, even if discourses have evolved and laws have been changed, there is a continuity between the racism of today and that of the past. State-sanctioned racism existed in France from the *Code Noir* in 1685 and circulated in endlessly reinvented ways until the final colonial independences of the 1970s. At that point it became systemic racism, and it persists today in different iterations that are often subconscious. Two hundred and fifty years of state-sanctioned racism is not so easily wiped away.[1] If history serves a purpose, it is clearly to identify what the present has inherited from the past, to understand it, to trace it step by step, to consider continuities and ruptures but also to underline new understandings.

Mention of this particular section of the exhibition was enough to silence several of those Pascal Blanchard and I spoke to. Showing that Black people were mistreated in the past is acceptable, but saying they continue to be so today is not – clearly, it's easier to keep turning a blind eye. As Reni Eddo-Lodge says, 'the covert nature of structural racism is difficult to hold to account. It slips out of your hands easily, like a water-snake toy.'[2] I'm not arguing here that there is still an intent to discriminate against non-Whites in French law, the constitution and the civil code. On the contrary, nowhere is it written that the French Republic requires its police officers to conduct ID checks on non-White people more often than White people or to speak less respectfully to them. Nowhere is it stipulated that the careers of non-Whites will be different, or that the justice system is obliged to be harsher in its sentencing of non-Whites than Whites. However, all these realties exist and are ordinary experiences for non-White people. And when nothing concrete is done to prevent them, they end up forming a system. This is also why we live in a society where patriarchy and sexism remain all-pervasive.

The sociologist Fabrice Dhume-Sonzogni, a researcher at Paris-Diderot University, explains this very well. For him, institutional racism is a 'racism that functions by using the capabilities, the

---

1 The *Code Noir* was passed in 1685 and the *Code de l'Indigénat* wasn't abolished until 1946. The latter was a set of laws and regulations, first introduced in Algeria, which formalised an inferior legal status for France's colonial subjects.

2 Reni Eddo-Lodge, *Why I'm No Longer Talking to White People about Race*, p. 64.

resources and the organisational methods of the state and in effect produces differentiated categories of citizens. This social order produces a hierarchy of individuals based on an ethno-racial logic'.[1] Put another way, the structures of the state are harnessed to set in stone discrimination based on skin colour.

When a police officer treats me, almost systematically, in a differentiated way, not because I pose an objective danger to society but because of the colour of my skin, it is nothing other than institutionalised racism. This police officer is part of the state machinery, was trained by the state and is paid with public funds. We're not talking about the excesses of one individual (even if that is sometimes the case); rather, it's about a set of practices that aren't coincidental: they are the product of our collective history, especially slavery and colonisation. As Fabrice Dhume-Sonzogni explains: 'I saw this institutional racism at work in a training college where I was doing some research on discrimination with future police officers. In one of the classrooms, a drawing of the map of France depicted the *banlieues* of the greater Paris area – where a lot of the trainees would probably end up working – as a zoo. Even if this map had been drawn by one individual, it represented a normalised discourse, widely shared by professional bodies, with an animalisation of social groups that is typical of the racist imagination.'[2]

Another sociologist, Fabien Jobard, quantified the reality of identity checks in five locations in Paris between 2007 and 2008. His conclusions are the result of meticulous data collected in the field: 'Compared to a White person, a Black man is between 3.3 to 11.5 times more at risk of being stopped, depending on the place, a North African between 1.8 to 14.8, and a passer-by of another minority between 3.5 and 19.5 times more at risk.'[3] This blatantly differentiated treatment, which is based on obvious criteria of skin colour, will only surprise those who want to be surprised by it.

---

1 Cited by Anne Chemin in 'Peut-on parler de racisme d'État?', *Le Monde*, 1 December 2017. Available at: https://www.lemonde.fr/idees/article/2017/12/01/peut-on-parler-de-racisme-d-etat-l-avis-d-un-sociologue_5222931_3232.html.

2 Ibid.

3 Fabien Jobard, Réné Lévy, John Lamberth, Sophie Névanen, 'Mesurer les discriminations selon l'apparence: une analyse des contrôles d'idenité à Paris', *Population*, vol. 67 (2012/13), pp. 423–51.

Non-Whites will shrug it off with an air of inevitability; they know it all already.

What exactly does it mean to be White in a public space? I can tell you that being Black in certain urban areas means having your identity papers checked several times a week. I know a lot of White people who would go crazy if they were subjected to this treatment, even if it was only for a week! But we're used to it because society makes us believe we have no choice. Likewise, a young woman needs to be aware that if she leaves her house with too much of her body uncovered, or too much covered, it will be perceived as being available. Because being a woman means you don't have the same privileges as men, starting with the right to be out in public without being shouted at because you're a woman. It's the same thing for non-Whites who are stopped by police because of racial profiling. And as a result, they rarely go out without their identity papers (just think about that term!). Everything needs to be in order so the situation doesn't turn bad. This is not something a White person will think about too often. And yet it's a regular experience: non-Whites find themselves out in the street and see police officers approaching them. There's an immediate undiluted reaction: 'It's me they're looking for...' Then a little rush of adrenaline before they quickly ask themselves: is there something about my appearance or the way I'm moving that might cause a problem? Often nothing happens. When a person is oppressed, they've a tendency to overinterpret signs of potential trouble and to play the 'paranoid' card. But the idea is firmly embedded, the idea that says if the police used violence against them – verbal, behavioural or physical – society would side with the police and blame the victim, whatever the context. I dream of a world where nobody but a thug would ever begin to think like this, not even for a split second.

A non-White person in a public place knows they are seen. Their presence is mentally registered. Could this feeling come from centuries of slavery and colonisation, where the implicit mission of every White person, whether in uniform or not, was to control everything they did? If for one reason or another young non-White people set off running down the street, for example if they're late for their bus, they risk being seen as delinquents who've committed a crime. If the police are in the area, there's a strong chance they'll decide to stop these citizens running to avoid being late and carry out an ID check. Dragging out the ID check is a way of letting these non-White people know quite explicitly that they are suspect by their very 'nature'.

It's rare, if not exceptional, for White people to be addressed informally during an ID check. On the other hand, non-White people can testify that they are very often spoken to in an insulting way, for example with the French informal 'tu' form of address. This example is offensive because it's not intended to establish the more usual familiarity associated with 'tu' but to reinstate a racial, even colonial hierarchy. Let's not forget that the systematic use of 'tu' to address indigenous populations in French was not just the customary practice at the beginning of the twentieth century, it was recommended (a comparable practice in English would be a White person's use of 'boy' to address a Black man so as to let him know he is not on an equal footing). Henri Quinot's 1926 *Petite grammaire de la langue Kilubu du Congo belge* [*A Short Grammar of the Kilubu Language of the Belgian Congo*] for employees in colonial businesses spells it out clearly: 'When ordering around the black man, use an impersonal imperative. Note that one always addresses the black man using the informal "tu" rather the formal "vous".'[1]

To different degrees, depending on the country, racism is one of the unchanging elements of the history of the White world. To give just one example: on 13 November 2018, in a town close to Chicago, twenty-six-year-old security guard Jemel Roberson intervened in a fight that had broken out in a bar. Roberson successfully subdued one of the aggressors with his service weapon and was pinning him to the ground when the police arrived. And what happened then? A police officer drew his pistol and shot the security guard. Roberson died in hospital shortly afterwards with the word 'Security' on his vest having offered him no protection. If, in the heat of the moment, the police officer immediately surmised that Roberson was the aggressor, it's not because the former was a dreadful racist or lacked judgement. It's the result of thinking that developed a long time ago and continues to impact on Black people's lived experience. It's the result of state conditioning that designates Black people as a permanent

---

1 Cited in Philippe Goddin, *Les Tribulations de Tintin au Congo* (Paris: Casterman, 2018), p. 10.

potential threat even when they are wearing a uniform with the word 'Security' emblazoned on it. People will say it was the United States, but if we're honest, this racist bias also exists in France. Too many young, non-White men have died during police interrogation: Adama Traoré, Lamine Dieng, Zyed Benna and Bouna Traoré, Abdelhakim Ajimi, Mamadou Marega, Amadou Koumé and more recently Cédric Chouviat. Just one name would be too many. I can't explain why, but I recognise my sons, my nephews, my friends in these men. White thinking, for its part, believes that the law is always right and says: 'When the police arrest somebody, as long as they hand over their ID and respect them, they won't find themselves on the ground and they won't lose their life.'

Do you know why the police use more violence in their interventions with non-White youths? In the collective unconscious it's because the latter are physically stronger than the White person and this provokes fear. Experience proves that when White people are shown non-Whites holding objects in their hands they very often identify the objects as guns. Thus, US researchers conducted a study using a simple video game:

> In the game, images of people who are either armed or unarmed, and either African American or White, appear unexpectedly in a variety of contexts. [...] Participants were told to 'shoot' armed targets and to 'not shoot' unarmed targets. [...] half of the targets were African American and half were White. [...] Clearly, the responses of participants to these stimuli depended at some level on the ethnic category of the target, with potentially hostile targets identified as such more quickly if they were African American rather than White and benign targets identified as such more quickly if they were White rather than African American.[1]

1 See J. Correll et al, 'The Police Officer's dilemma: using ethnicity to disambiguate potentially threatening individuals'. *Journal of Personality and Social Psychology*, 83.6 (2002), pp. 1314–18. See also the follow-up study, J. Correll et al, 'Across the thin blue line: police officers and racial bias in the decision to shoot'. *Journal of Personality and Social Psychology*, 92.6 (2007), pp. 1006–23.

The relationship the police form with certain young people in France is tainted with this same bias and can be fully explained. But the question is whether police officers are trained enough to understand that this concerns them. We need to conduct research on this inherited historical bias in a sector that is particularly sensitive and essential for the security of each and every one of us.

However, it's not just in policing that we find this systemic discrimination. A lot of research has made clear that it also exists in French state schools. The sociologist Georges Felouzis, who works on educational inequalities, has examined the way in which schools treat children with North African-sounding names. It's clear that ethnic-based segregation is much more pronounced than that linked to social or economic background. The children and grandchildren of immigrants are put on pathways that lead to 'lower quality' professions. The sociologist Stéphane Zéphir has observed how a disciplinary hearing unfolds in a French middle school. He shows how pupils with the name Issam or Kader and their parents are immediately judged to be poor at communicating and raising their children, whereas a Matthieu is given the benefit of the doubt: 'The repeatedly disagreeable behaviour of Matthieu towards teachers has not been the subject of written reports. As a result, the mother can defend her child effectively [...], the words of the mother and of her son are not questioned', unlike those of Issam, Kader and their parents.[1] We need to ask to what extent schools contribute to the shoring up of a discriminatory system and to the reproduction of inequalities that were already being criticised in the 1960s. Of course, this system is not unique to the French education system. There are countless studies concerning the system in England: 'According to the Department for Education, a black schoolboy in England is around three times more likely to be permanently excluded compared to the whole school population. [...] At the age of eleven [...], research indicates that he will be systematically marked down by his own teachers [...]. It will take anonymity to get him the grade he deserves.'[2]

This discrimination is also applied in public hospitals. Reni Eddo-Lodge cites a series of reports that clearly illustrate this:

1 Stéphane Zéphir, 'Catégorisation ethnoraciale en milieu scolaire. Une analyse contrastive de conseils de discipline.' *Revue française de pédagogie*, no 184 (2013).

2 Eddo-Lodge, *Why I'm No Longer Talking to White People about Race*, p. 66.

A 2003 NHS England report confirmed that 'there is a uniformity of findings that people of African and African Caribbean backgrounds are more at risk than any other ethnic group in England to be admitted to psychiatric hospitals under the compulsory powers of the Mental Health Act'. In the same year, an inquiry into the death of David Bennett, a black man who died in a psychiatric unit, added '[black people] tend to receive higher doses of anti-psychotic medication than white people with similar health problems. They are generally regarded by mental health staff as more aggressive, more alarming, more dangerous and more difficult to treat. [...] [T]hey are more likely to remain as long-term in-patients.'[1]

Once again, there is no equivalent data available for France. How can this be right? Surely a clear overview of all these forms of discrimination is needed. Are the police, schools, hospitals, museums capable of genuinely taking account of the White bias of our society and its consequences for the entire population?

During the memorial service for George Floyd, the African American man murdered in the United States on 25 May 2020, the Reverend Al Sharpton eloquently expressed this relationship between White thinking and Black people:

George Floyd's story has been the story of Black folks because ever since 401 years ago, the reason we could never be who we wanted and dreamed to be is you kept your knee on our neck. We were smarter than the underfunded schools you put us in, but you had your knee on our neck. We could run corporations [...], but you had your knee on our neck. We had creative skills, we could do whatever anybody else could do, but we couldn't get your knee off our neck. What happened to Floyd happens every day in this country, in education, in health

1 Eddo-Lodge, p. 71.

services, and in every area of American life. It's time for us to stand up in George's name and say get your knee off our necks. That's the problem no matter who you are. We thought maybe we had a complex. Maybe it was just us. But even Blacks that broke through, you kept your knee on that neck. [...] The reason why we are marching all over the world is we were like George, we couldn't breathe, not because there was something wrong with our lungs, but you wouldn't take your knee off our neck. We don't want no favours, just get up off of us and we can be and do whatever we can be.[1]

We need to start paying attention and understanding that the deaths of Adama Traoré, George Floyd and others are not just connected to police violence. The police serve White thinking, they didn't construct it. And let's not be naive and say racism exists only in the police force. It's there even where we least expect it. For example, it's there right now with the use of artificial intelligence in all kinds of everyday situations. According to Michel Wieviorka 'new technologies and social media function like a layer, a thickening, an extra screen between the prejudices circulating in society and their application in reality, especially in the form of discrimination'.[2] Algorithms are in the process of replacing humans for the allocation of social housing, bank loans, jobs, insurance and appraisals, and they are reinforcing prejudices and stereotypes, making it even more difficult to be aware of them and to fight against them.

FIGHTING FOR A SEAT AT THE TABLE

I wonder why, despite evidence from victims of discrimination, White thinking refuses to accept that systemic racism exists. Is it because fighting against an endemic, inherited racism in society means interrogating White privilege? Is it because making it visible would require starting out from the same place as non-White people

---

1 Reverend Al Sharpton eulogy, George Floyd memorial service, 4 June 2020.

2 Michel Wieviorka, *Pour une démocratie de combat* (Paris: Robert Laffont, 2020), pp. 175–76.

and therefore likely to mean losing out? Losing out on the job market, in housing, in terms of success; in short, losing out in terms of power? As Reni Eddo-Lodge says: 'Racism's legacy does not exist without purpose. It brings with it not just a disempowerment for those affected by it, but an empowerment for those who are not. That is white privilege.'[1] Because there's already significant competition between White people themselves. In this bitter fight, racism means the majority of non-White people are excluded and some people make sure that doesn't change. By denying the reality of racism, White thinking says that in the neoliberal struggle everybody, whether White or non-White, is equal.

The world of football illustrates this reality perfectly. The lower down the ladder you go, especially in junior football, the greater the number of non-White managers. The higher the level, and particularly at professional level, the more managers are White, even though there is a large percentage of non-White players in professional teams. Even a former key player for the French national team, Jean Tigana, confirmed that his application to become manager of the national team was rejected because of his skin colour. Within the French Football Federation some were saying, 'There are too many Black players in the French team now; we can't add a Black coach.'

We need only recall the 'racial quota' scandal exposed by the news organisation Mediapart in 2011 to see the extent of prejudice among several of the leading figures of the French Football Federation's technical board, including then director François Blaquart. These individuals had agreed to implement unofficial quotas designed to exclude 'dual nationals' – read Black and North African youths – from selection to youth training centres like the celebrated national academy in Clairefontaine. Shameful conversations were recorded and made public, such as this from Blaquart: 'We can set out, in an unspoken way, a sort of quota. But it needs to be done on the quiet. It needs to be purely a question of actions taken. So, we need to be careful. We have the lists, at some stage...'[2] And the conversation went on: 'We need to refocus, especially for boys of [twelve],

1 Eddo-Lodge, pp. 115–16.

2 Fabrice Arfi, Mathilde Mathieu, Michaël Hajdenberg,'Quotas dans le foot: la vérité au mot près', *Mediapart*, 30 April 2011. Available: https://www.mediapart.fr/journal/france/290411/quotas-dans-le-foot-la-verite-au-mot-pres?onglet=full

thirteen, fourteen [...]; we need to have other criteria, modified with our own culture.'[1] It's easy to see what's meant by 'culture' here: prioritise White players who might be genetically less strong but are strategically sharper. These prejudices won't come as a surprise to those who remember what I said about colonial history: the colonised are 'produced' solely to supply strong arms and legs whereas 'thinking minds' are naturally White.

Unfortunately, in the world of football this idea is all too widespread, as Willy Sagnol, the former manager of Bordeaux football club, casually revealed in a press conference: 'The advantage of the, how shall I say, typically African player is that he's not expensive, is usually ready for the physical battle; you could say he's strong on the pitch. But football is more than that. It's also about technique, intelligence, discipline. You need a bit of everything. You need Nordic players too.'[2] Indeed, one of my White teammates, unaware of his racist bias, would often say to me: 'Imagine if I had my intelligence *and* your physical qualities.' Of course, it wasn't him speaking; it was an entire history. Let me explain for readers who might not be familiar with the norms of football that the idea of physical strength versus intelligence makes no sense: all great players, whatever their position on the pitch, possess both physical prowess and footballing intelligence. When you tell all these people that their comments are racist, they get annoyed, genuinely angry. Being called a racist is the worst insult. And they end up telling you that you're the racist! They declare themselves not to be racist, but I wonder if they've even once said to themselves that they need to take care not to be racist. Françoise Héritier used to say to me, 'Every day I take care not to have racist prejudices.'

These comments never result in serious sanctions. They're made public, provoke various degrees of outrage, and are forgotten about within a few days. And if you think I'm exaggerating, ask what punitive measures were taken in the French Football Federation quotas affair: the national technical director received a warning and the right-hand man of the Federation's president

1 Ibid.

2 '"Joueur typique africain": les propos de Sagnol suscitent de nombreuses réactions', *Sud Ouest*, 5 November 2014. Available: https://www.sudouest.fr/2014/11/05/joueur-typique-africain-les-propos-de-sagnol-suscitent-la-polemique-1726757-766.php.

a six-day suspension, that's it. Why this baffling leniency? Is it because White thinking sees non-White success as White failure? If non-White people exceed an invisible quota of privileged social positions, there's always somebody to remind them to be careful, they mustn't forget they have no right to be there. They can be tolerated in small numbers but they mustn't think that their success is down to merit; it's only because White people want it. When a Black person succeeds, you always get the impression people are saying to them, 'You succeeded because we wanted it. So it's down to us.'

I recall a story a friend told me. He was extremely bright, so much so that he made it as far as the entrance exams for an elite French university. In the oral exam, he was certain he had put in an excellent performance, one that, in his view, meant he deserved to get in. But to his great surprise he wasn't offered a place. When he discovered the grades one of the examiners had given him, he was confused. What could he have said – or not said – that deserved such a mediocre grade? To understand why he had been marked down, he met up with one of the examiners, the very one who had been most harsh on him. He explained to my friend, 'Your performance was good but I didn't want my colleagues to think I had given you an unfair advantage because you're Black like me.' For me, this anecdote is a perfect illustration of what I would call the 'mentality of the oppressed'.

If a Black person is harder on another Black person, it's because they often feel judged by White society. Where does this fear come from? Do White people on admissions panels ask themselves whether they are giving a White candidate preferential treatment because of the colour of their skin? Isn't this the same problem women have when other woman deny them legitimacy because they don't want to be suspected of giving preferential treatment?

Of the graduates from France's soon-to-be-closed elite school for top civil servants, the École Nationale d'Adminstration (ENA), 69% have parents who are themselves management or executive-level professionals, as opposed to 4% who are working class. The remaining quarter come from backgrounds that are in between.[1] What is the percentage of non-White students at the ENA? Do you think ENA graduates have ever asked themselves 'if I hadn't

1 See Observatoire des Inégalités, 12 April 2017.

been White, would I have followed this path?' Do you think they might be bothered by their over-representation and the fact it proves their 'good' education and their parents' social networks were indispensable to their success, and that some of those competing for a seat at the table didn't have these advantages?

Once again, the experience of women can shed light on things for non-White people appalled by this injustice. Women have never, ever gained anything in their history that they didn't wrest from men. Rights aren't handed over, they're won.

The overrepresentation of White people within the establishment has to do with what sociologist Pierre Bourdieu referred to as *reproduction* and *distinction*, two concepts that are only rarely applied to White domination but which are very useful for understanding it.

In short, what Bourdieu says is that those who have power have established a system that serves to sanction their position. In other words, people are made to believe that those who achieve power do so solely thanks to their own efforts and those who do not are entirely to blame themselves because they haven't worked hard enough. This is what French state education is for. This is what elections are for. In theory, our schools should help to select the most intelligent, the most competent, so that when they are adults they will be given responsibilities worthy of their skills. But in fact, in seven out of ten instances, the offspring of professionals go on to become professionals and the offspring of industrial workers go on to become industrial workers.[1] That is *reproduction*: more often than not, children share the same fate as their parents without it bearing any direct relation to their true worth. This is because, from an early age, they've assimilated the knowledge and codes that power demands. The system is the same in the case of so-called democratic elections. In theory, any French citizen of the requisite age can present themselves for election. In practice, a large majority of elected representatives come from the most privileged backgrounds. In France's National Assembly, 31% of deputies were professionals prior to being elected, 18% belonged to the liberal professions and 22% were members of the civil service (often high-ranking). Between 2012 and 2017, the percentage of those who were professionals increased 8%, and that of liberal professionals

1 Statistics quoted in Chantal Jaquet, Gérard Brads (eds), *La Fabrique des transclasses* (Paris: PUF, 2018).

5%. In contrast, 3.5% of deputies were salaried employees and just one deputy came from a background as an industrial worker![1] As a result, the laws they pass are highly unlikely to favour workers and the poor; instead, there's a strong possibility they'll favour the groups they represent. That's what reproduction is.

Above all, as Bourdieu explains, the privileged organise themselves, more or less consciously, to exclude those who don't resemble them. This is *distinction*. If you come from 'good' families (that is to say, middle-class), you distinguish yourselves through 'good' manners, you know the correct words and the right cultural references, and you know when to use them. As a result, those who share the same background can identify you easily. You acquire the right to be part of the clique of those who matter.

This is how White domination works. Without necessarily being conscious of it, White people co-opt each other within spaces of power, not because they're racist in the literal sense of the term, but because they've more confidence in those they believe are like them. A lot of social psychology studies show how much people, more or less consciously, favour somebody who looks like them, behaves like them, has the same style, accent and, also, skin colour. It's the feeling of belonging that prevails. Broadly speaking, the reason why jobs requiring qualifications are more consistently given to men rather than women and to White people more than non-White people is because those doing the recruiting are almost always White men. It's the reason why it's harder for non-White people to rent accommodation: property owners and letting agency staff are most often White and they need to trust those they are employing or renting property to. But the question they should be asking themselves is why, precisely, they lack trust. Where does this strong sense of belonging to White identity come from? From history? Isn't it up to the people who lack trust to look for the reasons and cure themselves?

UNIVERSALISM

There's a very common mindset in Western societies that seeks to justify actions known to have harmful consequences. For example,

1 See https://www.publicsenat.fr/article/politique/une-assemblee-nationale-tres-csp-74986, 19 June 2017.

telling yourself that combating climate change is necessary but then continuing to consume in a mindless, wasteful fashion. The state of tension that allows us to do contradictory things subsequently leads us to invent all kinds of reasons for doing them, and especially to invent a double reality, an illusion. French philosopher Clément Rosset speaks of this tendency we have of pretending not to see that our behaviour contradicts what we say we're doing.[1] Like the way we declare all humans to be equal but then don't always recognise it in practice.

The 1948 Declaration of Human Rights is a case in point. In this case, fifty-three countries, under the auspices of the United Nations, solemnly declared the absolute universality of human rights, from cradle to grave, no matter a person's class, gender or skin colour. However, some countries, including my country, France, were still colonising parts of Africa, Oceania, America and Asia and, therefore, part of their prosperity was built on an intrinsically violent and racist politics. France had just brutally suppressed Madagascar's desire for freedom, leading to the death of more than 89,000 people, and was already engaged in the lengthy conflict in Indochina that is estimated to have resulted in 500,000 deaths.[2] Moreover, French women, half the population, were still being treated as inferior and had only just won the right to vote.

The French historian Valentine Zuber highlights the fact that 'in 1948 the two great colonising powers of the time, Great Britain and France, were fully aware of this paradox: they were reckless inventors who refrained from publicising this solemn declaration in their empires'.[3] This seems to be how the illusion or contradiction is handled: a country treats women and indigenous populations as subhuman in practice, but all the while proclaims their place within a universal humanity. So, certain actions need to be accompanied by a language that masks this dishonesty. After all, how can you accuse

1 See Clément Rosset, *Le Réel et son double* (Paris: Gallimard, 1976) and in translation *The Real and its Double*, trans Chris Turner (London: Seagull Books, 2012).

2 The number of deaths in Madagascar was quoted at the time in the French National Assembly and is referred to in Jacques Tronchon, *L'Insurrection Malgache de 1947* (Paris: Karthala, 1986). For more on the Indochina war see, Jacques Dalloz. *La Guerre d'Indochine (1945–1954)* (Paris: Seuil, 1987).

3 Quoted in Anne Chemin, '"70ᵉ anniversaire de la Déclaration universelle des droits de l'homme: la fin d'une utopie?": Entretien avec Valentine Zuber'. *Le Monde*, 8 December 2018. Available: https://www.lemonde.fr/idees/article/2018/12/06/70e-anniversaire-de-la-declaration-universelle-des-droits-de-l-homme-la-fin-d-une-utopie_5393556_3232.html.

the signatories of the Universal Declaration of Human Rights of being racist and sexist?

This illusion isn't just a feature of the 1940s. As a non-White person, it's still difficult today to try and explain to White people that France is a country of systemic racism. How is it even conceivable, they ask, that France could do such a thing. France, 'the cradle of human rights', 'birthplace of the Enlightenment', a generous nation that abolished slavery twice, brought colonisation to an end, implemented the politics of 'integrating' immigrants and their descendants. It's just not possible.

In my view, White thinking may dress itself up in the values of universalism, but every day, every minute, it flouts them in very real ways. It is a form of cultural imperialism that methodically destroys cultural norms that came before it: deities, languages, customs, accents. It practises the culture of annihilation I spoke about above. Western universalism doesn't present itself as one culture among others; it declares itself as *the one* that oversees and encompasses all others, all these other, more or less backward irrational beliefs that it demands disappear progressively to leave room only for it. As the Senegalese philosopher Souleymane Bachir Diagne rightly notes, universalism is 'the position of those who declare their own particularity to be universal by saying: "I have the particularity of being universal".'[1]

The Universal Declaration of Human Rights proclaims itself 'the common standard of achievement for all peoples and all nations'. It's a sort of collective goal, a state of perfection that's never really attainable, but which we must constantly strive to reach. We know well what this 'common standard' looks like in the minds of those who advocate for it: it's the Western model. In *The View from Afar*, anthropologist Claude Lévi-Strauss succinctly declares that 'a universalist doctrine evolves ineluctably toward a model equivalent to the one-party state'.[2] The genuine defender of one-party rule is convinced they are providing a significant benefit for humankind because they are bringing an end to disputes in the name of a greater good – a good which they themselves have outlined. Where there is a multiplicity of approach and vision, they see noise and disorder.

---

1 Souleymane Bachir Diagne, with Jean-Loup Amselle, *En quête d'Afrique(s): universalisme et pensée coloniale* (Paris: Albin Michel, 2018).

2 Claude Lévi-Strauss, *The View from Afar*, trans. by Joachim Neugroschel and Phoebe Hoss (New York: Basic Books, 1985 [1983]), p. 307.

At best, they can't see the point of it; at worst, they display outright contempt for it.

How should we conceive of things in a multicultural world worthy of the name? In the first instance, there must be an end to hierarchies of people and cultures. For Lévi-Strauss, 'Our science [social anthropology] reached its maturity the day that Western man began to understand that he would never understand himself as long as there would be on the surface of the earth a single race or a single people whom he could treat as an object.'[1] Although Lévi-Strauss's original words date from 1973, the White world is still a long way from applying them in practice. The White 'model' still sees itself as a subject – the one that observes, understands, lives, the driver of thought and action. It treats the rest of the world as object, as a passive spectator or imitator. Once again Lévi-Strauss reminds us: 'Tolerance is not a contemplative position, dispensing indulgence to what was and to what is. It is a dynamic attitude consisting in the foresight, the understanding, and the promotion of what wants to be. The diversity of human cultures is behind us, around us, and ahead of us.'[2] In a truly renewed universalism all cultures would be subjects. All cultures deserve the same level of attentiveness, but not in a way that looks down on and selects from on high. It's painstaking work to make sure everybody has the same 'speaking time'.

Valentine Zuber also explains:

> Instead of bringing them [non-Western countries] the 'truth', the cultural assumptions about human rights need to be deconsecrated, their history de-westernised and the story [...] that accompanies them demystified. The parareligious, indeed millenarian, solemnity surrounding human rights hinders their promotion. In today's world it is important to demonstrate instead that the philosophical and religious traditions of non-Western and non-Christian cultures are also attentive to human dignity and can serve as a common good for all humankind. [...] In future, human rights need

1 Claude Lévi-Strauss, *Structural Anthropology*, Vol. 2, trans. by Monique Layton (New York: Basic Books, 1976 [1973]), p. 32.

2 Lévi-Strauss, *Structural Anthropology*, Vol. 2, p. 362.

> to be conceived for what they are: shared rules, not
> specific philosophical values.[1]

True universalism should involve the calm acceptance of the diversity of the world's practices and beliefs. It should call on all the world's traditional systems of knowledge – Indian, African, South American, Asian, Oceanic, Caribbean, European – for what they have in common: a wise perspective on human realities, on life, the past, the relationship to time, to the Earth, the relationship with our ancestors, our children, between the sexes. It would represent the distinction established by philosopher Achille Mbembe between the 'universal' and the 'in-common': 'The universal implies inclusion in some already constituted thing or entity, where the in-common presupposes [...] the idea of a world that [...], to be sustainable, must be shared by all those with rights to it, all species taken together'.[2] In the first case, there's a corpus of Western-produced texts that other cultures are 'invited' or compelled to adopt unchanged; in the second, there's a collection, co-produced and co-constructed, on an equal and respectful basis, by all the world's cultures.

This traditional wisdom was given voice by the Lakota Chief, Sitting Bull (1831–90), a legendary figure still remembered today. This remarkable man made a number of speeches that denounced White imperialism and showed that the harmonious cohabitation of humans and nature is possible, indeed that it is the *only* kind possible.

We all belong to the same species and share the same space on this tiny, fragile planet. There's only one way to share it that makes sense: with intelligence, kindness, by learning to listen and engage in dialogue.

One day I met a woman and documentary maker from Burkina Faso who told me she had given birth in Brittany. After the delivery, she asked the surprised midwife where her child's umbilical cord was and was told it had been thrown away. The Burkinabe woman was devastated because, in her country, the cord is kept for burial in the courtyard of the family home to mark a connection with the earth, the fact that humankind belongs to the earth. I get the

---

1 Anne Chemin, 70ᵉ anniversaire de la Déclaration universelle des droits de l'homme: la fin d'une utopie?' op cit.

2 Mbembe, *Necropolitics*, p. 40.

sense that, in Europe, children are encouraged to think the opposite: the earth belongs to them. These two visions describe different relationships with the world. The question is how to be humble enough to listen to other cultures.

I remember going to the opening of the Museum of Black Civilisations in Dakar. The ceremony began with a dance in memory of the ancestors. It showed a certain respect for the past that seems infinitely precious to me but which I never detect in the West. Celebrating innovation and preparing for the future are all very well, but I suspect a civilisation loses its mind if it cuts the ties to its past. Doubtless, this explains, at least in part, how much our society has lost its way, even if there are some who reminisce nostalgically about their past as a glorious era – before then talking about decline.

I'm from the French Caribbean; I spent my childhood in France, and then lived throughout Europe. But I still find myself telling my sons: 'Remember the ancestors are with you. They've given you life, courage, a sense of survival; you represent them.' It's almost like I'm recalling something from far away, from Africa, the land of the ancestors. Those spirits are there, somewhere, so that things have meaning. And I don't think you can do whatever you like when, somewhere in a corner of your mind, you hang on to the feeling that those who came before are watching us. We too will become ancestors, and our descendants, in turn, will need to consult us. And they'll judge us for standing by and doing nothing.

3. WHO IS NOT WHITE?

One of the powers that White thinking possesses is to determine who isn't White. A mixed-race person of Black and White parents should be allowed to feel closer to one colour more than another, or to neither. But this White power to assign identity barely registers such feelings: the mixed-race person will automatically be placed in the category 'Black'. The person who is 'different', who isn't White, is immediately placed in the category of the 'other'.

There is a vast palette of darker skin tones, from the barely noticeable mixed race to the very dark. But there's no place for these subtleties in a world where White thinking dominates. The non-White is the different one, the one who doesn't fit the norm. Whether your skin is dark or lighter toned, you are a 'person of colour', and this classification guarantees a particular social order. In the United States, the one-drop rule that was formerly enshrined in law meant even the smallest amount of Black blood in a person's ancestry was sufficient for them to be classed as 'Black'. So former President Barack Obama is Black in the same way the actor Omar Sy is; the politician Christiane Taubira is Black in the same way the performer Beyoncé is. The power to include or exclude effectively gives rise to another, even more essential type of power: the authority to say who has the right to do things or not to do them, to have or not to have. That means proclaiming who has more rights than others.

TRACES OF THE COLONIAL

The situation of non-Whites in societies dominated by White people invariably returns the former to a particular experience of inferiority. The White world endlessly repeats the quiet refrain: 'It's much better than it was before. You should be happy.' And yet I'm reminded of what the Black actor Aïssa Maïga says in a film uploaded to social media:

> I remember one day when I was on a bus. A woman started to lash out at me and said that I shouldn't be there with my buggy. So I explained to her that, at the end of the day, everybody has the right to travel, even with kids. I stayed calm. And then she said, 'Yeah, that's right. Get your machete out. We know what you're like!' I remember for a few seconds just not being able to believe it. As far as I could tell, the comment came from nowhere. In fact, I'm fascinated by it because it's such a primal leap to make![1]

In truth, it's not as 'primal' as it seems: what Maïga experienced is the collective system of classification that White thinking imposes on non-Whites, which is a form of racialisation.

1 Agissons contre le racisme ordinaire, *Fraîches*, 12 February 2019: https://www.facebook.com/watch/?v=2694250147497146.

The woman on the bus equated a young black Parisian mother with a 'Rwandan' militia member because they had the same skin colour. It might seem unbelievable, but in fact such racialisation is our daily reality. Being forcibly ranked in the category marked 'others' is the first type of essentialisation that we are forced to encounter and we end up internalising it.

Many of you might not remember the Liam Neeson 'affair'. In an interview for *The Independent* in February 2019, the Irish actor recounted an incident from forty years earlier when one of his close friends told him she had been raped:

> I asked did she know who it was? [...] She said it was a black person. [...] I'm ashamed to say it. I went up and down areas with a cosh, hoping I'd be approached by somebody. I did it for maybe a week, hoping some 'black bastard' would come out of a pub and have a go at me about something, you know? So that I could... kill him. It was horrible, horrible, when I think back, that I did that.[1]

Neeson's admission caused an outcry in the English-speaking world; he was accused of being a racist, which he strongly rejected. It was said he'd been overwhelmed by a 'primal' impulse. But once again, Neeson's reaction isn't quite so primal: it's the result of a long tradition of racialised thinking.

When it comes down to it, what is shocking in Neeson's admission – something that few people raised – is not that he wanted to kill, but that for one week it wasn't the man who raped his friend he wanted to murder, but a random Black man. It's as if, in the mind of the young Liam Neeson, all Black men were interchangeable – killing any Black man would have avenged his friend. If, tomorrow, the police happen to be looking for a forty-year-old White paedophile, I don't think it would occur to anybody to take revenge for the latter's victims by seeking to kill a random forty-year-old White male. This is precisely what the essentialisation of Black people means: making all of them responsible for the wrongdoings of a

1 Clémence Michallon, 'Liam Neeson interview: rape, race and how I learnt revenge doesn't work', *The Independent*, 4 February 2019 [Available at: https://www. independent.co.uk/arts-entertainment/films/features/liam-neeson-interview-rape-race-black-man-revenge-taken-cold-pursuit-a8760896.html].

few. Believe me, when a murder hits the headlines and the killer has yet to be identified, a lot of Black people are praying it's not a Black person. They know that a comparison will quickly be made between the killer and them. Lots of Muslims will have the same feeling when the media are reporting on criminals with the name 'Rachid' or 'Kader'. In the words of journalist and novelist Tania de Montaigne, 'I've had experience of this phenomenon where, when you are put in a group, you feel responsible for everything that the people in it do.'[1]

Designating others as non-White is also, and above all, subjecting them to surveillance. It's about ensuring their presumed violence stays in check. When those who are despised and oppressed are in the public space, they must always be closely watched. Telling them they can do what they want, that there are no more categories, risks a considerable degree of disorder. Achille Mbembe provides a perfect explanation of this need to divide and to rank in order to rule better:

> In the colonial context, this permanent work of separation (and thus differentiation) was partly a consequence of the annihilation anxiety felt by the settlers themselves. Numerically inferior but endowed with powerful means of destruction, the settlers lived in fear of being surrounded on all sides by 'bad objects' that threatened their very survival.[2]

Even though colonisation has had its day, White people still seem to fear those territories where non-white people live.

Have you heard about the *police des Noirs* (police for Blacks) established by King Louis XVI in 1777 by royal declaration? Pressure from slave-owning planters prompted the king to forbid Black servants from the colonies from entering French metropolitan territory. As the legislation says:

> The number of blacks has so increased, especially in the capital, because of the ease of transportation between the Americas and France, that the number

---

1 Gladys Marivat, 'Tania de Montaigne: "Me reconnaître comme 'noire' n'allait pas de soi"', *Livres* supplement, *Le Monde*, 31 May 2018.

2 Mbembe, *Necropolitics*, p. 46.

of men necessary for the cultivation of lands is daily taken from the colonies at the same time as their presence in our Kingdom causes the greatest disorder; and when they return to the colonies, they bring with them the spirit of independence and indocility and become there more harmful than they are useful.[1]

The legislation did allow for Black servants to accompany their masters on the transatlantic voyage. However, as soon as they arrived in France, they were to be held in certain places until their masters had concluded their affairs. All of this was designed to buttress 'the general welfare (sic) of the colonies, the particular interests of its inhabitants and the protection we owe to the preservation of mores and good order in our Kingdom'.[2]

It's clear that in seeking to satisfy the economy, the political powers did everything they could to quash even the vaguest desire for equality between Whites and non-Whites.

During the era of apartheid in South Africa, the White population had a term for the fear of being overcome by a Black revolt: *swart gevaar* or 'Black peril'. This is also the crude reality painted by the 1900 Colonial Congress, one of the organisations involved in the Paris Exhibition, a world fair held in the same year. If the Congress opposed universal suffrage and education for the colonies, it was because, as one brochure explains with notable candour, 'the day when all our subjects know French like we do – or believe they do – they will want the same rights as us; as the French element finds itself everywhere the minority, it will quickly be absorbed by the indigenous element'.[3] Between these lines is a tacit sense of White thinking's considerable unease, the feeling of those who know they are a numerical minority yet sit atop an unjust system that benefits them.

It's not by chance that I've cited this example from the colonial era. I'm curious to know if the descendants of former colonisers continue to feel worried by, even afraid of the descendants of the former

1 'Déclaration pour la police des Noirs', *Recueil général des anciennes lois francaises, depuis l'an 420 jusqu'à la Révolution de 1789* (Paris: Belin-Leprieur, 1826).

2 Ibid.

3 Cited in Claude Liauzu, *Race et civilisation*.

colonised. The problem is not what the non-White person is doing in the public space, it's what they could do. Or as Achille Mbembe says, summarising the thinking of Frantz Fanon: 'The white [man] fears me not at all because of what I have done to [him] [...] but owing to what he has done to me and thinks that I could do to him in return.'[1]

Even as a child, in France, I felt this terror and it confused me. We, Black people, frighten White people. Recently, I asked my White childhood friend Éric why White people fear us, as it's something I've never actually understood. He replied: 'I remember, in the school playground, we had the impression you were stronger than us. That we wouldn't be up to it if there was a fight.' Why is it White people perceive Black youths to be taller, stronger, older than they really are, almost as if there's some kind of animalistic violence lurking beneath their Black skin? It explains why there are so many Black security guards. Disdain and fear combine in White people's attribution of violent tendencies to Black people. It begins in your early teenage years when you notice a change in atmosphere around you as soon as you put up the hood of your sweatshirt; you are the cause of a gnawing fear in the street or on public transport. It's a strange feeling: you've only put up your hood because you're cold or because you want to, just like any White youth would do. But you realise that even though that wasn't your intention, your action has an effect. I don't think it's an exaggeration to say the problem doesn't stem from young non-White youths in hoodies but from the socio-cultural judgements made about them. And no matter what they do, they're quickly judged to be responsible for the fear they provoke.

We rarely ask why White people might fear Black people. Perhaps it's because they know Black people have been mistreated and still are. Perhaps it's because there's such a social divide separating them that they imagine one day non-White people will rebel; perhaps it's because there's a risk the situation will be inverted, or that if it were them, White people wouldn't put up with it. Even if they don't want to confront it, every White adolescent, every White adult knows the history of relations between Whites and non-Whites. It's not *our* history, say White people. But how could it be my history without being yours, says the non-White person?

I've already said that too many non-White people are filled with institutional fear as soon as they leave their home: fear

1 Mbembe, *Necropolitics*, p. 133.

of being stopped for an ID check, fear of being refused a job, accommodation, fear of a system that at any moment can send them back to their presumed place. By the way, most non-White people who might have the possibility to speak out publicly don't do it. Why? Because they're afraid of White people's violent reaction. I myself, for that matter, am afraid of provoking White violence by writing this book. When I spoke about the project with my mother, she said, 'You won't have any problems because of this book, will you?' My friend Relik's advice was: 'As soon as it comes out, you're jumping in a plane!' And a taxi driver declared, 'You're going to attract a lot of anger!' My answer: 'White thinking is not the thinking of White people.' Why are they so afraid?

Aimé Césaire explains things wonderfully in his *Discourse on Colonialism*: 'I am talking about millions of men in whom fear has been cunningly instilled, who have been taught to have an inferiority complex, to tremble, kneel, despair, and behave like flunkeys.'[1] Black people, but also White people who have analysed and understood things, must tell it like it is so things will change, because a lot of people, White and non-White, are not aware of this reality.

What is indisputable is that non-White people have internalised the discourse of contempt concerning them and have no more faith in people who look like them than White people do. In most situations, this is the sad reality of oppressed individuals: like everybody else, they end up absorbing dominant discourses, and feel towards those who look like them a little of the hatred they themselves endure. As Achille Mbembe explains, 'A representative instance of the "white" took my place and made my consciousness its object. Henceforth, this instance breathes in my place, thinks in my place, speaks in my place, monitors me, acts in my place.'[2] This is why expressions of pride, which can seem unnecessary, even strange to White people, are so necessary for non-whites. It's why the African American slogan 'Say it loud, I'm Black and I'm proud', from the 1968 hit single performed by James Brown, is a way of opposing White thinking.

This is also what's happened with Gay Pride marches (which began after the Stonewall uprising of 1969). It's not about

---

1 Aimé Césaire, *Discourse on Colonialism*, trans. by Joan Pinkham. (New York: Monthly Review Press, [1950] 1972), p. 43

2 Mbembe, *Necropolitics*, p. 133.

declaring pride in a 'condition' you haven't chosen, like being 'non-White' or 'queer'. Nor is it about proclaiming some kind of non-White superiority in relation to White people, or of queer people in relation to heterosexuals. It's simply about asserting to a public whose minds are closed by contempt, that if you think we're worth little or nothing at all, well, that's no longer going to wash. We're no longer lowering our eyes. We're proud of who we are; there is no justification for shame. Shame can go and switch sides. It's a method that enables mentalities to change, opinions to mature, and also (and perhaps above all) it's a method, as Maya Angelou proves, that heals the wounded soul of the oppressed.

'Still I Rise by' Maya Angelou

You may write me down in history
With your bitter, twisted lies,
You may trod me in the very dirt
But still, like dust, I'll rise.

Does my sassiness upset you?
Why are you beset with gloom?
'Cause I walk like I've got oil wells
Pumping in my living room.
Just like moons and like suns,
With the certainty of tides,
Just like hopes springing high,
Still I'll rise.

Did you want to see me broken?
Bowed head and lowered eyes?
Shoulders falling down like teardrops,
Weakened by my soulful cries?
Does my haughtiness offend you?
Don't you take it awful hard
'Cause I laugh like I've got gold mines
Diggin' in my own backyard.

You may shoot me with your words,
You may cut me with your eyes,
You may kill me with your hatefulness,
But still, like air, I'll rise.

Does my sexiness upset you?
Does it come as a surprise
That I dance like I've got diamonds
At the meeting of my thighs?

Out of the huts of history's shame
I rise
Up from a past that's rooted in pain
I rise
I'm a black ocean, leaping and wide,
Welling and swelling I bear in the tide.

Leaving behind nights of terror and fear
I rise
Into a daybreak that's wondrously clear
I rise
Bringing the gifts that my ancestors gave,
I am the dream and the hope of the slave.
I rise
I rise
I rise.[1]

THE FRENCH FEAR OF COMMUNITARIANISM

During my playing days with a club in Italy, I remember my
manager calling out to me when we were sitting down for a meal.
'You Black players always have lunch together. Why do you always
stick together in your own corner?' He was highlighting the fact
that I always had lunch with a few Black players. I pointed to the
people seated in the tables around us and said: 'It's weird, all the

White people are eating together and you're taking us to task over it. There are a lot more of them. Do you ever ask them why they always hang out together?' He said nothing.

This kind of reaction can also be the preserve of so-called cultured society. I remember a working session for the previously mentioned exhibition on Black France, where the final section was to be about contemporary artists. Pascal Blanchard and I were coming up with some names when one of the people present warned us: 'Be careful all the same that it's not just Black artists. That would look like communitarianism.' I couldn't help myself turning to him and saying, 'You know what, I often go to museums, the theatre or the cinema, and I've just realised they're all communitarian spaces because the artists there are mostly or all White!' He became embarrassed and changed the subject. Is there such a thing as White communitarianism? As far as he was concerned, I suppose it goes without saying there isn't. But the most important thing is what he did think: there is a risk of a Black communitarianism.

I'm going to put this word 'communitarianism' in scare quotes because it's been so indiscriminately used its meaning is no longer clear. What is communitarianism, at least for those who want to condemn it? Solidarity, real or imagined, between individuals who seem to look alike to those who group them in what they call a 'community'. Because, of course, communitarianism is only ever the preserve of others.

People will say there's a Black community in the United States and in France, you only have to open your eyes to see it. Except that, where France is concerned, it's not true. In my opinion, there's no Black community, no more than there's a White community. On the other hand, those who claim or are convinced there's a Black community or a Muslim community in France, do they see themselves as part of a White community?

Even if they don't admit it to themselves, there are some people who seem to think all White people could unite on the basis of skin colour alone. Through this fantasy of a Black community, White thinking engages in a racialised conception of the world. Every time I hear so-called non-White communitarianism criticised, I know it indicates a resurgence of the idea of a White identity that needs to be protected.

Given that White people come from very different social and cultural groups and originate from a huge variety of countries, it would be stupid to consider them as a single community. It's no different where non-White people are concerned.

Moreover, it would be wrong to think that the prime instinct of non-White people who achieve professional success would be to draw in other non-White people like them. The few who accede to prestigious or powerful roles – where they are surrounded by White people – often feel suspected of empathising with non-White co-workers or influential colleagues. Why is this the case? Firstly, because as I've said already, 'seats at the table' obviously don't come cheap and White domination leaves little space for those who aren't White. A Black person who fails to accept the fate laid out for them by successfully accessing that space has no desire to be dislodged by somebody else potentially. They live with the dreadful, but understandable, idea that 'it's them or me'. Seats for non-Whites are counted out according to a sort of invisible quota that must not be exceeded – just remember the scandal around French Football Federation young-player quotas.

If systems of Black mutual support are simply not a factor, it's above all because of the weight of history and because White people dread solidarity between the oppressed more than anything. On 10 June 1705, a royal decree ruled on 'the reversibility of a slave's emancipation: a freed slave may be enslaved again if he provides a safe place for a runaway slave'.[1] Gatherings of oppressed people have been forbidden since slavery and the colonial era and continue to inspire fear. Needless to say, two White people from the same background who are alumni of the same elite university and who scratch each other's backs are free to do as they please. But careful: two Black people help each other out and there's a big risk of communitarianism. And it's a risk that straight away puts everyone on edge. White thinking immediately starts to ask questions: are you helping her out because she's your sister, because she's your cousin, because she's Black? Two Black people who stand together are always suspected of plotting and scheming. This is precisely what was written in the *Code Noir*,

1 Michelle Zancarini-Fournelle, *Les Luttes et les rêves. Une histoire populaire de la France de 1685 à nos jours* (Paris: La Découverte, 2016).

and it's why no Black person with a modicum of professional ambition wants to risk provoking suspicion.

I recall one day a former Black footballer who had become a TV pundit said to me: 'Lilian, you're obsessed with racism. I don't bother with it; I prefer to get ahead in life. My family always told me not to see myself as a victim and to rise above prejudice.' I was meant to understand that his professional success was a result of the attitude that, in the English-speaking world, is termed 'colour blindness'. According to its reasoning, 'if we really want to get beyond race, we have to stop talking race'.[1] This is common behaviour among a lot of White people. Tired of hearing about unpleasant things – such as persistent discrimination and violent racial harassment – that they don't feel responsible for or complicit in, they imply they don't see them all the better to make them disappear. But this feeling is sometimes shared by successful Black people, like the TV pundit. These are people who prefer to plough their own furrow without lowering themselves to think about the racist pettiness they encounter on the way. And they seem proud of it. 'But,' I answered him, 'have you noticed that the only non-Whites on TV have had to earn the right to be there by playing professionally at the highest level? How many of the journalists and consultants who didn't enjoy a professional career are non-White?' His answer was 'None! I hadn't been looking at it that way.' 'You're not asking yourself the right questions,' I replied. It seemed important to remind him that his individual case proved that a White person has to do far less than a non-White person to succeed. Because he didn't realise he had to work harder than others, he wanted us to believe, like those who don't succeed are so often made to believe, that 'where there's a will there's a way'. This hides the fact that some people start out with advantages others don't have. Without an awareness of the reality of his own situation, the TV pundit wasn't able to challenge the unequal system that had allocated him a place within it.

Challenging the system risks violent exclusion from it. History repeatedly teaches us that those who've tried to free themselves from White oppression and demanded more freedom have quickly been perceived as a danger to the social order. They've been observed,

---

1 Eddo-Lodge, *Why I'm No Longer Talking*, p. 82.

their actions scrutinised, then delegitimised, marginalised and categorised as 'radical' and 'irresponsible', just like women who tried to shake off the yoke of male oppression. I want to insist on this point: it's vital not to fall into the trap set by those who ask you not to see yourself as a victim because, behind this demand, they're trying to prevent you from developing any form of solidarity, any collective denunciation of injustices suffered. Show me the criteria that would allow anyone to say non-White people are not victims in this White world?

Martin Luther King and Nelson Mandela are venerated today, but let's not forget that in their time they were labelled traitors and racists. Their words were twisted and disparaged, their struggle mocked and despised, and they experienced the violent repression of White power. How many women, children and men were locked up, beaten and killed because White thinking forcefully resists any form of challenge? How can non-Whites be reproached for hesitating about rushing into a dialogue that is so complicated and dangerous? To take one example among many: Tommie Smith and John Carlos were inducted into the US Olympic Hall of Fame, the highest honour of the US Olympic and Paralympic Committee, fifty-one years after their suspension from the 1968 US Olympic team for denouncing White oppression.

ANTI-WHITE RACISM

Name me one country where there are political movements that incite violence against White people. Name me countries where political movements incite violence against non-White people. Those who spread the idea that there is such a thing as an anti-White racism are extremely dangerous because they sustain political parties that believe in a race war.

Anti-White racism today is a far-right concept; it's an argument raised by some of the people I speak with about racism. 'It's non-Whites who are racist against Whites.' This is classic transforming-the-victim-into-oppressor rhetoric. How many feminists in the 1970s were accused of 'hating men', an allegation hammered home in a way that meant people didn't have to listen to their demands? Let's be frank here about what's termed anti-White racism. To begin with, remember what racism is: an ideology that categorises people according to criteria – for example, skin colour, religion – that can vary across different societies. From these, innate qualities are deduced, hierarchies established, and policies and practices of segregation are put in place that lead to the harassment, at times death, of oppressed people who are considered as inferior and even non-human.

As far as I know, the people who denounce anti-White racism in France describe it with reference to five cases that occurred between 2010 and 2019.[1] Unlike the everyday racist practices encountered by non-Whites, which are part of a system, a report by the French National Institute for Demographic Studies (INED) notes that 'the racism of minority [groups] towards majorities [...] is not systemic and does not produce social inequalities'.[2]

What I know for certain is what's called anti-White racism in today's society has never prevented a White person from getting housing or work. Nor has it meant a White person has to move about in public fearing that a simple police ID check could end badly for them because of the colour of their skin.

The goal of those who play the anti-White racist card is to try and create an equivalence between so-called anti-White racism and racism in general and to discredit the struggle of those who are discriminated against in our society.

The power to oppress manifests itself in the right to name the person who is violent. The violence associated with non-Whites has become so ingrained in the minds of most of our fellow citizens, and the media above all, they have forgotten that it's above all non-Whites who are subjected to physical and psychological violence much more often than they perpetrate it. If we take the violence of France's *banlieues*, the first to experience it are the residents themselves. And who is the violent one in this instance? The original violence arguably stems from housing disadvantaged populations in what some people consider to be non-places. There are White people who would like to convince themselves that – we've all heard it before – non-White people are more racist than White people, we don't find racism where we think we will, and so

---

1 *Libération*, 18 September 2018; *Valeurs actuelles*, 4320, September 2019.
2 Ibid.

on. And while we're at it, why not add that women are more sexist than men and that queer people terrorise heterosexuals. All these ideas reveal a profound intellectual dishonesty.

As it happens, in France, in recent years, one practice has shocked public opinion: the creation of safe spaces for victims of racism. To be clear, these are meetings where only victims of racist prejudice are allowed to participate and everybody else is excluded. In Reims, in 2016, a four-day 'decolonial' summer school was held that described itself as being exclusively for 'people who had personal experience of institutional racism'. This meant White people were excluded. How should we react to this? It's entirely understandable that such an initiative should shock. I would be appalled and offended if a meeting was organised that expressly or implicitly excluded Black people. In my view, the Reims summer school was completely out of step with the times. Although I fundamentally disagree with this type of meeting, let me try to explain to you why I think French society shoulders some of the blame. When you haven't been listened to, when you haven't been understood, when you haven't been invited to discuss your lived experiences of discrimination and people go so far as to criminalise you before they've heard you, there's something logical about retreating into yourself and wanting to reflect on things solely with people who put up with the same types of harassment, even violence. It seems like a necessary condition for generating a political consciousness that can allow collective reflection on this feeling. The fact that it's not individual, that it's not the result of a weakness, or a psychological sensitivity. That it's not an error or mistake or some lack on your part but is part of an arbitrary social order. It's worth noting, too, that the Reims meeting was an opportunity for White people to experience what it feels like to be excluded from an institution or event. It's violent, it's hurtful. I wouldn't wish anybody to experience any form of exclusion, but I find it interesting that it might mean some people realise just how brutal such a rejection feels. From now on, pay attention to your surroundings and you'll see what you weren't seeing before: all too frequently in certain work spaces, meeting rooms and conventions there are only White people present. And yet nobody has said non-White people aren't allowed to be there.

Here's a question. Do non-White people have the right to assemble without the approval of White people? Today they can, but for centuries White thinking controlled the voice of non-White people. White people took offence at the idea that even the smallest thing could escape their watchful eye – this is a historical fact: 'We forbid slaves belonging to different masters to gather in the day or night […] on pain of corporal punishment […]. In cases of frequent violations […] can be punished with death' (see Article 16 of the Code Noir mentioned earlier).[1] Gatherings of the oppressed are invariably seen as 'suspect' or potentially threatening. When four White people meet, they're just individuals talking to each other; when four non-Whites do the same thing, they're a 'communitarian convention'. The former are never considered a cause for concern, whereas the latter are always suspected of posing a danger, of plotting. And let's not even mention what people would think of twenty non-White youngsters taking public transport on their way to a party.

It's important to try and understand why non-White people taking part in this summer school might believe they'd have licence to speak more freely about their pain and their hopes without a White person in the room. If women have the right to bring up patriarchal violence without men interfering, why shouldn't victims of racism have the right to state their preference to remain among themselves to talk about their experiences of discrimination. My own view is that if we're going to talk about racism, we should also do it with people who haven't experienced it and who could potentially be racist.

Sihame Assbague, one of the organisers of the Reims meeting, explains: 'We didn't want to engage in teaching aimed at white people – which can be useful and we can do it on other occasions. Instead, we wanted to focus on racialised people like us, who, experience the same oppression as we do and need to share their views on those questions.'[2]

It's important to understand that this desire to withdraw into oneself is first and foremost cathartic and allows people to move on from trauma. It's about letting your guard down with people who get what it's about and can understand you. I'm reminded of my friend, an artist of French Caribbean origin who has lived in lots of different countries, including Brazil and Switzerland. This friend is

---

1 See Garrigus translation of Code Noir: http://www2.latech.edu/~bmagee/louisiana_anthology/texts/louis_xiv/louis_xiv--code_noir_english.html.

2 'Les organisatrices du camp d'été décolonial', Vice.com, 19 December 2016.

able to fit in anywhere except in his own country, France, because he's tired of not being treated as French due to the colour of his skin. He suffers from the significant and unfortunately widespread angst of non-White people who would simply like people to stop seeing them as foreigners. He wants to be treated kindly, but it doesn't happen. His angst is also caused by the efforts he has to make to avoid offending and hurting White people by telling them all this. Telling the truth to a White person is complicated. You need to proceed with the greatest caution if you don't want to be seen as extreme or antagonistic. It's quite difficult, for a White person, to understand the violence of those who tell you 'whatever you do, whatever you say, you're not from here'. Just imagine for a moment somebody insinuating that you have no right to be here.

So, yes, let me repeat that safe discussion spaces can be necessary for therapeutic reasons. Victims need to unload the burden they carry; they need to be able to speak freely. I always remember that the great thinker Frantz Fanon was a psychiatrist. What is being played out in racist violence if not a neurosis? And what does it mean to be a victim of racism if it isn't experiencing trauma?

It's by compiling people's stories and comparing your own experiences with those of others that you really establish the truth of discrimination. One thing mustn't be underestimated: the idea that when you've constantly experienced a form of mental isolation or rejection since childhood you end up asking yourself if you're the cause of it. I don't mean that my skin colour is responsible, but my whole being and whatever people read into it. The oppressed wonders, 'Perhaps I am, despite myself, confrontational or awkward with people. Perhaps, objectively, I do look a little scary. Or maybe I'm simply more paranoid than average. Maybe I don't encounter more discrimination than my White friends and I just have a particularly heightened persecution complex that makes me see hostility where there is none.' I can assure you that a lot of non-White people have asked themselves all these questions at least once in their lives.

Publicly acknowledging your feelings and comparing them with similar feelings of other people allows you to understand that it's not about your personal perspective but the prejudices that are associated with your skin colour. You are on the side of truth, and knowing this is vital for preventing you from sinking into a depression.

From a more political perspective, these exchanges are absolutely essential because they allow the commonalities across different experiences of discrimination to be revealed. They allow distinctions to be made between individual cases and, as mentioned above, what is systemic. It's the best method for reflecting on everyone's experience. When accounts stack up and sound the same we forget what separates us politically and socially and discover together that an insidious process has been put in place that affects every individual who is discriminated against.

The question remains whether it's really necessary to exclude White people. I've always preferred to engage people, make them feel uncomfortable if needs be, even if it means getting involved in heated, polarising debates. It's also what this book is doing: I tell myself that people of a certain intellectual honesty will work their way through the arguments and that's how mentalities change. But there's a fundamental question that mustn't be neglected and that's whether keeping to 'one's own kind' provides better conditions for genuine dialogue. The answer is yes. All psychologists know that feeling free from judgement is very important for the process of telling your story. Speaking without White people present provides strength; it gives value and power to your words and your experiences. It provides the opportunity to find strength in your words so that you can express them in public and not be undermined by efforts to refute, qualify or treat them with disdain and indifference. It's why it's still so difficult for women who've been victims of male violence to report or speak about it to other men. Because even if they have the best intentions, men can sometimes fail to listen.

It's the same for victims of racism: White people, even those who listen, will never know the visceral feeling of being called a 'Black bastard'; in other words the feeling of being seen and perceived, now as always, as an inferior being with no right to the same dignity as a White person; to experience the contemptuous look that cuts into the deepest part of you and tells you you're nothing. We know that people who are subjected to degrading treatment experience a dreadful cocktail of anger, humiliation and shame. In this context, providing a personal account becomes very difficult if somebody doesn't feel supported and understood when they're disclosing it. A woman who's been assaulted will open up to a female police officer much more easily than to a male one. In an entirely different context, whether we like it or not, non-Whites don't speak with the same ease about what they experience daily when they know a White person is listening. Because for the person who is telling their story, the person who is listening could potentially judge them.

If White people were to attend meetings with victims of racism they shouldn't leave with a feeling of guilt, nor with the impression that accounts have been exaggerated. Victims of racism don't need White people's guilt; they need their courage to fight injustice. It seems to me that most White people would like non-White people to reassure them. They'd like them to say, 'It's true that from time to time I experience racism. But apart from a few exceptions, most White people are obviously not like that, and especially not you.' White people would like racism to be a deviant behaviour, limited to a few ignorant individuals, just like men would like to believe that sexism is the preserve of a small number of their kind. Victims and non-victims need to talk to each other; they need no-holds-barred conversations and what sociologists term 'unconscious biases' – the multiple minor hurtful behaviours and discriminatory remarks made by White people convinced they're not racist – to be exposed. In the same way that sexism happens in the 'minor details' (which aren't minor at all: e.g. interrupting women during meetings, instinctively allocating them menial tasks despite their qualifications), racism is made up of 'invisible' attitudes that are only too visible for those who are discriminated against.

In a famous preface he wrote to a poetry collection edited by the Senegalese poet Léopold Sédar Senghor, Jean-Paul Sartre wrote:

> When you removed the gag that was keeping these black mouths shut, what were you hoping for? That they would sing your praises? Did you think that when they raised themselves up again, you would read adoration in the eyes of these heads that our fathers had forced to bend down to the very ground?[1]

---

1 Jean-Paul Sartre, 'Black Orpheus', in *'What is Literature?' and Other Essays* (Cambridge, MA: Harvard University Press, 1988), p. 291.

Non-Whites need to learn to express themselves in the same way, with the same words, regardless of whether they're alone or in the presence of White people.

I remember being in a meeting in a large institution because we had to choose the designs for an exhibition on racism. At one point, a suggestion was made to get a Black designer to do the layout of the exhibition. But somebody said, 'Isn't there a risk she's too close to the subject?' Too close to it! One instinct might have been to think: if we choose a Black woman she'll know what she's talking about; she'll be able to make positive use of her lived experience of this complex subject matter and, whether she's of African or Caribbean origin, she'll be able to draw on things like her roots and her identity. But no: she was judged to be 'too close' to it. It's always White people who know best what the right level of 'closeness' to questions of racism is, even if they've barely thought about it. The right level of 'closeness' is theirs.

This is why I insist on the fact that the colour of a gathering can determine the tenor of the things that are said there. I've frequently been the only Black person at meetings and very often I've felt that what was being said was very White. In other words, it was being spoken with the casual self-assurance of those who don't imagine there might be other ways of thinking about things. Your thinking can be shaped by your gender, your sexuality, your social class, just as it can by the colour of your skin. A few years ago on social media there was a hashtag #SiLesNoirsParlaientCommeDesBlancs ['If black people talked like white people'], where comments by White people about non-White people were turned against them. Things like: 'I've nothing against White people, my caretaker's daughter even married one'; 'Ah come on, why aren't you dancing Lucy? It's a Daniel Balavoine song, he's from your country isn't he!'; 'Fabrice, did you know there's another *White* working here, on the third floor. You'd get on well.'

It's not enough simply to be non-White to get the condescending intention behind these remarks. You need to have thought about the issue for years, to have read authors that lead you towards this kind of reflection, to have understood the way oppression works through language. In my view, exchanges between victims and non-victims of White oppression allow all these elements to be put into words so they can be better understood and challenged.

ETHNICITY AND DATA

There are always two issues to take into account when it comes to data collection: the question of principle and the question of reality. For the defenders of principle, gathering data on ethnicity is invariably pernicious. The exceptions are the occasional times researchers are authorised to do so for limited projects by the CNIL, the French state body for regulating data protection. I've already spoken about 'colour blindness', which claims that speaking about race encloses people within artificial categories of identity, something that would justify different types of communitarianism. But, in reality, I've known from nine years of age that we're already pigeonholed according to our identity. Every Black person is conscious of being confined within a Black identity. It seems like White people are the only ones who don't know they're imprisoned within their skin colour.

It's difficult to find precise data in France relative to ethnicity-based discrimination: disaggregation on this basis is not permitted, and there are laws that penalise racist practices.[1] Nonetheless, in 2008, the French national office for statistics (INED) conducted an important survey, the results of which are telling. One of the report's authors, Patrick Simon, notes that:

> 'Ethnoracial discrimination' largely affects people of North African, sub-Saharan African and overseas territorial origin, whereas the effect on immigrants of European origin, and especially their descendants, is negligible. Relatively speaking, people of Asian origin are also spared. [...] Less visible, discriminatory practices have persisted and been adapted to the new legal and moral context. While rejection, marginalisation or violation of rights can still be explicitly formulated with reference to gender or origin, among other characteristics, the reality of discrimination now covers a wide range of practices essentially that are written into multiple decisions where the discriminatory character is not

1 See in particular the 1972 law that led to the modification of the Penal Code.

evident. The diffuse and systemic nature of these practices makes it difficult to identify them.[1]

Simon's research squarely demonstrates that among all the causes of discrimination (gender, religion, age), those based on skin colour are the strongest. Stereotypes and prejudice set non-White people apart and lead to a strong cognitive bias on the part of White people in relation to schooling, work, health and access to housing and other services. And yet our knowledge of these questions is limited.

Women know the importance of relying on accurate data because feminists, who had long demanded an objective overview of their representation within decision-making forums, were not listened to and were countered with: 'What for? In France all citizens are born equal. Whether male or female, rich or poor, tall or short, the French Republic grants you the same rights and treats you the same under the law. Why would you want to collect data on women? It's not necessary. French men are a little chauvinistic; they need time to get used to the idea that women have as much right as men to be in charge. Mentalities need to change. Let time take its course.'

Feminist activists refused this and insisted that an accurate picture of reality was needed. I share their position. Let's go back to the mid-1990s and the Palais Bourbon, the lower house of the French National Assembly. The person who rejects the need for gender data seems to believe that all is well. But of course, walking through the rows of seats in the debating chamber, it's easy to see that there aren't very many elected female representatives. In 1945, thirty-three women were elected to parliament, but when Charles de Gaulle became president in 1958 there was a backwards surge and only eight women were elected (or 1.4% of seats). Today, 224 women hold seats (39% of the total).

At some point, counting becomes necessary. For example, in the 1993–97 legislature of the French parliament, there were forty-two female deputies out of a total of 579 (i.e. 7%). A quick, inquisitive look at the French Senate, the upper house of Parliament, reveals that 5% of senators were female. It's important to know that in the mid-1990s, in a country that believed itself to be modern, 93%

---

1 Mirna Safi, Patrick Simon, 'Les discriminations ethniques et raciales dans l'enquête *Trajectoires et Origines*: représentations, expériences subjectives et situations vécues.' *Économie et statistique*, n° 464-465-466 (2013).

of directly elected representatives and 95% of senators were men. Let's be frank: 93% is the indisputable sign that action is required. It's the sign that the glass ceiling preventing women from assuming legislative roles has nothing to do with the so-called mentality of French men. It's to do with a political system that is sectioned off by men and makes women ineligible.

Figures make it infinitely easier to confirm this. Between the end of the 1950s and the mid-1990s, the percentage of elected female representation increased by just 5.6%. In the space of forty years, women had, through their efforts and their demands, won a significant number of rights and freedoms. But these rights stopped at the doors of power. A calculation based on the average rate of feminisation of the French parliament tells us it would have taken 356 years to achieve an equal number of male and female representatives! And that's only the National Assembly, which wasn't the most misogynistic of France's elected authorities. The only way to know this is by consulting the data.

It was political decisions that enabled practices to change. On 6 June 2000, a law on gender parity was passed. It didn't wait for mentalities to evolve. The law shook up institutional sexism and allowed for progress towards equality. In 2002, seventy-seven women (13% of seats) were elected to France's lower house of parliament. In 2012, there were 155 women (26% of seats). In the 2017 elections, 224 women were elected (39% of seats). This suggests parity should be achieved by the mid-2020s. In concrete terms, this is the purpose that data serves: to pass legislation that achieves in twenty years what would otherwise have taken 356. In terms of parliamentary gender parity today, France has achieved almost double the global average of 23%. Nonetheless, although it is the world's seventh most powerful nation, France is only seventeenth for the overall percentage of women in national parliament – on a list topped by Rwanda.[1]

France didn't stop there. Following on from the National Assembly 'case', efforts were made to measure female representation in all decision-making bodies: town halls, regional prefectures, regional and departmental councils but also the heads of large companies, senior public service, universities, the military, broadcasting. What was discovered, of course, was that the same glass ceiling existed

1 See http://archive.ipu.org/wmn-e/classif.htm.

for women in these domains too. That the sexist system and male privilege that blocked their entry to parliament excluded them everywhere.

Those who reject ethnicity data may hide behind statements such as: 'Everyone is afforded the same opportunities by the French Republic' or 'We mustn't distinguish between citizens'. It's obvious that refusing the collection of ethnicity data serves above all to protect certain interests and to prevent discrimination from being clearly exposed. This assessment was true where low levels of female representation were concerned, and it remains true for the glass ceiling that non-White people are coming up against.

Society compiles statistics for all kinds of things from yoghurt consumption to belief in aliens. It does this because we need a precise and quantified understanding of situations in order to take effective action. The job of 'ethnicity' data is simply to show us the facts. And the facts I'm talking about here are White political and cultural domination. It's domination that's expressed through an over-representation of White people in institutions of power: elected assemblies, corporate management, honorary roles, high-status professions (such as doctors, lawyers, journalists). If we were to produce an organisational chart of these spaces of power, it would be possible to determine precisely what so few notice: that is to say, the proportion of White people. I don't state this in order to present it as unfair. I'm very aware that the majority of French people are White. What I would like above all is if we could acknowledge it and ask ourselves why it is so. This 'keeping to one's own kind' is not a coincidence: it's telling. It's a sign of how our society has been constructed and how it functions today. We could then speak about it calmly, the way we do in relation to gender equality.

Ethnicity data would allow the issue to be discussed and to determine whether there's a difference between what we say we want to do and what we are doing in reality. If we say that what we want to do is achieve equality, are we really doing it? Isn't there an unacknowledged racial segregation in our society that is getting worse even while we're making a different kind of progress within our formal power structures?

Why did the composition and balance of the National Assembly increase from 7% to 40% female representation in a little over twenty years? It's because legislation established an objective of absolute parity. In other words, it laid out a clearly delineated direction of travel where progress could be measured in stages. It didn't do away with all the forms of discrimination women suffer from, far from it. But at least women can say that elected representatives look like the men and women who vote for them. Moreover, when issues relative to abortion, contraception, domestic violence, sexism come up for debate, there are enough female legislators to ensure these questions aren't hijacked by men. And the same goes for all the other issues that concern the entire population, half of which is female. Because women's perspectives ensure a diversity of opinion that helps to better grasp the complexity of things.

We need to reach the same level of non-White representation in all decision-making bodies. So that when questions relevant to race are tackled such as police training, education policy, data collection, there will be a certain number of politicians involved who don't see these as just 'details' or the inventions of supposed victims. As with women, it's not about confining non-White people to particular areas of interest but about enabling everybody to benefit from their unique experience. I'm not claiming that will get rid of everyday racism. Nonetheless, it will be more difficult, generally speaking, to have prejudices about non-White people and their 'abilities' when your mayor, departmental prefect, deputy or senator is not White, when your university chancellor is not White, when the expert speaking on the television is not White, when the prime minister or president of your country is not White.

3

BECOMING HUMAN

1. RACE SUICIDE

From the moment we are born, we are raised to be White, Black, Senegalese, Armenian, French, British… to be a man, a woman; our parents raise us in this religion or that religion, society gives us different roles to play, determines what groups we belong to. Do we question these feelings of belonging in order to avoid being imprisoned by them? Can we exist without these masks? Are there not some masks that we never remove? Is it not, in fact, very difficult to be truly free?

These were the questions I asked when I took people to visit the exhibition *Real and Imaginary Depictions of the Orient: A Matter of Gazes* that my foundation organised in collaboration with the Musée National Eugène-Delacroix in Paris in 2018. I continue to ask these kinds of questions when I meet with young people today to raise their awareness of the ways in which we are conditioned by our environment. I tell them that one of the most powerful ways in which we are conditioned is through religion. I ask them: 'Which of you has the same religion as your parents?' Generally speaking, the vast majority, if not all of them, raise their hands. Then I add:

'This evening, when you go home, tell your parents that you want to change religion.' I'll let you imagine the reactions from the young people who experience a sense of panic... I calm them down by advising them *against* doing this and then tell them that society finds it difficult to accept people who want to act differently, people who want to free themselves from behaviours that are imposed, often from one generation to the next. You, yourselves, experience a feeling of betrayal if you don't reproduce some of these behaviours, some of these ways of doing or of saying things. And I explain to them that, depending on our religion, the colour of our skin, depending on whether we're male or female, societies ask us to reproduce particular intellectual frameworks and hierarchies. That's why it's vital to challenge them. You're going to have to force yourself to break free from the multiple masks that you're made to wear. And you really run the risk of being misunderstood because society doesn't like free spirits. But that's who brings about change in society. After all, are all inventors of religion not, in fact, true revolutionaries who have broken with pre-existing beliefs and ways of being?

Needless to say, it's extremely complicated, but many have succeeded and their success shows us that it is, nevertheless, possible. Amílcar Lopes da Costa Cabral was a politician from Guinea Bissau and the Cape Verde Islands. He founded the African Party for the Independence of Guinea and Cape Verde (PAIGC) before being assassinated by a former PAIGC veteran, in Conakry, in 1973, under the orders of the Portuguese political police. It was Cabral who coined the notion of the 'suicide' of the revolutionary intellectual: 'The revolutionary petite bourgeoisie as a class must be able to commit suicide in order to return to life as revolutionary workers who identify completely with the profound aspirations of the people to which they belong.'[1] The petite bourgeoisie has always been haunted by the spectre of bourgeois tendencies, tendencies that call upon it to betray the Revolution, whether by impeding it or by hijacking it. For Cabral, only one solution was possible: death by 'suicide'. The expression 'class suicide' is interesting, as Achille Mbembe pointed out to me, in relation to the fight against racism, and I find myself wanting to

1 Cited by Demba Moussa Dembélé in 'Amílcar Cabral, quarante ans après', *Frantz Fanon International*, 2013.

talk about the need for 'race suicide'. Should we not all practise a form of race suicide in order to free ourselves from the identities of colour within which history seeks to imprison us?

When I look for the women and men who have brought about profound change not only in their own lives, but also in the lives of many others by trying to drag society towards a life that is more just for the oppressed, there are many to be found.

I'm reminded, for example, of what former French Justice Minister Christiane Taubira said in the parliamentary report that led to the 2001 French law that recognised the slave trade and slavery as a crime against humanity. She referred to the *Cahier de Doléances* in Champagney, in the Haute-Saône *département* that called for the abolition of slavery. But this *commune* was not the only one to do so: we could add the *Cahier de Doléances* of the town of Charolles or of Toulon-sur-Arroux, for example. These *Cahiers* were established by royal edict as a means of compiling and recording public grievances and suggestions which were then passed on to the Estates-General. Of 164 *Cahiers* written by the Third Estate, twelve issue a plea for the abolition of the trade, of which four call for the abolition of slavery and eight condemn its practices; of the fifty *Cahiers* written by the nobles, three wish to see the abolition of the trade, two of which also call for slavery to be abolished; and finally, of 155 *Cahiers* written by the clergy, eight call specifically for the trade to be abolished, of which four also call for slavery to be abolished. The inhabitants of Toulon-sur-Arroux ask that 'under the French empire, no vestige of slavery shall remain! that measure of public fortune should no longer be calculated on the number of misfortunates! and that slavery be abolished in the colonies, that the nation renounce forever the trade in Negroes, and that the King, following the movement of his heart, deigns to invite all nations to renounce this monstrous commerce, by a general pact for which Humanity calls out!'[1] 'Race suicide' has long been at the heart of the struggle for equality.

The French priest and abolitionist Abbé Grégoire understood and wasted no time in speaking out against it. Along with Condorcet, Brissot, Mirabeau and Lafayette, he defended Jews just like he defended Black people. He knew only too well that Article 1 of the 1685 Code Noir forced Jews to leave islands that had been colonised

1 Article 10 of the *Cahier de doléance de Toulon-sur-Arroux*, Saône-et-Loire archives.

by France. For him, Black people and 'Jews are members of this universal family, which must establish fraternity among all peoples'.[1]

I am also reminded of Olympe de Gouges, author of the *Declaration of the Rights of Woman and the Female Citizen*, who published an astonishing book in 1788 entitled *Reflections on Negroes*. 'I have always been interested in the deplorable fate of the Negro race. [...] People I asked did not satisfy my curiosity and my reason. They called those people brutes, cursed by Heaven. As I grew up, I clearly realised that it was force and prejudice that had condemned them to that horrible slavery, in which Nature plays no role, and for which the unjust and powerful interests of Whites are alone responsible.'[2] She wrote an anti-slavery play, *The Black Market*. She explained, in a letter: 'What did I say to the colonisers? I urged them to treat their slaves with greater kindness and generosity. But they do not want to lose even the smallest part of their revenues. That lies at the heart of their fears, their rage, their barbarism.'[3]

And then, of course, we have Georges Clemenceau, who I've already spoken about, this politician who fought against Jules Ferry and his attempts to justify colonialism. In his letters on Black slavery, Clemenceau states that the motto 'Liberty, Equality, Fraternity' should apply to *all*: 'That Black people should soon have the right to vote, from the moment slavery is abolished, should no longer be in doubt. That must be so and will be so' (*Le Temps*, 10 January 1866). In recounting his journey to America, he notes with surprise:

> I remark that in all discussions here, there is no question of universal suffrage being established. Each State is to be given the right to establish its own electoral law. The only stipulation is that,

1 Rabbi Michael Williams, 1996, 'Peut-on rendre les juifs plus utiles et plus heureux en France?' *European Judaism. A Journal for the New Europe.* Vol. 29, No. 2, p. 53.

2 Olympe de Gouges, 1788, *Reflections on Negroes*. Online English translation available via the University of Georgia's Francophone Slavery webpages: http://slavery.uga.edu/texts/literary_works/reflections.pdf.

3 'Departure of M. Necker and Mme de Gouges, farewell to the French/France', in Benoîte Groult, *Ainsi soit Olympe de Gouges. La Déclaration des droits de la femme et autres textes politiques* (Paris: Grasset, 2013), p. 150; Olympe de Gouges, *Écrits politiques*, presented by Olivier Blanc, Volume 1, p. 149; Benoîte Groult's 1986 and 2013 editions cut several pages from the work published by Olivier Bland (Paris: Côté-femmes Éditions, 1993).

within this law, no distinction shall be made between Black people and White people. [...] But these rules and restrictions on suffrage must be the same in the minds of everyone. There are many lowly White people in the Southern states who are no more capable of exercising the right to vote than the most stupid of Black people. (*Le Temps*, 11 October 1865)

For Clemenceau, '[...] Absolute equality of all citizens, without exception, in the eyes of the law' (*Le Temps*, 29 January 1867) was vital. Humanity is universal and 'this race war has been going on for a long time; it started the day a White man bought a Black man. [...] Yes, without a doubt a war between the races: But who started it? And who is prosecuting it?' (*Le Temps*, 29 November 1867).

On this last point, I have to object: there has never been a war between the races. The invention of race seeks to shatter solidarities, to construct an enemy who makes it easier for the majority to be exploited by the oligarchy.

In his famous address to the Chamber of Deputies on 30 July 1885, Clemenceau once again condemned Jules Ferry's expansionist colonial policies. In the speech, he set out two fundamental arguments in favour of decolonisation: the financial problem and the scale of French losses. Was this a strategy to hide his profound belief in equality among all men (but not women, who still hadn't gained the vote)? It was more than just that, and I have already quoted part of his speech:

Superior races? Inferior races, that's easy to say! Personally, I am less inclined to believe in any such thing, since I heard German scholars scientifically prove that France must surely lose the Franco-Prussian War because the French belong to an inferior race than the Germans. I must admit that, since that time, I hesitate before turning to a people or a civilisation and stating: inferior people, inferior civilisation. The Hindus [Indians], an inferior race? With their great, refined civilisation whose origins are lost in the mists of time! With its great Buddhist religion that left India for China, with this great efflorescence of the arts, the traces of which we can still see today! The Chinese, an inferior race! With their civilisation whose origins are unknown and which appears to have been pushed to its extreme limits. Confucius, inferior! Allow me to reveal the truth that, still today, when Chinese diplomats are locked in talks with certain European diplomats… (*laughter and applause across the benches*) they make a good impression, and if one were to consult the diplomatic annals of certain peoples, one would discover documents that assuredly prove that the yellow race is, when it comes to competent negotiation, or the safe handling of extremely sensitive matters, by no means inferior to those who rush to proclaim their supremacy.[1]

In this way, I hope what I mean by 'race suicide' is clearer: it is to accept the need to question what it is to be White. Why is it so difficult to remove the mask of Whiteness?

Without the Quakers, the abolitionist Harriet Tubman would not have been able to escape from slavery. Nicknamed the 'Moses of her People' for her role in the struggle to abolish slavery in the nineteenth century, Tubman helped many slaves to escape their fate. What I'm particularly interested in here is that she received assistance from a group of Quakers and abolitionists from the Underground Railway resistance network. As slavery was banned there, British North America (which would become Canada) was one of the principal places of refuge. Many roads led there and there were numerous points of access on the border, but the journey itself was dangerous. Estimates put the number of slaves who escaped thanks to this clandestine network at around 100,000.[2] This case shows that these Quakers never accepted that they should wear the mask of Whiteness of the era.

---

1 Speech delivered in the French Chamber of Deputies, 30 July 1885.

2 James Banks, *March Toward Freedom. A History of Black Americans* (Belmont: Fearon Publishers, 1974).

In a 1956 essay, 'Colonialism is a System',[1] Jean-Paul Sartre responds to the arguments put forward by colonisers in favour of French Algeria and lays bare the economic and social violence that underpins such a system. For Sartre, colonisation was responsible for the impoverishment of the Algerian people, a situation that exclusively profits the colonisers and their capitalist economy. Sartre also demonstrated the mechanisms behind the 'fabricating'[2] of the native, a native who, in order to survive, can see no alternative but the development of an Algerian nationalism. Sartre's words undoubtedly put him in the line of fire of the far-right paramilitary organisation the OAS (Secret Armed Organisation) and his Paris apartment was bombed twice.

In this essay, Sartre states, in terms reminiscent of Aimé Césaire's *Discourse on Colonialism*, that colonialism is:

> our shame; it mocks our laws or caricatures them. It infects us with its racism [...], it obliges our young men to fight despite themselves and die for the Nazi principles that we fought against ten years ago; it attempts to defend itself by arousing fascism even here in France. Our role is to help it to die. Not only in Algeria but wherever it exists. People who talk of the abandonment of Algeria are imbeciles. There is no abandoning what we have never owned. It is, quite the opposite, a question of our constructing with the Algerians new relations between a free France and a liberated Algeria.[3]

Sartre's preface to Fanon's *The Wretched of the Earth* renders the relationship between coloniser and native explicit: 'I, a European, am stealing my enemy's book and turning it into a way of healing Europe. Make the most of it.'[4] Do those who have tried to remove or to refuse the mask of Whiteness not make society better?

---

1 First published in *Les Temps modernes*, No. 123, 1956.

2 Taken from 2001 translation of Sartre's essay published in *Interventions: International Journal of Postcolonial Studies*, Vol 3(1), pp. 127–140. Translated by Azzedine Haddour, Steven Brewer and Terence McWilliams.

3 Ibid., p. 140.

4 Jean-Paul Sartre, 'Preface', in Frantz Fanon, *The Wretched of the Earth*, trans. by Richard Philcox (New York: Grove Press, 2004 [1961]), p. xlix.

And, of course, I must also cite White civil rights activists, from Jean Seberg to Jane Fonda and others, whose activism led them to be persecuted in many ways.

On 8 September 1979, Jean Seberg was found dead in the back of her car; to all intents and purposes, she appeared to have died of an overdose. Her second husband, French author and director Romain Gary, accused the FBI of being responsible for her death by suicide. Seberg had become involved with the struggle for the rights of Native Americans and African Americans at a very young age and, in 1970, the FBI had placed her under surveillance as part of an operation, the aim of which was to investigate dissident political organisations. During the press conference Gary gave a few days after the discovery of Seberg's body, he revealed an internal FBI document that provided evidence of a campaign of defamation and harassment the actress had been subjected to by the FBI, the sole aim of which was to slander and neutralise her.

We can see here that freeing oneself of the mask of White thinking is viewed as a betrayal by White forces of power. It takes courage to break with this ideology.

And what can we say about Denis Goldberg, the anti-apartheid activist imprisoned for 22 years, along with other key figures of the movement? This White South African was sentenced to life imprisonment, like Nelson Mandela, on 12 June 1964. 'It was an honour to risk your life alongside Nel [as he refers to Mandela]. To fight alongside a man who was capable of such determination and such humanity forces you to be dignified in your actions. Even in the face of death. First we smiled, then we shouted with joy. We were expecting to be hanged. To survive was a miracle. [...] Life imprisonment. Life! It's wonderful!' 'How does one take on the anti-Apartheid cause when, as a White person, you have so much to lose and so little to gain? the journalist asks. 'It was what the situation required!' is his straightforward response. 'It is possible to give greater importance to the ideal of liberty than one gives to one's own life [...]. In my opinion, an individual can't be free if others aren't.' Like Mandela, he believes that 'both the oppressor and the oppressed are dispossessed of their humanity.'[1]

1 Interview published in the French daily newspaper *La Croix*. Marie Boëton, 'Denis Goldberg, mon combat auprès de Mandela', 12 June 2019.

And I can also picture Francis Jeanson and his network of support for the Algerian National Liberation Front (FLN). After the outbreak of the Algerian War, he joined the anticolonial struggle and in 1955, with his wife Colette, he published *L'Algérie hors la loi* (*Outlaw Algeria*), in which he affirmed the legitimacy of the Algerian people's struggle for freedom. Two years later, he founded the 'Jeanson network' in order to offer support to Algerian fighters, the so-called 'suitcase carriers' who raised funds to help the militants move around and pay for accommodation. Considered a 'traitor' to France, he justified his involvement in the 1960 book *Notre Guerre* (*Our War*) which was seized on publication and distributed clandestinely while his network was dismantled and its members tried. At the end of a trial with far-reaching consequences, Jeanson was sentenced in absentia to ten years in prison. He was pardoned in 1966, and French Minister of Cultural Affairs André Malraux invited him to play a role in the newly established 'Maisons de la Culture', a network of cultural centres set up in each French *département* in order to widen access to the arts and, in particular, theatre, cinema, music and the visual arts. Jeanson went on to serve as Director of the Maison de la Culture in Chalon-sur-Saône from 1967 to 1971.

For me, this trial offers an explanation of what stops many White people from abandoning their White mask: being seen as a traitor, being thought, by some, to have switched sides.

And then there's Nellie Bly, the American journalist who, at the beginning of the twentieth century, pioneered undercover journalism in order to don the skin of another, to live and understand the realities of those who are not permitted to express themselves and whose very thoughts are misrepresented. By feigning mental illness, Nellie Bly got herself interned in the asylum on Blackwell's Island, New York. Her account was serialised in the *New York World*, causing great scandal and leading to root-and-branch reform of the institution. Nellie Bly repeated the experiment by taking on the role of a maid trying to find work. When she died in 1922, the press expressed their sorrow at the loss of 'the finest journalist in America'.

Some White people have taken up where Nellie Bly left off, disguising themselves as non-Whites in order to bear witness in the most just way possible to the violence imposed on the latter by the White world.

The first to have carried out this experiment was John Howard Griffin, whose *Black Like Me* is the tale of what he lived through over a period of several months in 1959 and 1960, having chemically altered the colour of his skin to try to pass as a Black man.[1]

Griffin describes an American society in which segregation reigned supreme. There was no great surprise in that. The public sphere was clearly divided in two with everyone keeping to the confines of their allocated space. It was a form of discrimination that could be found not only in the physical domain, since the extreme economic insecurity in which Black people lived was the subject of innumerable prejudices spread by White people, according to whom Black people were dishonest, violent, untrustworthy, etc. Griffin, however, for his part, painted a picture of people who were concerned for their future, who sought to succeed as far as was possible, a far cry from the image of Black people languishing in their own misery that tended to be propagated by White thinking. Prejudices were also whirling around about sexuality and Black people, according to which Black people were lascivious and, yet again, closer to wild animals than to humans. An important point that Griffin makes is that these ideas are expressed honestly to him by White people who, in other domains, had acted respectfully towards him, in some instances even helping him out. In other words, discrimination is entrenched, insidious, perfidious. Black people continue to be treated as inferior under the guise of equality: separate but equal.[2] In this way, Griffin saw his initial hypothesis confirmed: you have to be Black to understand the segregation to which Black people are subjected. What is sad in this story is that it's always necessary that it be told in the words of a White person in order to convince other White people of the violence experienced by non-White people. And that is most definitely due to a particular

---

1 John Howard Griffin, *Black Like Me* (1961: London: Serpent's Tail, 2019).

2 See the 1896 US Supreme Court ruling on the Plessy Case, which essentially made the Jim Crow laws legal.

racist bias to which it is difficult to admit: a non-White person's word cannot be fully trusted.

Following the publication of his work, Griffin received death threats. Once again, for some here was a traitor, a traitor to his race. And yet he was praised internationally and became a human rights activist.

Günter Wallraff, someone I had the good fortune to meet in 2011, used the same set-up as Griffin had done but this time in Germany where Wallraff passed as a Turkish guest worker over a two-year period. *Lowest of the Low* (the German title *Ganz unten* literally means 'Right at the bottom') recounts the journalist's undercover investigations and was published in Germany in 1985 (and later translated into French and English).[1] While living as a Turkish man, Wallraff above all came face-to-face with the everyday racism experienced on a daily basis by immigrant workers in the early 1980s in former West Germany. Wallraff highlighted the appalling living conditions of these workers, the grey zones in their working environment, stuck between exploitation, the absence of social security and the refusal to provide the basic safety equipment necessary to carry out some of their jobs. Are today's undocumented workers not also subject to the same forms of violence? Do they not also have to face the same fears and the same humiliation?

Coming from the sporting world, there is another case that I find deeply touching in the strength of its symbolism and for just how rare an example it is, namely that of Peter Norman. Norman was a White Australian athlete, five-time Australian champion and silver medallist at the 1968 Mexico City Summer Olympics. On 16 October 1968, on the podium after the 200 metre final in Mexico, Norman showed his support for the African American athletes Tommie Smith and John Carlos by pinning an Olympic Project for Human Rights badge to his jacket. This demonstration of solidarity led to the Australian being excluded from the 1972 Olympics. Once again, he was considered a traitor, a traitor to his race. When they learned that he had not been invited to attend by the Australian

---

1 Günter Wallraff, *Lowest of the Low*, trans. by Martin Chalmers (1988, London: Methuen).

organisers, the American federation invited Norman to the 2000 Sydney Olympics. At his funeral in 2006, John Carlos and Tommie Smith agreed to be pallbearers, prompting his nephew, Matt Norman, to state: 'It made sense that they should be together again one last time. His gesture in Mexico had created a bond between them for life and Peter wholeheartedly shared the convictions of his fellow sprinters on equality and the fight against racism. He was a man of faith, raised in a family that had, for generations, been active in the Salvation Army. And the racism Black people were enduring in America reminded him of the condition of Aboriginal Australians, who had to wait until 1967 for White politicians to recognise them as true citizens. Peter was conscious of all that. And it was with great pride and a great awareness that he stood in solidarity with the two Americans.'[1]

I'd also like to mention one of my idols, Megan Rapinoe, captain of the US football team which won the World Cup in France in 2019, and subsequently named FIFA Women's Player of the Year. She wasn't afraid to talk about taboo subjects. For example, she gave her backing to Colin Kaepernick – the American football player who spoke out against police brutality against Black people in the US – by taking a knee during the US national anthem before one of her matches. 'I'm going to keep taking a knee. I'm trying to find another way to speak out but, in the meantime, this is my way of making my voice heard.' When FIFA criticised her, she replied: 'We have to look at everything our flag and our anthem represent: does this anthem and this flag really protect everyone?'[2]

It was a gesture I reprised, myself, when I was awarded an honorary doctorate by the University of Stockholm in 2017.

Cédric Herrou is a farmer from Nice who is also an activist working to help refugees and asylum seekers. He made headlines in France and elsewhere following his arrest in 2016 for having helped more than 150 migrants to cross the Franco-Italian border. When his trial began in Nice in January 2017, he was welcomed by applause from hundreds of members of the public who supported his actions. He was found guilty in the lower courts,

---

1 As cited in Annick Cojean, 'Des amis de trente-huit ans et vingt secondes', *Le Monde*, 18 November 2006.

2 As cited in 'États-Unis: Rapinoe boycotte à nouveau l'hymne américain' , *L'Obs*, 16 September 2016.

but then won his case at the Constitutional Court on 6 July 2018, thereby underlining the primacy of the constitutional principle of fraternity and the freedom to help others to humanitarian ends. In transposing this legal judgement, the French Parliament softened the law that seeks to stop those who help others gain entry to France illegally or who help individuals who are classed as illegal immigrants, although such actions remain punishable by law. The farmer was acquitted by the Court of Appeal in Lyon on 13 May 2020. A 2016 *New York Times* article made him famous worldwide. Since then, Cédric Herrou's actions have been in the public eye. With other activist citizens from Nice and its environs, Herrou founded the association Roya Citoyenne, which works in partnership with other associations such as the Auberge des Migrants in the Calais region, first and foremost in order to defend citizens from around the world.

Organisations and people like Cédric Herrou, along with thousands of anonymous individuals such as those who work as ambassadors for the Human Rights League or Education without Borders, working to help migrants get the right paperwork, to find employment, accommodation or self-esteem, or the European maritime humanitarian organisation SOS Mediterranée, or PAUSE, the French national programme for the urgent aid and reception of scientists in exile, and so many others, are all working to repair and to maintain the ties that bind us as humans. What is at stake is not the humanity or the lives of *migrants*, but first and foremost our own humanity.

Recently, I have spoken out about racism in football, particularly in Italy. I said that the fans who make monkey noises when they watch Black players do so because they think they are superior as White people. In part, what I was saying was reported as 'White people think that…' and I wasn't at all surprised by some reactions in France that accused me of essentialising White people. History shows us that Black people are under scrutiny. It would have been naive of me to think that wouldn't also be the case for a Black person who leads a foundation that fights against racism. I discussed it with a friend, a former footballer who happens to be White: I told him that, in France, we are lagging behind in terms of reflecting on what it means to be White and I suggested that he should check out some of Gregg Popovich's statements.

Gregg Popovich is an American basketball coach. When he was invited to speak about Black History Month which the NBA marks every February, he responded as follows before his own team San Antonio's match against Utah:

> The league is made up of a lot of Black guys. To honor [Black History Month] and understand it is pretty simplistic. How would you ignore that? But more importantly, we live in a racist country that hasn't figured it out yet. And it's always important to bring attention to it, even if it angers some people. The point is that you have to keep it in front of everybody's nose so that they understand it, that it still hasn't been taken care of, and we have a lot of work to do.[1]

On 27 September 2017, in a video recorded and edited by the French online media platform channel Brut, he reacted to anti-racism protests within American sport: 'Yes, because you were born White, you have advantages that are systemically, culturally, psychologically there! Whether it's the LGBT movement or women's suffrage, race, it doesn't matter. People have to be made to feel uncomfortable. And especially White people because we're comfortable. We still have no clue of what being born White means. Yes, because you were born White, you have advantages! [...] And they have been built up and cemented for hundreds of years. But many people can't look at it. It's too difficult. It can't be something that is on their plate on a daily basis. People want to hold their position. People want the status quo. People don't want to give that up. And until it's given up, it's not going to be fixed.'[2]

After watching the video, my friend sent me the following text:

> I've been lucky enough to meet this guy and I completely agree with what he says. You have my support, Lilian. What you said triggered me

1 *Guardian Sport*, 'Black History Month vital in 'racist country' like US, says Spurs' Gregg Popovich', 13 February 2018. Available online at: https://www.theguardian.com/sport/2018/feb/13/gregg-popovich-black-history-month-nba.

2 See Gregg Popovich, 27 September 2017: https://www.youtube.com/watch?v=ydAQ2PycOWs.

because, in my view, it could have added to this gap between Black and White (even though you told me it had been taken out of context). In fact, what I think, is that there are things that you can't say because you're Black. But Popovich, who's White, can say them. It's in terms of the bigger picture that you can and must intervene. You need White people to say the things that are going to get a reaction. If you do it, you're going to look like the guy who's out for revenge. A White guy who does it will look like a traitor in the eyes of racists. But he'll also get people who want it to stop to do something. When I listen to Popovich, I think 'f**king sh***y society! How can we still accept such inequalities?' You've got to come down hard: he's in a position of neutrality that means it's possible for him to say certain things. I hope I've been clear and that there's no ambiguity in what I've said. You, in fact, are the instigator and your White friends are the ones who need to hit where it hurts: the truth. That's just my opinion.

To me it seems very interesting to analyse this text: it's the first time that I've heard such a sincerely expressed view from a White person, telling me that the fact that I'm Black gives meaning to the stances I adopt. And that I need White people to come with me. These words strengthen the idea that the key to change is for White people not to see that process of accompanying as a betrayal but as a struggle to establish new forms of solidarity. Did you notice that my friend said that Popovich is in a position of neutrality? Why do White people so often think of themselves as neutral?

Because all the women and men I've spoken about above are important, indeed vital to bring out the human in each of us.

I recently had the opportunity to speak about this topic with Achille Mbembe:

A.M.: We must find women and men who are ready to accompany us. Perhaps they won't undertake the whole journey with us. Some will only accompany us for 20, 50, 75 of the 100 kilometres we have to travel. It doesn't matter because to be able to move forward, we need companions. We need to know how to welcome them in the knowledge that each and every one of them will bring with them what they can. What is important is the movement, the setting in motion, the setting out.

L.T.: But I want to emphasise that the people I've spoken about are only those who happen to find themselves in the media spotlight or under the gaze of the historian. In reality, there are many more of them, these unknown individuals who have always rejected the mask people have tried to force them to wear. Everyone can refuse to wear the White mask to open up the possibility of non-racial thinking. The latest sociological research shows that the so-called 'silent' majority, the majority of French people or of so-called White people, are not against non-White people, and that xenophobia is not central to their concerns, although it is difficult to measure racist offences objectively,[1] in particular due to a kind of 'bureaucratic subconscious' that underestimates offences involving people who are victims of racism.

A.M.: The only way we will stop being Black or White is if we learn to be human, first and foremost, and to be nothing but human. To become human is to invent, tirelessly, every day, new possibilities for encounters with our fellow humans on the basis of an acknowledgement that we are all 'like everyone else'. It's a case of approaching the other, from the outset, by placing oneself in a position of fundamental equality. What I'm saying is, in fact, deeply aligned with the values of the French Republic. Humanist. To put it into practice requires us to go back to our roots, to the very essence of the term 'universality' because equality is the sine qua non of universalism. Of course, universalism means world-making with others. Not without them, for them or against them. Fanon and Césaire already said the same thing in their time. I think we need to insist on the 'becoming'. It's a horizon, a tending towards a horizon that we will never reach but that orients us, that gives meaning to our actions.

---

1 See the 2018 study carried out by the French national statistics bureau INSEE, 'Cadre de vie et sécurité'.

L.T.: But the institutions – economic, financial, political, media – refuse to allow us to adopt that position and constantly reconstruct the categories of 'them' and 'us'. You've only got to look at what's happening to Muslims today: when Muslim individuals are stigmatised, it is in order to reinforce this White identity that remains unspoken.

A.M.: That's why we need the story that this book tells. White identity, in and of itself, doesn't exist. Just as Black identity doesn't exist. The only White identity that exists is a constructed one. If, on all sides, we lose sight of the long history of this construction, we won't understand anything or very little. But it's going to take a long time. And once we have understood, we'll need to put in place strategies for today's context, equivalent to the struggle for civil rights in the US or the anti-apartheid struggle in South Africa, all the while recognising that France is neither the United States nor South Africa. But the struggles that played out in both these countries remain important because they were universally significant. They were universal struggles because their aim was a collective rise in humanity. What alliances can we form today to face our own challenges?

L.T.: There are so many forces working against us, and they're on the rise at the moment.

A.M.: The big picture is that of human emancipation. Of how humanity can become more and more free and able to take responsibility for itself, with no God, if necessary, and especially with no master. We have to learn how to exercise responsibility towards all of humanity, to all look after all humans and non-humans in order to make the world the manifestation of that freedom. In order to understand what is standing in its way: racism, sexism, inequalities of all types, this desire for separation that is eating away at our present. The forces that don't want this great convergence to happen are very powerful and they have the wind in their sails. Everywhere, they are reactivating a desire for White supremacy and ethnic and religious nationalisms of all types.

L.T.: But how can we not see that that is also a form of self-destruction? That this state of affairs gives rise to new confrontations?

A.M.: In the US, right at the start, as the colonies were being founded, poor White people lived side-by-side with Black people. They all belonged to the subaltern classes. Objectively, they had the same interests as Black people and other people of colour, and there was a solidarity between poor people of all colours. The White authorities were afraid that this class-based solidarity would turn against them. They wanted to create division among the subaltern classes and to bring them into opposition with each other. In order to do this, they granted privileges to poor White people that were first symbolic and then material. That's how, for White people, skin colour became a bonus, an added advantage. The system guaranteed one thing for them: they would never be treated like 'Negroes'. There would always be a section of the population that would be inferior to them, below them. This is no longer the case today. In our contemporary neo-liberal context, very few people escape the treatment that was once inflicted on 'Negroes'. This is what I mean when I've spoken elsewhere about the becoming-Black of the world. For the bulk of poor White people, the great threat today is of being taken for and being treated like 'Negroes'. What they fear is seeing the border between them and others being erased. White people are increasingly afraid of suffering the fate that has thus far been reserved for Black people. To repair the bonds of solidarity that have been broken: that's the challenge. But in order to repair, we need a strategy. Especially when numerous capitalist forces are working against us. Look at Facebook, and other social media, creating false connections, and letting people think that they're really creating links when all they're doing is reinforcing individual solitude. It turns each of us into a body as border. There are more and more walls in in the world, more and more enclosures. As a result, violence and fear increase and they enclose each of us in a state of pseudo-security.

L.T.: The White world has had many violent encounters with the rest of the world. White thinking will continue to provoke violence everywhere. You've only got to look at its interest in the arms market. That's preparing people for violence outside but also at home.

One final remark to conclude here and to explain what it could look like if White people accompanied non-White people in their struggle against racism: when journalists ask Black players about the abuse they endure in football stadiums, they should be sent to speak to White players, to ask them why they don't intervene. White people need to be invited to stop pretending to be neutral. To be neutral is to sanction racism. White people have to have the courage to remove the mask through which they observe such scenes. In order to intervene, they have to stop being White and become just human. To be human is to go beyond the colour of one's skin.

2. PWOFITASYON[1] ('PROFITATION')

Becoming human begins when we acknowledge what our contemporary world is really like. The global population is over 7 billion. If I ask people what percentage of that global population is White, some reply 40%, others go as high as 70%, and most have no idea. Let's be clear that when they say 'White', they mean White Europeans, White North Americans, White Australians... The reality is that the vast majority are non-White. And yet, we live in a world where the dominant discourse has, for centuries, been constructed by a White elite, primarily to its own advantage. 'Although the West[2] only accounts for 16.6% of the global population, it creates 35.1% of the waste we produce every year, is responsible for 36% of CO_2 emissions, occupies 38.2% of the land mass, accounts for 41% of energy consumption, as well as representing 52.3% of wealth production and containing 54.5% of all world heritage sites.'[3]

---

1 The Creole term *'pwofitasyon'* is the contraction of 'profit' and 'exploitation'. It took on a political dimension in the context of the Guadeloupean social movement LKP during the general strike on the island in 2009 (Liyannaj Kont Pwofitasyon – Stand Up Against Exploitation). For details, see http://news.bbc.co.uk/1/hi/world/europe/7925553.stm.

2 When we refer to 'the West' here, in historical and geopolitical terms, we refer to the United States, Canada, Australia, New Zealand, and all European countries, including Russia, but excluding Turkey. Sources: United Nations, *World Population Prospects*, 2019; *BP Statistical Review of World Energy*, 2019; World Bank, 2019; *Encyclopedia Universalis*, 2018; UN Food and Agriculture Organisation (FAO), 2019; UNESCO, 2019.

3 Tarik El Aktaa, Deputy Director of Foresight Studies and Cartographic Analysis Laboratory (LEPAC).

Furthermore, if we consider the division of resources among the global population, we can note that the 800 million people who are living on less than $1.90 per day are all non-White; that the 10% of the global population without access to drinkable water are all non-White; that the 70 million forced to leave their lands and to seek refuge elsewhere due to the conflicts raging across the globe in 2017 were, for the most part, non-White.[1] A handful of billionaires – 26 of them, to be specific, of whom only two are women – has as much wealth as the poorest half of humanity; that's to say the same amount as 3.8 billion people. In 2016, they were 43.[2] Who are they? Of the 26 richest human beings on the planet, 18 are White Westerners, that's to say almost 70% of them.

White people have dominated most of the global land mass since the end of the fifteenth century. The fabrication of White identity, the processing and legitimising of White domination the world over, have not come about by chance: they underpin a very specific logic that began with the early days of capitalism, a logic of appropriation, on an economic front, of course, but also symbolic. This logic has spread its hierarchies to serve the needs of the White world: can we really deny it?

This White thinking does not bring peace, as it claims, but quite the opposite: it brings war by everyone on everyone. The billionaire Warren Buffett sanctimoniously acknowledged as much in a *New York Times* interview: 'There's class warfare, all right, but it's my class, the rich class, that's making war, and we're winning.'[3] The official theme of the 2018 World Economic Forum in Davos was 'Creating a Shared Future in a Fractured World' and that of 2017 was 'Responsive and Responsible Leadership.' It has been a constant in world history, whose logic we have only too clearly understood, thanks to the first half of this book. Slavery in Antiquity, the massacre of Native Americans, the slave trade and colonisation have always been underpinned by ideologies that

1 Cited in UN Refugee Agency's annual Global Trends study. See Adrian Edwards, 'Forced Displacement at Record 68.5 Million', 19 June 2018, available online: https://www.unhcr.org/news/stories/2018/6/5b222c494/forced-displacement-record-685-million.html.

2 Figures from Oxfam cited in 'Qui sont les 26 milliardaires pesant autant que 3,8 milliards de personnes ?'. Forbes.fr, 21 January 2019.

3 Ben Stein, 'In Class Warfare, Guess Which Class Is Winning', *The New York Times*, 26 November 2006.

have sought to justify predation and its associated acts of violence: a mission dictated by God Himself, a desire to civilise savage and inferior peoples, to pacify them or to develop them economically in order to enable them to access consumer society... Nobody in the course of the history of White thinking has ever admitted that they were only acting in their own interests. There has always been a discourse to mask the reality of the acts of violence. And this violence is growing, taking over the whole planet. White thinking, and the colonisation that went with it, has won out.

When Columbus landed in the Americas, believing that he had landed in the Indies, it was not out of any particular pleasure in encounters with other peoples or to serve the Spanish Crown, but first and foremost to seek his own fortune. When Europeans established the Black slave trade, they committed a crime that was both economic and utilitarian; in other words, a form of extermination that was not destined to eliminate men and women, but to offer a means of enriching themselves. When Jules Ferry defended colonisation and the 'duty to civilise inferior races', he explained in no uncertain terms: 'Colonial policy is the daughter of industrial policy. For rich states [...], exports are an essential factor in public prosperity, and the use of capital, like the demand for work, is measured by the size of foreign markets.'[1] Once again, it was a case of enriching oneself.

In order for these elites to be able to appropriate the world around them, a racist ideology had to be constructed, one that would break and continue to break the bonds of solidarity between human beings who challenge these economic and political structures. We can see clear illustrations of this in the history of the Americas, notably around the Haitian Revolution of 1791–1804 and the American Civil War of 1861–65. During these two conflicts, rebel slaves found key allies: Léger-Félicité Sonthonax and Étienne Laveaux, in the first case, and Abraham Lincoln and the soldiers and officers of the Federalist army in the second. These alliances contributed in profound ways to the abolition of historical slavery, first in Saint-Domingue in 1793, then by the National Convention in 1794. The entire 'Reconstruction' project in the United States promised a

1 William D. Bowman, Frank M. Chiteji and J. Megan Greene (eds), 'Le Tonkin et la Mère-patrie', in *Imperialism in the Modern World: Sources and Interpretations* (London & NY: Routledge, 2007), p. 18.

radical transformation of society on the basis of racial equality. In both cases, the reactions to these alliances were brutal. In the US, Reconstruction was destroyed with the violent introduction of the Jim Crow laws. This racist system was built on a symbolic process that forced White Southerners, many of whom had been opposed to Secession, to consider themselves the heirs of that movement, particularly via the construction of monuments to the glory of the 'Confederate' army, which have become the subject of tremendous conflict in numerous locations across the US, such as Charlottesville. For me, these two examples show how institutions erase historic solidarities and would have us believe that violence and barbarism are the norm.

To reinforce its propaganda and to control the imagination of those it seeks to dominate, White thinking erects monuments in the public sphere in honour of its great men (I would note, in passing, that very few women have been honoured in this way). Everyone who frequents these spaces is thus forced to approve the discourse of White thinking. The statues of the nineteenth-century French abolitionist Victor Schœlcher in the French Caribbean are part of this strategy. I'd like you to be able to change perspective and to understand the recent toppling of such statues. Firstly, to attack symbols in the public sphere is an ancient and global practice: we need look no further than the Vendôme Column, a symbol of power and imperialism in the heart of Paris, dismantled by the Commune in 1871. And then, ask yourselves whether it is right to see Schœlcher as a hero? If he is a hero for White thinking, can he be one for the descendants of enslaved people? Let us not forget that Schœlcher compensated slave owners, using French taxpayers' money, when slavery was abolished and that he forced former enslaved people to come back to work on the plantations.[1] Toppling these statues is a means of showing that, contrary to what the state would have us believe, it is, indeed, the oppressed who freed themselves and who forced the oppressors to change their behaviour. And this is something the statues of Schœlcher radically deny. Black people do not have to thank White people for having freed them. Just as the workers do not thank their bosses for having given them the right to strike, a right that they fought for and won through their own struggles.

---

1 27 April 1848 Decree on the abolition of slavery in the French colonies.

3. BECOMING BARBARIAN

Appropriating that which belongs to us all was already considered by Jean-Jacques Rousseau as the beginning of barbarism:

> The first man who, having enclosed a piece of ground, to whom it occurred to say *this is mine*, and found people sufficiently simple to believe him, was the true founder of civil society. How many crimes, wars, murders, how many miseries and horrors Mankind would have been spared by him who, pulling up the stakes or filling in the ditch, had cried out to his kind: 'Beware of listening to this imposter; you are lost if you forget that the fruits are everyone's and the fruits no one's.[1]

Do processes of colonisation not show that Rousseau was right? For centuries, has White thinking not declared itself to be the owner of the world? As the Innu author An Antane Kapesh has so rightly said:

> The White man never said to us: 'You the Innu, do you agree that I join you in your territory? Do you agree that I exploit your territory? Do you agree that I destroy your territory? Do you agree that I build dams on your rivers and that I pollute your rivers and lakes? Before agreeing to what I am asking you, think hard and try to understand. You might come to regret in the future that you have allowed me to join you, because if you agree that I go into your territory, I will go so as to open a mine. Once the mine is open, I will then have to exploit and ruin your land, to its whole extent. And I will dam all your rivers and dirty all your lakes. What do you think? Will you like drinking polluted water?'[2]

---

1 Jean-Jacques Rousseau, 'Discourse on the Origin and Foundations of Inequality Among Men', in *Rousseau: The Discourses and Other Early Political Writings*, ed. by Victor Gourevitch (Cambridge: Cambridge University Press, 1997), p. 164.

2 An Antane Kapesh, *I am a Damn Savage; What Have You Done to My Country/Eukuan nin matshi-manitu innushkueu; Tanite nene etutamin nitassi?* Bilingual edition, trans. by Sarah Henzii (Waterloo, ON: Wilfried Laurier Press, 2020), pp. 13, 15.

Is it right and what does it say about us if we are willing to accept such a state of affairs? Does that not make us barbarians? Who are more barbaric: the 16.6% who own 52% of the world's wealth or the rest? It is the colonisers who are the most barbaric. Is one who oppresses their fellow humans still human? Do we not accept this domination because White thinking has broken the bonds of recognition between humans, because we have been raised to think that skin colour represents a border? That religions are a border? In establishing racial hierarchies, have the elites not placed White people 'outside humanity'?

According to Aimé Césaire:

> I think that these heads of men, these collections of ears, these burned houses, these Gothic invasions, this steaming blood, these cities that evaporate at the edge of the sword, are not to be so easily disposed of. They prove that colonisation, I repeat, dehumanises even the most civilised man; that colonial activity, colonial enterprise, colonial conquest, which is based on contempt for the native and justified by that contempt, inevitably tends to change him who undertakes it; that the coloniser, who in order to ease his conscience gets into the habit of seeing the other man as an animal, accustoms himself to treating him like an animal, and tends objectively to transform himself into an animal. It is this result, this boomerang effect of colonisation, that I wanted to point out.[1]

The exploitation of those it considers inferior, different, is at the very heart of White thinking: Amerindians, Black people during the slave trade, colonised peoples, as well as the women or children who are employed for miserly wages, those who are declared insane and who are excluded from humanity and yet made to work, prisoners...

Since 1968, when the civil rights of Black people were recognised in the US, exploitation has continued to lurk where we least expect it. On this front, I would highly recommend the 2016 documentary *13th* by Ava DuVernay which shows, with figures to back up its

---

1 Aimé Césaire, *Discourse on Colonialism*, trans. by Joan Pinkham (New York: Monthly Review Press, 1972), p. 41.

assertions, that 40% of inmates in the American prison system are Black. 40%! This mass incarceration is the fruit of historic racism and of an economic targeting because the Thirteenth Amendment of the American Constitution which gives the documentary its title dates from 1865 and abolishes slavery, with one exception: 'for crime whereof the party shall have been duly convicted'. In no uncertain terms, a century and a half after having abolished slavery, the American state continues to accord itself the right to exploit individuals who have been imprisoned.

For 150 years, African Americans have been criminalised, in order that they might be put behind bars and, in this way, constitute a low-cost workforce. Some economic lobby groups, such as the American Legislative Exchange Council, have deliberately sought to strengthen the severity of the country's penal policy. As Kyung-Ji Kate Rhee, of the Center for NuLeadership on Urban Solutions, working in the field of juvenile justice, puts it in DuVernay's film: 'All the legislation you could think of [is designed to ensure] a steady influx of bodies to generate the profit that would go to the shareholders.' Profit is born of the very fact that prisoners are paid peanuts. Today, there are more African Americans in prison than were enslaved in the 1850s!

How have Black people come to be criminalised to such an extent that many people find their over-representation in prison statistics to be normal? This point is extremely well explained in the documentary *13th*. First, it has happened because of the depiction in American popular culture (and cinema, in particular) of Black men as dangerous, slaves to their sexual and homicidal tendencies. People who must be imprisoned immediately at the first offence, even if it is a minor one, in order to stop them causing further damage to society. And then it has happened through the introduction of particularly harsh penalties for certain practices, such as the use of crack cocaine, a destructive drug primarily used by those in the poorer sections of society. For Ronald Reagan's administration, Black people were criminals who should be thrown in jail: in reality, they represented a workforce that was easy to exploit because it was large, feared and despised.

Why do so many White people subscribe to this kind of discourse? Because there is a symbolic interest in them pledging allegiance to it, which places them at the top of the hierarchy of human civilisations. It always feels good to be described as superior, and whether this superiority comes from God, nature or the market economy is immaterial. A form of authority that labels you as 'above the masses', and as running the risk of being fleeced by those inferior 'others' who threatened to take from you what little you have, has everything it needs to keep you in a state of terror.

That's why some of the poorest in society believe in the theory of the 'Great Replacement' that I discussed earlier. Because they often come from sections of society who have been dealt the worst hand, the least well paid or protected by the state, they don't have much left from which to draw some sense of pride, other than their belonging to a White 'elite' that all these 'subaltern ethnic groups' want to knock off its perch. After all, belief in White superiority has a basis that is not solely symbolic. All White people have a concrete material interest in supporting the order that is dictated by White domination, not only because many of them are victors in the 'fight for a seat at the table', which ensures that they will have access to positions of responsibility and to reward before most non-White people, even those who have the appropriate qualifications, but also because, materially, the globalisation of international commerce offers dominant countries a level of comfort that is unendingly seductive.

In the eighteenth century, Voltaire very clearly summarised what triangular trade relations and the slave system represented: 'This is the price at which you eat sugar in Europe.'[1] This phrase is uttered by the 'Negro' of Surinam to the young Candide, who is appalled to learn, through his words, of the horrors of slavery: 'When we work at the sugar-canes, and the mill snatches hold of a finger, they cut off the hand; and when we attempt to run away, they cut off the leg.'[2] An atrocious way to treat people that has two outcomes: financial profit for the investors and the material benefit of Europeans who were wild about sugar. In *Candide*, sugar naturally comes to embody a summary of all the pleasures with which the consumer society overwhelms us. In Voltaire's day, that meant coffee, cotton, spices, silk, tobacco, exotic wood... Nowadays, the products have changed but the principle remains the same. Indeed, Jean-Paul Sartre appeals to the Western reader in his preface to Frantz Fanon's *Wretched of the Earth*:

---

1 Voltaire, *Candide* (New York: Boni & Liverright, 1918), p. 91. Available at the Gutenberg Project: www.gutenberg.org/files/19942/19942-h/19942-h.htm.

2 Voltaire, *Candide*, p. 91.

> You know well enough we are exploiters. You know
> full well we have taken the gold and minerals and
> then oil from the 'new continents', and shipped them
> back to the old metropolises. Not without excellent
> results in the shape of palaces, cathedrals and centres
> of industry [...]. [F]or us, a man means an accomplice,
> for we have *all* profited from colonial exploitation.[1]

What is the modern-day equivalent of this sugar for the West? Our
drawers, our cupboards, our fridges are overflowing with it and I
could give more than a thousand examples here of these products
that delight us as consumers but that we know, with a greater or
lesser degree of certainty, are still often the output of a human and
environmental catastrophe on the other side of the planet. Achille
Mbembe calls this dark side, this violent and savage exploitation
that enables inhabitants of our democracies to enjoy good products
at accessible prices 'the nocturnal body of democracy'.[2] Among a
thousand other examples, it is, for instance, the cobalt used by some
multinational companies to make the batteries in our smartphones,
our tablets and our computers, as well as in the batteries for our
electric cars. In 2016, the *Washington Post* revealed that 60% of
the world's cobalt comes from the Democratic Republic of Congo,
one of the poorest countries in the world. This cobalt is sold on
by a multinational company with a hundred thousand Congolese
workers, including thousands of children, in conditions of quasi-
slavery, not too far removed from those described by Voltaire.

What's more, the smartphones we all use every day are filled with
other rare minerals, ripped from the earth: tin, lithium, tantalum,
tungsten, neodymium, gold, coltan... So many minerals that the
local populations, working in conditions of subjugation in these
mines, more often than not have to extract without benefitting from
basic fundamental rights. This greed has led to conflicts in China,
Bolivia, Chile, the Democratic Republic of Congo. Victor Hugo's
observation that 'the paradise of the rich is made out of the hell of
the poor' retains its relevance today.

Collectively, we are prisoners of a model of consumption upon
which we have all become dependent. In concrete terms, though,

---

1 Sartre, 'Preface' to Fanon, *Wretched of the Earth*, p.lviii.

2 Mbembe, *Necropolitics*, p. 15.

few people truly measure what that means in human terms nor in terms of its impact on the climate. Just one figure here: the carbon footprint of the average French person is 10.8 tonnes of CO_2 per year. If that same French person wanted to respect the terms of the agreements signed at COP21, with the aim of ensuring that global warming will never increase beyond 2°C higher than pre-industrial temperatures, their maximum carbon footprint should be... two tonnes.[1] A fifth of the current rate, at most!

I have discussed these problems at great length with Virginie Raisson-Victor, expert in geopolitics and foresight studies: she explained to me that, if all of humanity adopted the European diet, current global farming production could only feed 4 billion people, and yet there are more than 7 billion of us. We would thus need to double our current agricultural output in order to feed the world which would, in turn, accelerate deforestation and thus climate change, water shortages, biodiversity loss and epidemics. However, if we were to adopt the diet of Bhutan, a country we refer to as the 'Kingdom of Happiness', we could feed 12 billion people with current production methods. All we would need to do would be to lower our meat consumption, for example, to bring it in line with the inhabitants of Bhutan who eat 4kg per year, the equivalent of a small steak every ten days. In that scenario, there would be no need to pursue practices of deforestation. Rather, we would just need to improve our use and distribution of resources. Raisson-Victor added that we should also be aware that our fears of what some term a 'demographic time bomb' and its impact on the planet result from rather weak analysis. In South Asia and in Africa, where demographic growth is currently strongest, people don't eat much meat and people don't drive much, unlike in the countries of the global North. In other words, even if we were to wipe sub-Saharan Africa from the surface of the earth, it would not lower CO_2 emissions or other greenhouse gases, since very few of them are produced there. Does this fantasy not also derive from a vision of the White world that makes non-White people the source of all our ills? In reality, the situation is even more cynical, since we know, at the global level, that the countries who will be most affected by climate change are those who will have least contributed to its development!

---

1 Based on estimates from the French low carbon and climate change consultancy firm Carbone 4.

But we have been conditioned by White thinking that fabricates our opinions and forces us to only look in one direction: we end up thinking what it wants us to think. For example: there is no such thing as global warming. And besides, we have the tools to find solutions. The White world denounces the 'crimes' of 'dictators' who stop them ruling over certain strategic territories. In so doing, it also deflects our gaze from the acts of violence it carries out. And, of course, its own violence is never recognised as such but rather, depending on the context, is referred to as 'regaining control', 'peacekeeping' or 'liberation'. And yet, would 'the violent defence of one's interests' not be closer to the mark? Throughout history, Western powers have sustained themselves in this way, by labelling that which goes against their interests as violent or illegitimate while, at the same time, being in possession of the most destructive military potential on the planet.

The United Nations Security Council brings together the US, China, France, Russia and the UK as its permanent members. The official mandate of the Council is 'to maintain international peace and security'. However, we often forget to mention that the US, Russia, France and China are, respectively, the first, second, third and fifth largest arms dealers in the world. We also forget to note that, from 2013 to 2017, arms sales increased by 10% in volume compared to the five previous years. Those who are in charge of this arsenal and who, as a result, profit from exporting it are also those who, in our international system, are charged with 'maintaining international peace'. The latter could be phrased more precisely: a particular kind of peace, one that does not disturb a certain number of interests – in other words, a peace that guarantees privileged access to primary global resources at an attractive price – or a particular hierarchy.

However, the most serious thing, from my perspective, would seem to be precisely this widespread violence that is engendered and sustained by White thinking. Has it not turned us into the very barbarians we think we are holding off at the border? Behind the ever more numerous walls it has built – I'm thinking, in particular, of Native American reservations – and that it continues to build all over the place, in the camps where it holds the women, men and children who are trying to escape poverty and war in their own countries? Thinking White constructs borders on its own turf, but elsewhere, too, in order to stop those it perceives as potential invaders from coming to its lands. It even goes so far as to pay governments such as those of Turkey or Libya to imprison people who are guilty of nothing, who only want to improve their own lives. Its hypocrisy is astounding since it always foregrounds the 1948 Universal Declaration of Human Rights, article 13 of which nevertheless states: 'Everyone has the right to freedom of movement and residence within the borders of each state. Everyone has the right to leave any country, including his own, and to return to his country.' It is not other people who are the barbarians, but rather White thinking which has settled into utterly ineffective defensive actions, since it is within its own confines that barbarism can be found. White thinking claims to be human, civilised, universal: how could that be the case?

I feel as though we are slipping closer and closer to a form of inhumanity, full of anger, meanness, brutality. We no longer speak to each other as we should, and we no longer give others a space in which to be listened to and to be afforded the kindness they deserve. White thinking is not possible without violence, without breaking bonds.

I have already described the culture of erasure brought about by Western materialism. This culture, it seems to me, is now encouraging the weakening of the basic bonds that previously existed between individuals. Everything that unites us, beyond our differences, seems to me to be genuinely under threat. We are living in a generalised state of depression because we have erased that which connects us. Have we not entered an era of resentment and of fear? How many anxiety-inducing messages do we receive every day via our so-called 'news' media? Or rather 'fake news'? How many positive exchanges do we experience in a day? These observations should lead us to take great care because the shift towards violence can come extremely quickly if we make this or that 'other' responsible for the malaise that we are experiencing.

The mechanisms for excluding the other are at work all around us, including against ourselves. For example, how many people in the White world are convinced, taking their lead from former US president Donald Trump, that 'shithole countries' live in a state of mismanagement and corruption because they are quite simply incapable of taking charge of their own destiny? On what criteria do we describe a country as a 'shithole'?[1] Which countries' lifestyles pose a greater threat to the existence of biodiversity and, thus, humanity? Haiti and African countries or the US?

Let's look at my own country, France. A 2019 OECD report estimated that 16% of jobs in France will be threatened by automation over the next twenty years, particularly so-called 'low-skilled' jobs.[2] Is that not an infinitely more dangerous and more violent process than the arrival of migrants within our borders, instrumentalised in order to stoke fear within a section of public opinion?

What will become of our department stores once digitisation has removed the need for flesh-and-blood individuals? A nightmarish space where customers won't cross paths with a single human interlocutor, apart from perhaps the occasional security guard. Do we stop to think for even a second about the key social role played by cashiers in towns and in the countryside, especially for older people? And what will become of this 'unskilled' and low-skilled workforce who will be refused employment elsewhere, even on a precarious footing? This automation promises a relentless throwing onto the scrapheap of a section of our society, a section that is considered neither 'useful' nor 'productive' enough for the system. The section of society that is said to not adapt quickly enough to the changes brought about by globalisation, that isn't 'mobile' enough or 'flexible' enough or 'agile' enough. People who we judge to be useless in today's world.

Economists such as Daniel Cohen have been expressing their concern about this for several years: 'We don't need to integrate the lower sections of society any more, the elites are working all by themselves.'[3] Before, the economic system had many faults but it also had the merit of making each social class useful in its own way. Although the working classes soaked up the least gratifying and the least well-paid jobs, they were no less useful to the general functioning of the economy than their hierarchical superiors. But we have entered what Cohen calls the 'post-industrial era', which

1 Patrick Wintour, Jason Burke and Anna Livsey, '"There's no other word but racist": Trump's global rebuke for "shithole" remark', *The Guardian*, 13 January 2018, available online at: www.theguardian.com/us-news/2018/jan/12/unkind-divisive-elitist-international-outcry-over-trumps-shithole-countries-remark.

2 Marie Charrel, 'La robotisation devrait faire disparaître 14% des emplois d'ici à vingt ans, selon l'OCDE', *Le Monde*, 25 April 2019.

3 'L'analyse. L'émergence d'une "nouvelle aristocratie" mondialisée', *Le Temps*, 1 November 2005.

quite simply no longer has any use for them. As Cohen explains: 'Yesterday, machines made the workers more productive. Today they make them useless, just as concierges were replaced by intercoms.'[1]

This grasping, exclusionary economy has made us insensitive and indifferent towards other people. It promotes rivalry, confrontation, competition and individualism rather than defending cooperation and solidarity. It's about making money, above all else. We are told over and over that the best will rise up from such confrontation, that is to say, the highest-performing. Is this not the return of social Darwinism? Even more so when we raise our children to have a 'killer' mentality, is it not tragic because what would become of a society in which there were nothing but 'killers'? A fearful society where each individual would be alone and would end their life in madness?

Elite sport also lends legitimacy to this widespread competition. In its own way, the glorification of sporting achievement has contributed to the legitimation of the system in which we find ourselves. That's why it has become a business above all else, whether for its financial backers, those in charge or for those who take part. That was clear at the Australian Tennis Open in 2020, where the organisers insisted on the qualifying matches going ahead despite the heat and the pollution, leading some players to feel unwell and others to experience breathing difficulties. To me, that is an indication that money has won out over the human element.

It's the very principle of hyper-competitivity that we need to challenge. As the geneticist Albert Jacquard observed: 'The idea that, in every discipline, someone must come first, second and third, is an aberration.'[2] Who said that competition between different groups was better than peaceful cohabitation? Do we ever reflect on the horror that would emerge if we asked each individual to attain perfection? And yet, is that not precisely what is implicitly asked of us, sometimes even explicitly? Thinking White does not respect human imperfections. It doesn't respect life.

---

1 *L'Obs*, 30 August 2018.

2 Interviewed in *L'Entreprise*, December 2004.

I believe that the greatness of a civilisation lies in the space it offers to those who are considered its most vulnerable, as different from a standard model. In the possibilities it opens up for them, despite the challenges they face. In this context, I find myself thinking of Romeo. Romeo was the kit man for Juventus when I played for them. He was the one who made sure our boots were in the right place, who cleaned the changing rooms, who drove us about in the minibus, who saw to the 101 daily little needs of us as busy sportspeople. I often said to him: 'Romeo, you're the most important man at Juve!' These words made him laugh, but it was no joke: without his patient work, without the care he took in looking after us, in satisfying our little whims, we would never have been able to offer a footballing spectacle of such quality to the fans. It's something that we always have to be aware of, those of us who go to work in offices, who eat in restaurants, sleep in hotels, take public transport, use public toilets... there are women and men, real flesh-and-blood beings, who are our equals and who expend a tremendous amount of energy, who sometimes push themselves to breaking point, to ensure that these spaces are clean and pleasant for those who use them. Their job is often not very pleasant to carry out, and we must remember that nothing they give us comes without cost or pain for them. They deserve a little more than our respect. Perhaps it's because my mother was a cleaner, but I've always remembered that professional success for the most 'brilliant' employees, ideas from the most 'ground-breaking' creative thinkers, are only possible thanks to this multitude of people toiling away in the shadows, and who, generally speaking, don't receive even the simplest word of thanks. Let's spare a thought for all those who, far from where we find ourselves, are labouring to ensure that our standard of life can be maintained. Does White thinking not teach us to no longer see the poorest in society?

4. THE IN-COMMON

Everything in the discourse that our society has developed – not only in the sporting domain – conditions us to be blinkered and to only look towards individual success. The only things that count these days are our individual interests, our little privileges and making money by whatever means. Solidarity has become a secondary notion. It's one of the ways the system has found to continue to keep us divided: we are so obsessed by the idea of preserving our circumstances, of passing them on to our children, that we refuse to look at how our less-well-off neighbours are living. Thinking White has made us forget the struggles we had to go through in the past to obtain the right to join a union, the right to strike, the right to benefit from education and health systems worthy of the name, whatever our social background.

Thinking White would have us believe that only the richest human beings are worthy of respect and of being allowed to live, while the poorest are seen as nothing. Even Charles Darwin, founder of the theory of the evolution of species, never wrote such a thing.[1] Not only does he have nothing to do with what we refer to as 'social Darwinism', the idea that human society is a jungle where only the fittest should survive – a purely political theory without the slightest founding in scientific fact – but on many occasions in his works, particularly in *The Descent of Man and Selection in Relation to Sex*, he emphasised that the process of natural selection has led to the emergence of morality and civilisation in humans, that is to say the development of cooperation and devotion to others. Even if we can practise them in an entirely disinterested way, these feelings have enabled us to survive, as much as guile and physical aptitude have, in difficult environments, as zoologists know only too well. Animals also demonstrate empathy and altruism, and practise mutual assistance when they 'gain' nothing from it directly. It's one of the traits of the natural world that we also find in the realm of plants and of trees.[2]

Should we not tell other stories, stories of solidarity rather than competition? The history of the fight for equality is not told often enough to schoolchildren. As a result, when they grow up, it does not occur to them that solidarity and being united are the most formidable destructive weapons against social injustice that the people have at their disposal.

We know nowadays that many species of trees, such as the beech, only live a long and healthy life if they grow in groups and

1 Philippe Testard-Vailland, 'Charles Darwin: de l'origine d'une théorie', *CNRS Le Journal*, 2015.

2 See Pablo Servigne and Gauthier Chapelle, *Mutual Aid: The Other Law of the Jungle*, forthcoming with Polity Press in late 2021, translated by Andrew Brown.

redistribute the resources, the nutrients, they require equally among themselves, via the underground networks of their roots. All the trees in a beech wood receive the same quantity of nutrients and the same access to sunlight, whether they were born of good or poor soil, whether their access to water is abundant or limited. Similarly, we know that, when acacias and oaks are attacked by insects or by any herbivorous animal, they warn the trees of their species around them in order that their leaves take on a bitter taste and so they can all repel the predator together.[1]

In 2007, for the exhibition *The Saga of Man, Episode 1: Man Exposed* at the Musée de l'Homme in Paris, I had the honour of seeing a model of my skull presented next to the skull of an Early Modern European human and that of the philosopher René Descartes.[2] We represented modern man. Like many people, I know his famous statement: 'I think, therefore I am.' I had always wondered whether he was only talking about White people. René Descartes is known as one of the founders of European modernity, one of those who established scientific rationalism as a means of thinking about humanity's place in nature. He wrote that the development of thought and of science should lead us to become 'masters and possessors of nature'.[3] It seems to me that Descartes's model of thinking consolidated White predation: the predation of women, of men, of children, the colonisation of America, the slave trade, the colonisation of the world, the predation of nature and, today, globalisation and patterns of over-consumption. As anthropologist Claude Lévi-Strauss stated: 'The problems raised by racial prejudice reflect, on a human scale, a far wider problem whose solution is all the more urgent: the problem of the relationship between Man and other living species [...] the respect we seek to obtain from Man towards his fellows is but one specific case of the respect he should feel for all living things.'[4]

1 Peter Wohlleben, *The Secret Life of Trees* (London: HarperCollins, 2017).

2 Rachel Mulot, 'Le nouveau visage du musée de l'Homme', *Sciences et avenir*, February 2007, pp. 8–15.

3 René Descartes, *Discourse on the method of rightly conducting the reason, and seeking truth in the sciences*, Alex Catalogue (Ebooks), p. 26.

4 Claude Lévi-Strauss, opening speech at the conference on 'Race and Culture' at UNESCO (1971).

We can see the extent to which it is toxic to think of ourselves as masters of nature. As astrophysicist Aurélien Barrau has emphasised: 'We often think of nature solely via the prism of what we can "gain" from it, what nature "dispenses" (as was the case with colonised people). [...] Must we continue to see the spaces we take over as being "at our disposal"?'[1]

For White thinking, no life, not even human life, deserves to be looked after, listened to, respected. We only need to look at the disdain with which it treats the animals that feed us, raised in concentrationary spaces, slaughtered in abominable conditions.

Thinking White has convinced us all that there is a nature that is external to us. What does the word 'nature' mean? Is thinking White not the only way of thinking that draws a watertight border between nature and humans? Even the word 'environment', if we think about it, reduces nature to a kind of backdrop that is external to us.

In the 1960s, the historian Lynn White Jr famously traced the origins of the growing ecological crisis in a pioneering article:

> In Antiquity every tree, every spring, every stream, every hill had its own *genius loci*, its guardian spirit. [...] Before one cut a tree, mined a mountain, or dammed a brook, it was important to placate the spirit in charge of that particular situation [...]. By destroying pagan animism, Christianity made it possible to exploit nature in a mood of indifference to the feelings of natural objects. [...] The spirits *in* natural objects, which formerly had protected nature from man, evaporated.[2]

Thinking White has killed the idea that humans and nature are one: it has killed the invisible presences that surround us. Call them 'spirits' if you want to. It makes no difference. By forgetting the spirits, White thinking forgets to be vigilant of what it inflicts on

---

1 Aurélien Barrau, *Le Plus Grand Défi de l'histoire de l'humanité*, (Paris, Michel Lafon, 2019).

2 Lynn White Jr, 'The Historical Roots of our Ecologic Crisis', *Science*, Vol. 155, No. 3767, 10 March 1967, p. 1205.

'the environment', on these places where, for example, the ancestors live. Fortunately, the ancient concept of nature as Mother Earth has continued to develop. Nowadays, in many societies, this idea is growing stronger. Is this not our good fortune?

I was talking to a man I met in a restaurant. He repeated the kind of discourse that is currently very widespread: 'There are too many of us on Earth, we're using up all the natural resources, we're killing the climate with our polluting emissions.' But, I asked him, picking up on what Virginie Raisson-Victor had told me (see p. 181), who is this 'we' that there are too many of? If we all lived as frugally as people in Senegal, there could be 15 billion of us on Earth without the planet suffering in any particular way. 'Oh yes, you're right,' he agreed. 'The problem is the Americans. They consume too much petrol.' This man had very obviously forgotten that he lived in France, a country that also contributes a good deal to the using-up of the planet's resources. I reminded him that, if everybody decided to live like the French, we'd need almost three planet Earths to be able to cope.[1]

Thinking White too often tends to deny its responsibility in processes of climate change, in the destruction of biodiversity, in acts of violence, displacements of peoples and the epidemics it gives rise to. The climate emergency is a direct and tangible consequence of this thinking White, based on the exploitation, without limits, of human beings and of nature. Is the Anthropocene of which we speak so often not a *White* Anthropocene?[2]

We need to shift from the human condition to what Achille Mbembe calls the 'terrestrial condition'.[3] That's to say, we need to be fully conscious of the fact that we, humans, are one with ecosystems, plants and animals. Are we not elements of a single great 'all' that must live together? Otherwise humans will disappear, since nature can survive without us. For the anthropologist Philippe Descola:

---

1 2018 WWF Report, 'L'autre déficit de la France', available online at 180504_rapport_jour_du_depassement_france.pdf (wwf.fr).

2 Kathryn Yusoff, *A Billion Black Anthropocenes or None* (Minneapolis: University of Minnesota Press, 2018).

3 Mbembe, *Necropolitics*, p. 13.

We need a psychological revolution: humans have no rights over nature, it is nature that has rights over us. As strange as that may seem, it is a common idea with which anthropologists are very familiar. In the Andes, the indigenous peoples see themselves as members of collectives formed of humans and non-humans. When a member of the collective, a mountain or a stream, is attacked, all its members must defend it.[1]

Just as it is imperative, as we have said, that thinking White stops, in the name of universalism, imposing its culture as though it were unique and soared above the rest of humanity, it is also necessary for it to understand that its allegedly rational 'management' of planetary resources is nothing but a catastrophic form of hoarding that emerges from the same arrogance. When I think about this topic, I listen to what the specialist in geopolitics Pascal Boniface has to say: 'Only cooperation on a grand scale, that is to say a multilateral politics, will enable us to confront climate change, terrorist threats, demographic challenges, greater access to global public goods and the establishment of a genuine international security system. In a world that is increasingly interdependent, multilateralism is neither a choice nor an option, rather it is absolutely vital. Avoiding it and thinking that we can do without it simply leads to a worsening of the dangers that weigh heavily on humanity.[2] We not only need cooperation between humans but we need to rebind the ties between humans and nature. To echo the Senegalese intellectual Felwine Sarr's question: 'How do we re-enter into a relationship with the rest of the world, with the living world, other communities, a relationship that is not instrumental? Europe must rethink the dogmatic framework of its relation to the world. Before it is political or economic, it is a question of the relational imaginary, of the way we conceive of our relationship with others.'[3]

So much wasted time!

---

1 Interview published in *Le Monde*, 31 January 2019.

2 Pascal Boniface, *Requiem pour le monde occidental* (Paris: Eyrolles, 2019), p. 112.

3 'Felwine Sarr, Heinz Wismann. Le pluriel et l'universel', *Philosophie Magazine*, May 2019.

We should listen to what those African peoples who practised *ubuntu* said: '*Umuntu ngumuntu ngabantu*', or 'I am what I am because you are what you are', or, more literally, 'I am what I am thanks to what we all are'. It is a Bantu term that was adopted at the end of the Apartheid regime in South Africa. In 1995, the Truth and Reconciliation Commission, chaired by Archbishop Desmond Tutu, was trying to find a way to rebuild the ties that had been broken over so many years. The vicious circle of violence had to be stopped and the desire for vengeance had to be countered by a genuine reconciliation capable of founding the 'Rainbow Nation'. Those who had carried out human rights violations committed to reveal their actions in their entirety, thus developing a genuine consciousness of the past and were thus able to move beyond it. This process echoed the 1993 Constitution, which described a 'need for *ubuntu* but not for victimisation'.[1] In 2013, at Nelson Mandela's funeral, Barack Obama said in his speech:

> My humanity is inextricably linked to yours. [...]
> We are all bound together in ways that are invisible
> to the eye; that there is a oneness to humanity; that
> we achieve ourselves by sharing ourselves with
> others, and caring for those around us. We can
> never know how much of this sense was innate in
> him, or how much was shaped in a dark and solitary
> cell. But we remember the gestures, large and
> small – introducing his jailers as honoured guests
> at his inauguration; taking a pitch in a Springbok
> uniform; turning his family's heartbreak into a call
> to confront HIV/AIDS – that revealed the depth of
> his empathy and his understanding. He not only
> embodied Ubuntu, he taught millions to find that
> truth within themselves. It took a man like Madiba
> to free not just the prisoner, but the jailer as well
> – to show that you must trust others so that they
> may trust you; to teach that reconciliation is not
> a matter of ignoring a cruel past, but a means of

---

1 Constitution of the Republic of South Africa Act 200 of 1993.

confronting it with inclusion and generosity and truth. He changed laws, but he also changed hearts.[1]

And Desmond Tutu has further clarified: 'A person with Ubuntu is open and available to others, affirming of others, does not feel threatened that others are able and good, for he or she has a proper self-assurance that comes from knowing that he or she belongs in a greater whole and is diminished when others are humiliated or diminished, when others are tortured or oppressed.'[2]

The philosopher Souleymane Bachir Diagne distinguishes two dimensions within *ubuntu*: the first consists in 'destroying the walls that separate humans from their own humanity', identitarian tensions that he calls ethno-nationalisms. The second consists in assessing the scale of human beings' responsibility to the Earth, to nature. For Diagne, the Earth has been entrusted to us and we must respect it for itself and for future generations. We can no longer be 'masters and possessors of Nature', but we must act as God's lieutenants, that is to say those who stand in God's place, going back to the etymology of the word 'lieutenant', which Diagne, in turn, relates to the term 'caliph', meaning 'steward' or 'successor', giving it a meaning that is far removed from the madness of Islamist terrorists. For Diagne, that is our responsibility as humans, not to fade away among other living beings, but to feel responsible and to act in consequence, using both our reason and our sensitivity, which he calls religion, which ties us to our neighbour who is not necessarily the person closest to us. Today, he insists on our responsibility towards migrants in relation to whom the appropriate response is one of hospitality, refusing an inward turn towards our own 'tribe'.[3]

It is also interesting to listen to the contemporary philosopher Zhao Tingyang, who has revived the ancient concept of '*tianxia*', a system

1 Full text of President Obama's speech available online at: https://www.bbc.co.uk/news/world-africa-25250278.

2 Desmond Tutu, *No Future without Forgiveness* (London: Rider, 1999), p. 35.

3 See the Apm YouTube video 'Souleymane Bachir Diagne: *Ubuntu*' (28 September 2018).

of political thought established over 3,000 years ago in China during the Zhou dynasty. He suggests that 'there are methods that would enable us to incorporate *any* other in a system of coexistence. [...] A politics of confrontation respects neither humanity nor the world and we must, therefore, replace it with a political idea centred on coexistence. In a word, politics must respect the world.'[1]

Why didn't we listen to the words of the Hopi chief, Dan Katchongva?

> The white man, through his insensitivity to the way of Nature, has desecrated the face of Mother Earth. The white man's advanced technological capacity has occurred as a result of his lack of regard for the spiritual path and for the way of all living things. The white man's desire for material possessions and power has blinded him to the pain he has caused Mother Earth by his quest for what he calls natural resources. And the path of the Great Spirit has become difficult to see by almost all men, even by many Indians, who have chosen instead to follow the path of the white man.[2]

Given the rise in inequalities and poverty, even in richer countries, given that the planet has started fighting back – yes, it's not out of control, it's fighting back – is there not now an urgent need for us to rethink the world?

---

1 Zhao Tingyang, *Tianxia, tous sous le même ciel* [*Tianxia, All under the same sky*], trans. by Jean-Paul Tchang (Paris: Éditions du Cerf, 2018), pp. 16–17.

2 From a letter addressed to then-President Richard Nixon in 1970 by a group of Hopis to oppose coal extraction on Najavo and Hopi terrirory by the Peabody Coal Company, a subsidiary of the Kennecott Copper Company. Dan Katchongva, 'The Hopi Story', in *Techqua Ikachi: Message from the Guardians of Land and Life* (No publisher, 1999), p. 45 (can be consulted at: archive.org/details/ChuckingIt.com-15/page/n1/mode/2up?q=insensitivity).

CONCLUSION

*Here are black men standing, looking at us, and
I hope that you – like me – will feel the shock of
being seen. For three thousand years, the white
man has enjoyed the privilege of seeing without
being seen.*

Jean-Paul Sartre, 'Black Orpheus'[1]

Guilty?

One day, a friend borrowed a book from me. It was a book I've
mentioned several times here, *White Ferocity* by Rosa Amelia
Plumelle-Uribe. A few days later, my friend came back to see me.
She was really upset:

'I couldn't finish it...'

'Why not?' I asked her.

She almost broke down in tears and explained that the book
was too hardgoing for her. 'I'm White,' she said, 'but I haven't
done anything wrong! This book tells of unbearable horrors, but
I'm not guilty!'

Among other things, *White Ferocity* is a meticulously detailed
inventory of the acts of violence that have been carried out in the

---

1 Jean-Paul Sartre, 'Black Orpheus', in *'What Is Literature?' and Other Essays*
(Cambridge, MA: Harvard University Press, 1988), p. 291.

name of the superiority of the White 'race' over the centuries. It brings to light the actions and behaviours of a minority of men who were ready to go to any lengths for power and wealth. My friend knew nothing of these actions and behaviours: how could she be to blame? Nobody had taught her about them at school. She felt as though she'd been dragged in front of a court. Because she found the truth of the raw facts unbearable. Her positive White identity was crumbling. She felt a sense of guilt. Exactly like the individuals in Plato's cave that I spoke about at the start of this book: she was blinded by the brutal light of truth and preferred to hide away in the cave.

If you wear the White mask, must you feel guilty for the crimes and offences of White thinking that I have described in these pages? Did you think that was the aim of this book? My answer to both of these questions is no, absolutely not. I know only too well, from personal experience, what impact coerced guilt has on most people: it makes them shut down, it makes them feel tense. Someone who feels they are being forced to repent will turn against you, quickly feeling under attack, and they'll refuse to play that particular game. 'It's got nothing to do with me! As an individual, I haven't done anything!' It's what the feminist political scientist and historian Françoise Vergès calls White people's 'fabrication of innocence'. 'Many recognise the existence of colonial crimes, affirming that not everyone is guilty. OK, but they must ask themselves how they managed to profit from them all the same,' she explains.[1]

I would like to reiterate here that thinking White is an ideological filter that has been imposed on us all via a story told by a greedy minority, acting in its own interest. However, and this is where things are more delicate, that has happened with the more or less passive, more or less hesitant complicity of a majority of those who benefit from it. Because, just as men have benefitted from male domination for centuries, whether they have contested it or not, White people have benefitted and continue to benefit from the systematic diminishing of non-White people. It's not a case of setting oneself up as a judge and gravely declaiming: do you admit your guilt? It's a case of asking: do you accept that things be given their true name? Are you ready to hear that your individual and collective responsibility is implicated and that you're going to have

1 'Françoise Vergès: 'Les droits des femmes sont devenus une arme idéologique néolibérale', *Le Monde Afrique*, 17 February 2019.

to face up to it? Do you accept that the fact that non-White people have been treated as inferior enabled your ancestors, and continue to enable *you*, to enjoy significant advantages in the 'fight for a seat at the table' in today's world?

Such reflection demands a good deal of humility and a certain courage. These questions must be faced now in the same way as elite sportspeople face criticism and have to challenge themselves. Nobody can reach an elite level if they take things for granted. Athletes' performances, when they're training or during matches, are observed down to their tiniest details, torn apart, critiqued. And of course, such comments are supposed to be helpful, to help to them evolve, correct their mistakes, rid themselves of anything that might stem from negligence. If such remarks are taken as insults, they're of no use, as I often tell my sons, Marcus and Khephren, both of whom are professional footballers. Constructive criticism helps us become better and, seen from this angle, the harshest of critics, those who don't lie to themselves, are obviously athletes when they observe their own performances.

But nobody is accusing you, yourself, of being racist. That's not what I'm saying. And besides, today more and more White people observe the world around us with a critical gaze that proves that what has been constructed can also be deconstructed. The famous 'widespread repentance' makes the White, identitarian essayists who are so closed to any form of criticism towards the West's colonial past and its systemic racism scream. Who has said anything about 'repentance'? Not the victims of racism, that's for sure. In whose interest would it be to make people believe that all White citizens are obliged to feel a sense of guilt? All the victims of racism want is to create a space for dialogue where their suffering can be acknowledged and where it stops. Some would have us believe that we cannot criticise, in any way, the history of colonial greed and its blindness. They invite us to forget. And yet it is precisely this forgetting that stops us from 'moving on'.

Who said that all White people were guilty of the acts that have been perpetrated, whether past or present? Who has mentioned anything about a sense of shame that should hold them all in its grasp? Who has called for atonement for the past? Not me. That would be as futile an attitude as that which states that all men have committed sexual assaults. As far as I'm concerned, the only duty of any value for White people acting in good faith is to try to understand what has happened over the centuries and to note what remains of it in today's behaviours. To recognise what the mechanics of White domination have looked like, how they have been put in place progressively, over the course of centuries, the most seductive ways in which they have been justified, and, in the present day, to note where they still resonate. What are today's 'good reasons' that justify rendering non-White people inferior or the wilful exploitation of parts of the globe or the pillaging of natural resources?

Why do we fall back on an age-old discourse to perpetuate disagreement between people of all colours in whose better interest it would be to be united? As the great African American thinker James Baldwin stated: 'What White people have to do is try to find out, in their own hearts, why it was necessary to have a "nigger" in the first place, because I'm not a nigger, I'm a man. [...] If I'm not the nigger here and you invented him, you the White people invented him, then you've got to find out why.'[1]

This is the task the philosopher Pierre Tévanian sought to undertake in his reflections on 'White privilege'. He explains very clearly how, to begin with, he first had to accept, with difficulty, that he was one of these White people, and thus one of the privileged members of society: 'What is unbearable, firstly, is the simple fact of being "particularised" [that is to say, put in the "White" box] because we have been raised, from the cradle, to believe that we represent the universal, the human. [...] To be White is to be doubly an impostor because of the benefits of privilege and the denial of that privilege.'[2] And to ensure that something that could seem abstract becomes genuinely concrete, he explains that to be White is 'to be raised in the idea that we are not dominant, that we are like everybody else, that we live in a society that is globally equal

---

1 Cited in Raoul Peck's 2016 film, *I Am Not Your Negro*.

2 Pierre Tévanian, 'Réflexions sur le privilège blanc', in *De quelle couleur sont les Blancs?*, Sylvie Laurent and Thierry Leclère (eds) (Paris: Éditions la Découverte, 2013), pp. 23–33.

and that our success is the fruit of our gifts and of our individual efforts'.[1] But he decided to take his reflection on his own condition even further, in order to go beyond the easy truths from which, he recognises, he took comfort:

> I don't recall, during my childhood or my adolescence, having had any real doubts that my educational, professional, intellectual or even my existential ambitions were well-founded. Unlike a non-White person, I didn't have to fight against the idea that such and such a course of study, such and such a job, such and such an activity [...] wasn't for me. I never even really asked myself the question [...]. I can aspire to do pretty much anything without lowering myself to becoming 'ambitious' [...] a particular career is available to me even if I'm not career-driven, I can 'start something up' without necessarily being an 'upstart'. Some will reply with the famous notion of merit [...] I know that, in order to succeed in the same kind of ways, a non-White person [...] will need to mobilise twice as many personal qualities [...]. I've had to make half as much effort to succeed in what I've undertaken but beforehand I had to make ten times less effort just to think about undertaking it.'[2]

This is what I have tried to show over the pages dedicated to our history: there has always been a discourse that was different to the imperialist and dominating one. Barbarism, even when it is justified through the most noble of motivations, can never fully escape the scrutiny of those who take the time to look it in the eye. Some of the voices that the majority didn't want to hear, couldn't hear, have shown us that there is another way of thinking. The most violent critiques of the fate meted out to Native Americans by the Spanish conquistadors came from Las Casas in the first years of the sixteenth century. The Black slave trade and its indignity were torn to shreds by Raynal as early as the nineteenth century. The French colonial empire was an object of indignation for Clemenceau in the nineteenth

1 Ibid.

2 Ibid.

century. Those thinkers were not superhuman, but rather they were, quite simply, individuals who opposed the consensus of the time.

That's the other thing we have to understand: racism is an illusion. It shatters solidarities in order that the few might exploit the many, regardless of the colour of our skin. Because, in this system, White people are exploited too: an enemy, the non-White person, is offered up to them in order to avoid them turning against those who are truly exploiting them. 'When a wise man points at the moon, the fool looks at his finger.' However, in order to be able to see it clearly, they would have to refuse the White mask. As Frantz Fanon puts it in the introduction to *Black Skin, White Masks*: 'The White man is sealed in his whiteness.'[1] Or we might turn to Sartre: 'Our whiteness seems to us to be a strange livid varnish that keeps our skin from breathing – white tights, worn out at the elbows and knees, under which we would find real human flesh the colour of black wine if we could remove them.'[2]

You have been allocated a White identity: there is a filter that forces those who are in a dominant position to reproduce this domination in the name of a superiority that is declared 'natural'. To question this White bias, to note that one applies it blindly and that one could refuse to do so, is to decide to be a free-thinking individual and to take responsibility for one's actions.

To become a free being is not to lose one's power or one's status. On the contrary, it's an invitation to resist. As Pierre Tévanian has written: 'It's not about hating yourself but hating your privilege.'[3] And to understand its double cost: the price of privilege, paid by others on whom we impose an existential violence, and the price of understanding White thinking which requires us to inform ourselves, to listen, to reflect and thus to invest time in it.

The White American basketball player Kyle Korver undertook this task in a brilliant article published in the American sports press. I would have so liked to have found a White French sportsperson who could demonstrate the same courage! I hope this book will be consciousness-raising. Korver begins his article with reference

---

1 Frantz Fanon, *Black Skin, White Masks*, trans. by Charles Lam Markmann (London: Pluto, 2008), p. 3.

2 Sartre, 'Black Orpheus', p. 291.

3 Tévanian, op. cit.

to a number of racist incidents he has witnessed over the course of his career: a Black teammate who was beaten up by the police in New York for no reason, another who was subjected to insults from the stands, another still whose mother feared for his safety after particularly tense matches. Kyle Korver explains so well the malaise he felt for so long at having seen these things happening without really seeing them. Above all, he explains how he became aware of the enormous privilege he enjoyed, as a White person, namely the right to be indifferent to such things:

> I can say every right thing in the world: I can voice my solidarity with [my Black teammate] Russ after what happened in Utah. I can evolve my position on what happened to [my other Black teammate] Thabo in New York. [...] I can condemn every racist heckler I've ever known. But I can also fade into the crowd, and my face can blend in with the faces of those hecklers, any time I want.[1]

And then Korver asks himself precisely what he can do to no longer just stand by and watch everyday racism. And the answers he gives are very interesting: he can learn more about the history of his country (and thus the foundations of a racism he refers to as 'systemic'), he can listen to what non-White people have to say to him, he can give his backing to politicians who want to work towards equality:

> But maybe more than anything? I know that, as a White man, I have to hold my fellow White men accountable. We all have to hold each other accountable. And we all have to *be* accountable – period. Not just for our own actions, but also for the ways that our inaction can create a 'safe' space for toxic behaviour. [...]. We have to be active. We have to be *actively* supporting the causes of those who've been marginalized. [...] By identifying that less visible, less obvious behaviour as what it is: *racism*. [...] what's happening to people of colour in this country – right now, in 2019 – is

---

1 Kyle Korver, 'Privileged', *The Players' Tribune*, 8th April 2019: www.theplayerstribune.com/articles/kyle-korver-utah-jazz-nba.

wrong. The fact that Black Americans are more than five times as likely to be incarcerated as White Americans is *wrong*. The fact that Black Americans are more than twice as likely to live in poverty as White Americans is *wrong*. The fact that Black unemployment rates nationally are double that of overall unemployment rates is *wrong*. The fact that Black imprisonment rates for drug charges are almost six times higher nationally than White imprisonment rates for drug charges is *wrong*. The fact that Black Americans own approximately one-tenth of the wealth that White Americans own is *wrong*. The fact that inequality is built so deeply into so many of our most trusted institutions is *wrong*. And I believe it's the responsibility of anyone on the privileged end of those inequalities to help make things right.[1]

In this article, Korver sets out a route for all White people acting in good faith to follow. He is part of what gives me hope in relation to our common future. Korver questions what it is to be White, what it is to put an end to denial, to admit that society acts unjustly towards non-White people.

Given the state of our planet, the climate emergency, the pollution of land and sea, the scarcity of water and the wars it leads to, given the displacement of people on a scale hitherto unseen, the conflicts and wars over natural resources, the growing tensions of identity politics for some… more than ever, we should unite to recreate the 'in-common', 'to recreate the community of humans in solidarity with all living things', to quote Achille Mbembe.[2]

Indifference and neutrality are no longer possible. Let's have the courage to take off our different masks, be they Black, White, male, female, Jewish, Muslim, Christian, Buddhist, atheist, homeless, poor, rich, old, young, straight, gay… in order to defend the only identity that counts: human identity. 'I' am 'Us'.

---

1 Korver, 'Privileged'.

2 Achille Mbembe, *Brutalisme* (Paris: La Découverte, 2020).

BIBLIOGRAPHY

Ajari, Norman, *La Dignité ou la mort: Éthique et politique de la race* (Paris: La Découverte, 2019).

Anselin, Alain, *Le Refus de l'esclavitude: Résistances africaines à la traite négrière* (Paris: Duboiris, 2009).

Balibar, Étienne, 'La construction du *racisme*', *Actuel Marx*, 38.2 (2005), pp. 11–28.

Bancel, Nicolas, Pascal Blanchard, Sandrine Lemaire (eds). *Culture post-coloniale 1961–2006* (Paris: Autrement, 2006).

Bancel, Nicolas, Thomas David, Dominic Thomas (eds). *L'Invention de la race* (Paris: La Découverte, 2014).

Bancel, Nicolas, Pascal Blanchard, Dominic Thomas (eds). *The Colonial Legacy in France*, trans. by Alexis Pernsteiner (Bloomington: Indiana University Press, 2017).

Banks, James, *March Toward Freedom: A History of Black Americans* (Belmont: Fearon Publishers, 1974).

Barrau, Aurélien, *Le Plus Grand Défi de l'histoire de l'humanité* (Paris: Michel Lafon, 2019).

Bat, Jean-Pierre, *La Fabrique des 'barbouzes': histoire des réseaux Foccart en Afrique* (Paris: Nouveau Monde éditions, 2015).

Battle, Michael Jesse. *Reconciliation: The Ubuntu Theology of Desmond Tutu* (Cleveland: Pilgrim Press, 2009).

Benot, Yves. *Massacres coloniaux, 1944–1950: la IVe République et la mise au pas des colonies françaises* (Paris: La Découverte, 1994).

Blanchard, Pascal, et al. (eds), *Human Zoos: Science and Spectacle in the Age of Empire* (Liverpool: Liverpool University Press, 2008).

Blanchard, Pascal, Sandrine Lemaire, Nicolas Bancel (eds), *Culture coloniale en France* (Paris: CNRS éditions/Autrement, 2008).

Blanchard, Pascal, 'Décolonisons nos mentalités'. *Revue internationale et stratégique*, 73 (2009), pp. 121–26.

Blanchard, Pascal, Gilles Boëtsch, Nanette Jacomijn Snoep (eds), *Human Zoos: The Invention of the Savage*, Exhibition Catalogue (Paris: Musée du Quai Branly/Actes Sud, 2012).

Blanchard, Pascal, Françoise Vergès, Nicolas Bancel, *La Colonisation* (Paris: Milan, 2012).

Blanchard, Pascal, Nicolas Bancel, *et al.*, *Sexe, race & colonies* (Paris: La Découverte, 2018).

Blanchard, Pascal, Nicolas Bancel, Sandrine Lemaire, *Décolonisations françaises: La chute d'un empire* (Paris: La Martinière, 2020).

Boniface, Pascal, Védrine, Hubert, *Atlas des crises et des conflits* (Paris: Armand Colin/Fayard, 2016).

Boniface, Pascal, *Comprendre le monde: Les relations internationales expliquées à tous* (Paris: Armand Colin, 2019).

Boniface, Pascal, *Requiem pour le monde occidental* (Paris: Eyrolles, 2019).

Boniface, Pascal, *Géopolitique illustrée* (Paris: Eyrolles, 2019).

Boniface, Pascal, *Atlas des relations internationales: 100 cartes pour comprendre le monde de 1945 à nos jours* (Paris: Armand Colin, 2020).

Brazza, Pierre Savorgnan de, *Le Rapport Brazza. Mission d'enquête au Congo: rapports et documents* (Paris: Le Passager clandestin, 2018).

Brice, Pascal, *Sur le fil de l'asile* (Paris: Fayard, 2019).

Bruno, G., *Le Tour de la France par deux enfants* (1877; Paris: Tallandier, 2012).

Brunschwig, Henri, *Partage de l'Afrique* (Paris: Flammarion, 1971).

Césaire, Aimé, 'Introduction à Victor Schœlcher', in Victor Schœlcher, *Esclavage et colonisation* (Paris: PUF, 1948).

Césaire, Aimé, *Discourse on Colonialism*, trans. by Joan Pinkham (New York: Monthly Review Press, 1972).

Chollet, Mona, *Sorcières, la puissance invaincue des femmes* (Paris: La Découverte, 2018).

Déclaration des intellectuels d'Afrique et de la diaspora sur les réformes du franc CFA, Dakar, January 2020: https://blogs.mediapart.fr/fanny-pigeaud/blog/070120/declaration-dintellectuels-africains-sur-les-reformes-du-franc-cfa.

Coppens, Yves (ed.), *Devenir humains* (Paris: Autrement/Muséum d'Histoire naturelle, 2015).

Correll, J., B. Park, C. M. Judd, B. Wittenbrink, 'The police officer's dilemma: Using ethnicity to disambiguate potentially threatening individuals'. *Journal of Personality and Social Psychology*, 83 (2002), pp. 1314 –29.

Correll, J., B. Park, C. M. Judd, B. Wittenbrink, M. S. Sadler, T. Keesee, 'Across the Thin Blue Line: Police officers and racial bias in the decision to shoot', *Journal of Personality and Social Psychology*, 92 (2007), pp. 1006–23.

Cugoano, Ottobah, *Thoughts and Sentiments on the Evil of Slavery* (1787; London: Penguin, 2007).

Dalloz, Jacques, *La Guerre d'Indochine (1945–1954)* (Paris: Seuil, 1987).

Defoe, Daniel, Robinson Crusoe (1719; London: Penguin, 1994).

Delacampagne, Christian, *Une histoire du racisme* (Paris: Le Livre de Poche, 2000).

Descartes, René, *Discourse on the method of rightly conducting the reason, and seeking truth in the sciences*, Alex Catalogue (Ebooks) [1637].

Diagne, Souleymane Bachir, with Jean-Loup Amselle, *En quête d'Afrique(s): universalisme et pensée coloniale* (Paris: Albin Michel, 2018).

Diallo, Rokhaya, *La France tu l'aimes ou tu la fermes?* (Paris: Textuel, 2019).

Diop, Birago, *Leurres et lueurs* (Paris: Présence Africaine Éditions, 1960).

Diop, Birago, 'Sarzan', in *The Tales of Amadou Koumba*, trans. by Dorothy S. Blair (London: Longman, 1965).

Dorigny, Marcel, Gainot, Bernard, *Atlas des esclavages: De l'Antiquité à nos jours* (Paris: Autrement, 2013).

Dorlin, Elsa, *La Matrice de la race: Généalogie sexuelle et coloniale de la Nation française* (Paris: La Découverte, 2009).

Dulucq, Sophie, David Lambert, Marie-Albane de Suremain, *Enseigner les colonisations et les décolonisations* (Paris: Canopé Éditions, 2016).

Eddo-Lodge, Reni, *Why I'm No Longer Talking to White People about Race* (London: Bloomsbury, 2018)

Eza, Emmanuel Chukwudi (ed.), *Postcolonial African Philosophy: A Critical Reader* (Oxford: Blackwell, 1997).

Fanon, Frantz, *Black Skin, White Masks*, trans. by Richard Philcox (1952; London: Penguin, 2021)

Fanon, Frantz, *The Wretched of the Earth*, trans. by Richard Philcox (1961; New York: Grove Press, 2004)

Ferro, Marc (ed.), *Le Livre noir du colonialisme, xvie-xxie siècle: de l'extermination à la repentance* (Paris, Hachette, 2004).

Firmin, Joseph Anténor, *The Equality of the Human Races*, trans. by Asselin Charles (NY & London: Garland, 2000).

Garrigues, Jean, *Les Grands Discours parlementaires: De Mirabeau à nos jours* (Paris: Armand Colin, 2017).

Gassama, Makhily (ed.), *L'Afrique répond à Sarkozy: Contre le discours de Dakar* (Paris: Philippe Rey, 2008).

Gobineau, Arthur de, *The Inequality of Human Races*, trans. by Adrian Collins (London: Heinemann, 1915).

Goddin, Philippe, *Les Tribulations de Tintin au Congo* (Paris: Casterman, 2018).

Gouges, Olympe de, *Écrits politiques*, présentés par Olivier Blanc, tome I (Paris: Côté-femmes Éditions, 1993).

Gouges, Olympe de, *L'Esclavage des nègres*, version inédite du 28 décembre 1789, suivi de *Réflexions sur les hommes nègres*, février 1788. Edited by Sylvie Chalaye and Jacqueline Razgonnikoff (Paris: L'Harmattan, 2006).

Gouges, Olympe de, *Reflections on Negroes* (1788). Online English translation available via the University of Georgia's Francophone Slavery webpages: http://slavery.uga.edu/texts/literary_works/reflections.pdf.

Grèzes, Julie, Safra, Lou, 'L'origine de l'expression des émotions', *Nuit sciences et lettres*, ENS, 7 June 2019.

Griffin, John Howard, *Black Like Me* (1961: London: Serpent's Tail, 2019)

Groult, Benoîte, *Ainsi soit Olympe de Gouges: La déclaration des droits de la femme et autres textes politiques* (Paris: Grasset, 2013).

Guengant, Jean-Pierre, John F. May, 'L'Afrique subsaharienne dans la démographie mondiale', *Études. Revue de culture contemporaine*, 415.10 (2011), pp. 305–16.

Héritier, Françoise, *Masculin/Féminin II: Dissoudre la hiérarchie* (Paris: Odile Jacob, 2002).

Horel, Stéphane, *Lobbytomie. Comment les lobbies empoisonnent nos vies et la démocratie* (Paris: La Découverte, 2018).

Hugo, Victor, *L'homme qui rit* (Paris: Albert Lacroix: 1869).

Irvin Painter, Nell, *The History of White People* (NY & London: W.W. Norton & Company, 2010).

James, C.L.R., *The Black Jacobins: Toussaint L'Ouverture and the San Domingo Revolution* (1938; Allison & Busby, 1980).

Jaquet, Chantal, Gérard Bras (eds), *La Fabrique des transclasses* (Paris: PUF, 2018).

Jobard, Fabien, Lévy, René, Lamberth, John, Névanen, Sophie, 'Mesurer les discriminations selon l'apparence: une analyse des contrôles d'identité à Paris', *Population*, 67.3 (2012), pp. 423–51.

Kapesh, An Antane, *I am a Damn Savage; What Have You Done to My Country/Eukuan nin matshi-manitu innushkueu; Tanite nene etutamin nitassi?* Bilingual edition, trans. by Sarah Henzii (Waterloo, ON: Wilfried Laurier Press, 2020).

Khosrokhavar, Farhad, Michel Wieviorka, *Les Juifs, les musulmans et la République* (Paris: Robert Laffont, 2017).

Koch, Alexander, Chris Brierley, Mark M. Maslin, Simon L. Lewis, 'Earth system impacts of the European arrival and Great Dying in the Americas after 1492', *Quatenary Science Reviews*, 207 (1 March 2019), pp. 13 –36.

Laurent, Sylvie, Thierry Leclère (eds), *De quelle couleur sont les Blancs?* (Paris: La Découverte, 2013).

Lavisse, Ernest. *Histoire de France, cours élémentaire* (Paris: Armand Colin, 1913).

Le Bon, Gustave, *The Psychology of Peoples* (New York: Macmillan, 1898).

Le Cour Grandmaison, Olivier, *De l'indigénat* (Paris: La Découverte, 2010).

Leroy-Beaulieu, Paul, *L'État moderne et ses fonctions* (1890; Paris: Guillaumin & Cie, 1900).

Lévi-Strauss, Claude, *The View from Afar*, trans. by Joachim Neugroschel and Phoebe Hoss (1983; New York: Basic Books 1985),

Lévi-Strauss, Claude, *Structural Anthropology*, Vol. 2, trans. by Monique Layton (1973; New York: Basic Books, 1976).

Liauzu, Claude, *Race et civilisation: L'autre dans la culture occidentale* (Paris: Syros, 1992).

Lombé, Lisette, *Black Words* (Amay: L'Arbre à paroles, 2018).

Maalouf, Amin, *The Crusades through Arab Eyes* (NY: Al Saqi Books, 1984).

Mabanckou, Alain, *Huit leçons sur l'Afrique* (Paris: Grasset, 2020).

Mabon, Armelle, *Prisonniers de guerre 'indigènes': Visages oubliés de la France occupée* (Paris: La Découverte, 2019).

Mann, Charles C., *1491: New Revelations of the Americas before Columbus* (NY: Vintage, 2006).

Markowitz, Gerald, David Rosner, *Children, Race, and Power* (Abingdon-on-Thames: Routledge, 2000).

Martial, Jean-Jacques, *Une enfance volée* (Paris: Éditions Les quatre chemins, 2003).

Mbembe, Achille, *On the Postcolony* (Berkeley: University of California Press, 2001).

Mbembe, Achille, *Necropolitics*, trans. by Steven Corcoran (Durham, NC & London: Duke University Press, 2019).

Mbembe, Achille, *Brutalisme* (Paris: La Découverte, 2020).

Menut, Nicolas, *L'Homme blanc: Les représentations de l'Occidental dans les arts non européens* (Paris: Éditions du Chêne, 2010).

Moro, Marie Rose, *Enfants de l'immigration, une chance pour l'école* (Paris: Bayard, 2012).

Morrison, Toni, *The Origin of Others* (Cambridge, MA: Harvard University Press, 2017).

Mukwege, Denis, Guy-Bernard Cadière, *Réparer les femmes: Un combat contre la barbarie* (Brussels: Mardaga, 2019).

Mulot, Rachel, 'Le nouveau visage du musée de l'Homme', *Sciences et Avenir* (February 2007), pp. 8–15.

Nubukpo, Kako, Martial Ze Belinga, Bruno Tinel, Demba Moussa Dembélé (eds), *Sortir l'Afrique de la servitude monétaire: À qui profite le franc CFA?* (Paris: La Dispute, 2017).

Nubukpo, Kako, *Urgence africaine* (Paris: Odile Jacob, 2019).

Pétré-Grenouilleau, Olivier, *Les Traites négrières* (Paris: Gallimard, 2004).

Peyrat, Jérôme, *Poing noir* (Méjannes-le-Clap: Éditions Salto, 2018).

Pigeaud, Fanny, Samba, Sylla Ndongo, *L'Arme invisible de la Françafrique: Une histoire du franc CFA* (Paris: La Découverte, 2018).

Plumelle-Uribe, Rosa Amelia, *White Ferocity: The Genocides of Non-Whites and Non-Aryans from 1492 to Date*, trans. by Virginia Popper (Dakar: CODESRIA, 2020).

Proctor, Robert N., & Linda Schiebinger (eds), *Agnotology: The Making and Unmaking of Ignorance* (Stanford, CA: Stanford University Press, 2008).

Raynal, abbé, *Histoire des deux Indes* (Amsterdam: NP, 1770).

Reclus, Élisée, *Les Grands Textes*, edited by Christophe Brun (Paris: Flammarion, 2014).

Robert, Maurice, *'Ministre' de l'Afrique* (Paris: Seuil, 2004).

Rosset, Clément, *Le Réel et son double* (Paris: Gallimard, 1976).

Rousseau, Jean-Jacques, 'Discourse on the Origin and Foundations of Inequality Among Men', in *Rousseau: The Discourses and Other Early Political Writings*, ed. by Victor Gourevitch (Cambridge: Cambridge University Press, 1997).

Safi, Mirna, Simon, Patrick, 'Les discriminations ethniques et raciales dans l'enquête "Trajectoires et Origines": représentations, expériences subjectives et situations vécues', *Économie et statistique*, nos. 464-465-466 (2013).

Sala-Molins, Louis, *Le Code Noir ou le calvaire de Canaan* (1987; Paris: PUF, 2015, 12th edition).

Sarr, Felwine, and Bénédicte Savoy, *Restituer le patrimoine africain* (Paris: Philippe Rey/Seuil, 2018).

Sarraut, Albert, *Grandeur et Servitude coloniales* (Paris: L'Harmattan, 2012).

Sartre, Jean-Paul, 'Black Orpheus' [1948], in *'What is Literature?' and Other Essays* (Cambridge, MA: Harvard University Press, 1988), pp. 289–330.

Saussure, Léopold de, *Psychologie de la colonisation française dans ses rapports avec les sociétés indigènes* (Paris: Félix Alcan éd., 1899).

Scheck, Raffael, *Une saison noire: Les massacres de tirailleurs sénégalais* (Paris: Tallandier, 2007).

Schmidt, Marie-France, *Christophe Colomb* (Paris: Gallimard, 2011).

Servigne, Pablo, Gauthier Chapelle, *Mutual Aid: The Other Law of the Jungle*, trans. by Andrew Brown (London: Polity Press, 2021). Forthcoming.

Spivak, Gayatri Chakravorty, 'Can the Subaltern Speak?', in *Marxism and the Interpretation of Culture*, ed. by Cary Nelson and Lawrence Grossberg (Urbana & Chicago: University of Illinois Press, 1988), pp. 271–313.

Subrahmanyam, Sanjay, *The Career and Legend of Vasco de Gama* (Cambridge: Cambridge University Press, 1997).

Techqua Ikachi: Message from the Guardians of Land and Life (No publisher, 1999).

Thérenty, Marie-Ève, *Femmes de presse, femmes de lettres. De Delphine de Girardin à Florence Aubenas* (Paris: CNRS Éditions, 2019).

Thuram, Lilian, *My Black Stars: from Lucy to Barack Obama*, trans. by Laurent Dubois (Liverpool: Liverpool University Press, 2021).

Thuram, Lilian, *Nelson Mandela* (Paris: Hachette enfants, 2017).

Tingyang, Zhao, *Tianxia, tous sous le même ciel*, trans. by Jean-Paul Tchang (Paris: Éditions du Cerf, 2018).

Todorov, Tzvetan, *Insoumis* (Paris: Robert Laffont, 2015).

Traoré, Aminata, *Le Viol de l'imaginaire* (Paris: Actes Sud/Fayard, 2002).

Tronchon, Jacques, *L'Insurrection malgache de 1947* (Paris: Karthala, 1986).

Vergès, Françoise, *The Wombs of Women: Race, Capital, Feminism*, trans. by Kaiama L. Glover (Durham, NC & London: Duke University Press, 2020).

Volney, Constantin-François de Chassebœuf, comte de, *Travels through Syria and Egypt in the Years 1783, 1784 and 1785*, Vol. 1 (London: G.G.J. and J. Robinson, 1787)

Voltaire, *An Essay on Universal History, the Manners, and Spirit of Nations* (1755; Charleston, SC: Nabu Press, 2011).

Voltaire, *Candide* (1755; New York: Boni & Liverright, 1918).

Wallraff, Günter. *Lowest of the Low*, translated by Martin Chalmers (London: Methuen, 1988).

Wieviorka, Michel, *La Tentation anti-Semite: Haine des Juifs dans la France d'aujourd'hui* (Paris: Robert Laffont, 2005).

Wieviorka, Michel, *Antiracistes* (Paris: Robert Laffont, 2017).

Wieviorka, Michel, *Pour une démocratie de combat* (Paris: Robert Laffont, 2020).

White, Lynn T., 'The Historical Roots of our Ecologic Crisis', *Science*, Vol. 155, No. 3767 (10 March 1967), pp. 1203–7.

Wohlleben, Peter, *The Secret Life of Trees* (NY: Harper Collins, 2017).

Yussof, Kathryn, *A Billion Black Anthropocenes or None* (Minneapolis: University of Minnesota Press, 2018).

Zancarini-Fournel, Michelle, *Les Luttes et les rêves. Une histoire populaire de la France de 1685 à nos jours* (Paris: La Découverte, 2016).

Zéphir, Stéphane, 'Catégorisation ethnoraciale en milieu scolaire: Une analyse contrastive de conseils de discipline', *Revue française de pédagogie*, 184 (2013), pp. 81–94.

Filmography

Calmettes, Joël, *Berlin 1885, la ruée sur l'Afrique*, 2011.

DuVernay, Ava, *13th*, 2016.

Peck, Raoul, *I Am Not your Negro*, 2016.

INDEX OF NAMES

Héritier, Françoise: 3, 59, 121
Herrou, Cédric: 165–66
Hervé, Georges: 44
Hippocrates: 18
Horel, Stéphane: 11n
Hovelacque, Abel: 44
Hugo, Victor: 180
Hussein, Saddam: 12

I

Isabella, Queen: 23

J

Jacquard, Albert: 185
Jaquet, Chantal: 123n
Jaucourt, Louis de: 36
Jauréguiberry, Jean Bernard: 53
Jeanson, Colette: 162
Jeanson, Francis: 162
Jefferson, Thomas: 48
Jobard, Fabien: 113

K

Kaepernick, Colin: 165
Kane, Coumba: 104n
Kant, Immanuel: 13
Kapesh, An Antane: 176
King, Martin Luther: 3, 141
Koch, Alexander: 25
Koch, Robert: 88
Korver, Kyle: 200–2
Koumé, Amadou: 116

L

Lafayette, Gilbert du Motier de: 156
Lambert, David: 35n
Lamberth, John: 113n
Larousse, Pierre: 62
Las Casas, Bartolomé de: 22–23, 26–27, 199
Laurent, Sylvie: 93n, 198n
Lavisse, Ernest: 66
Le Bon, Gustave: 48
Le Cour Grandmaison, Olivier: 53n, 54–55, 56n, 57n, 58n

Leclère, Thierry: 93n, 198n
Ledesma Valderrama, Martín de: 36
Lemaire, Sandrine: 50n, 58n
Leroy-Beaulieu, Paul: 62
Lévi-Strauss, Claude: 126–27, 188
Lévy, René, 113
Lewis, Simon L.: 25
Liauzu, Claude: 38n, 44n, 49n, 61n, 65n, 133n
Lincoln, Abraham: 174
Lombé, Lisette: 60–61
Londres, Albert: 53
Louis XIV: 34, 38
Louis XVI: 132
Lumumba, Patrice: 74

M

Maalouf, Amin: 14
Mabon, Armelle: 67n
Macron, Emmanuel: 73, 77, 82, 109
Madiba: see Mandela, Nelson
Maïga, Aïssa: 130
Maigne, Jules: 65
Malraux, André: 162
Mandela, Nelson: 89, 141, 161, 192
Mann, Charles C.: 21
Manuel I: 59
Marega, Mamadou: 116
Marivat, Gladys: 132n
Markowitz, Gerald: 104n
Martial, Jean-Jacques: 81
Maslin, Mark M.: 25n
Mbembe, Achille: 48n, 90–91, 128, 132, 134, 135, 155, 169–71, 180, 190, 202
McKeen Cattell, James: 48
Mirabeau, Honoré-Gabriel Riqueti de: 156
Miró, Joan: 89
Montaigne, Tania de: 132
Montesquieu: 13, 35–37
Moreau, David: 78–79
Morrison, Toni: 3, 42, 45n, 94
Morton, Samuel George: 43
Motolinia: 30
Mulot, Rachel: 188n
Mukwege, Denis: 68–69

ACKNOWLEDGEMENTS

Benoit Arnould, Mohamed Belkacemi, Laly Bernard, Roland Berthilier, Basma Bonnefoy, Vania Bonneton, Jean- Pierre Bontoux, Jackie Vernon Boyd, Eva Bravo, James Burnet, Juan Campmany, Jean-Christophe Camus, Mario Canonge, Emmanuel Chelli, Julien et Thomas Cohen, Évelyne Colas, Emmanuelle Collignon, Myriam Coneim, Grâce Dahié, Elizabeth De Loysa, Paul Demougeot, Souleymane Bachir Diagne, Elsa Dorlin, Laurent Dubois, Pierre Durieu, Tarik El Aktaa, Sony Eleore, Éric Fassin, Juliette Fievet, Thierry Gary, Muriel Gauthier, Henriette Girard, Julie Grèzes, Caroline Gueye, Pascale Iltis, Brother Jimmy, Cristina Johnston, Thierry Joor, Mélanie Leblanc, Lamine et Laurence Lô, Fary Lopes Brito, Wilfrid Marignan, Joffrey Martin, Achille Mbembe, Sophie Merle, Anne Meudec, Lucie et Philippe Miclot, David Murphy, Maguy Nestoret, Aedín Ní Loingsigh, François Njike, Kelly Njike, Kako Nubukpo, Sylvie Ofranc, Guy Ontanon, Josep Ortado, Stephen Ortega, Éliane Ouka, Sif Ourabah, Rodolphe Perchot, Sandra Piana, Damien Potdevin, Christophe Prémat, Virginie Raisson-Victor, Shirley Ribeiro, Lou Safra, Mahamadou Lamine Sagna, Rodney Saint-Éloi, Louis Sala-Molins, Felwine Sarr, Gianna Schelotto, Marick Selgy, Christine Siméone, Patrick Simon, Véronique Simon, Maria Sjöström Gisslen, Bruno Skropeta, Françoise Sule, Annick Tangorra, Denitza Thuram Ulien, Éric Toledano, Agnès Tricoire, Fabien Truong, Gilles-Marie Valet, Maria Vallès, Dominique Vénéré, Rafael Vilasanjuan, Marc Voinchet, Jean-Pascal Zadi.

And the members of the Foundation's advisory board: Yves Coppens, Pascal Blanchard, Pascal Boniface, Pascal Brice, Élisabeth Caillet, Doudou Diène, Patrick Estrade, Évelyne Heyer, Ninian Hubert Van Blyenburgh, André Magnin, Marie Rose Moro, Pierre Raynaud, Françoise Vergès, Michel Wieviorka.

In memory and recognition of all they taught me: Françoise Héritier, Alain Anselin, Tzvetan Todorov, Jean-Christophe Victor.

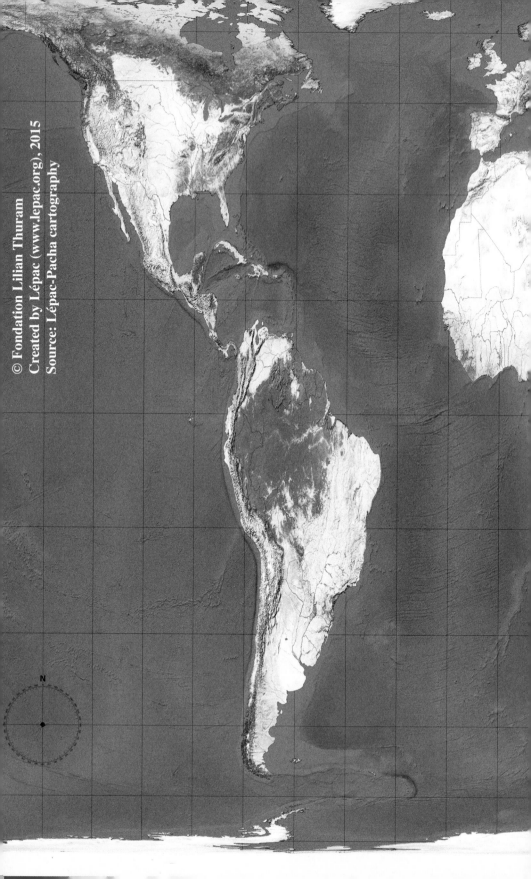

N